John E. Brownlee
A Biography

by Franklin L. Foster

Foster Learning Inc.

First published by
Foster Learning Inc.
2904 - 58 Ave.
Lloydminster, Alberta
T9V 1X8

Copyright © Franklin Lloyd Foster 1981
Copyright © Foster Learning Inc. 1996

ISBN 1-55220-004-3

Canadian Cataloguing in Publication Data

Foster, Franklin L., 1945-
    John E. Brownlee: A Biography

    Includes bibliographical notes and index
    ISBN 1-55220-004-03

1. Brownlee, John E., 1883-1961. 2. Politicians - Alberta -
    Biography. 3. United Farmers of Alberta - History. 4. Alberta
    - Politics and government - 1921-1935. 5. United Grain
    Growers Ltd. - History. I. Title.

Lithography by Screaming Colour, Edmonton, Alberta
Printed by Print Stop Inc., Edmonton, Alberta
Hard cover and binding by Atlas Book Bindery, Edmonton,
Alberta

Dedicated to:

my wife, Dorothy Foster

**who always believed
I could take the next step**

Contents

List of Figures

Preface to the Reader

History is grounded in stories. This is a story filled with paradox, triumph and tragedy. It penetrates the sweep of history and reveals how history often turns on the seemingly minor but often the most revealing of details. This book aims to engage the general reader. Thus, the scholarly foundation on which it rests has been moved discreetly out of the way so that all the twists and turns of the plot and all the fascinating and colourful characters can take centre stage. Readers are assured though, that this story is based on solid research; that every assertion, every direct quotation can be documented and verified. Readers who wish to confirm for themselves the facts presented are referred to the sources mentioned in the bibliographical note.

For the rest of us - let the story begin.

Introduction

As early as 4:00 AM they started to gather. Already daylight was well established in the north-east sky, for it was late June, 1934, in Edmonton. They came hoping to see the main characters in a riveting and sensational drama. They hoped against hope that they would be one of the lucky few to get a seat inside the courtroom. While they waited, they swapped rumours in excited stage whispers since the details were so scandalous.

By 8:00 the newspaper reporters and cameramen congregated. First, were the "heroes" of the local <u>Edmonton Bulletin</u>, who had incurred fines and prison sentences to publish page upon page of the shocking testimony. Next, to confirm the sensationalism, there were reporters from Toronto, Chicago, New York City. Even the British papers were covering "one of the great scandal trials of the decade".

Then they surged forward as the principals appeared. Court officials, clerks, and then, Justice Ives. Diminutive, distinguished by his wavy, silver hair, pencil thin mustache, crisp walk and commanding air.

Next, a new wave of excitement. The crowd jostling, needing to be restrained now. "She" was arriving. "Her" lawyer, the rumpled, loud-mouthed Neil MacLean, and his entourage of political hangers-on. "Her" parents and yes, "she" herself - Vivian MacMillan. They craned their necks and jostled to catch a glimpse, to decide for themselves, to hold in their minds simultaneously all the salacious details they heard and the details of what they could drink in of her appearance. She was no farm girl. Stylish, sophisticated business dress, black, shapely, thrusting curves. Startlingly white, well turned calves. What of her face? Tucked down, chin lowered, partially veiled by black netting on this season's hat. What of her eyes, her lips ... but she was gone, swallowed into the interior of the courtroom where only those lucky few would hear today's details. "Could she have done all that? ... Must of, no young lady could make up a story like that. No woman would invite being handled like that, over and over."

Then it was "him". There was "his" lawyer, A. L. Smith. Well over-weight but clearly with the finest suits. There was "his" wife, Florence. Courage in the face of adversity. Steeling herself with her dignity. The firm step of resolution betrayed by the vacant stare of someone in shock. Pastey pale, too tall, too thin, too shaken.

And there "he" was. They thought they had known him. He was John E. Brownlee, Premier of Alberta. They had known him for his competence. They had heard his lectures on fiscal restraint, the need to balance the budget. They had thought of him as simply another boring corporation lawyer doing well for himself in politics. But now they saw him anew, as a man. They realized now, he was a big man - well over six foot three - well over 230 pounds. The "sober faced seducer" some were calling him. Could he have "had his way with 'her'", so often, so many ways? "Not John Brownlee. He's all work and no play. ... I'm not so sure. There was always something shifty about him, like he was thinking about three things but only telling you about one."

* * *

John Edward Brownlee's career was indeed one of many paradoxes A native of Ontario, he became a determined and effective advocate of Alberta's economic rights. A lawyer who never farmed, he was the dominant political figure in the United Farmers of Alberta during that organization's entire fourteen year reign as the Government of Alberta. Although an unquestioned leader of Canada's most radical agrarian group, he never lost his commitment to reason, moderation and compromise. And while regarded by many as cool and aloof, his political career ended amidst one of the most sensationalized "scandal" trials in Canadian history.

Brownlee had notable and significant achievements in law, politics, agriculture and business. Less than ten years after being called to the Bar, he was the Attorney General of Alberta. He was a central figure in the evolution of Western grain marketing helping to form both United Grain Growers Limited in 1917 and the Alberta Wheat Pool in 1923, and helping to negotiate the Second and Third International Wheat Agreements in the 1950's.

Premier of Alberta he scored several major successes, most far-reaching of which was his negotiation of the transfer to the Province of control over its natural resources -- a development which laid the groundwork for the future prosperity of his adoptive province and of all of its future residents.

However, despite these and other impressive contributions, Brownlee has gone unmentioned in the general histories of Canada. Even the regional literature dealing with his period gives him little more than a stray footnote. This story fills an obvious biographical void by telling, for the first time, the full story of John Brownlee's life. It has its mystery and intrigue, and yes, a sensational scandal. However, this story aims mainly at conveying the context and significance of his achievements and failures. By understanding him, warts and all, I hope we can finally allow John Brownlee to take his rightful place as one of the major figures in the story of Canada.

Chapter 1: The Early Years

Young's Creek cuts a sharp notch in an almost cliff-like portion of the north shore of Lake Erie. Its waters glide leisurely into a shallow harbour protected by a small point of land to westward. The steep eastern flank of its tiny, heavily treed valley provides what at first appears an almost grudging site for the village of Port Ryerse. However, for those whose homes nestle among the tiers of trees, the slow moving creek completes the picture of the small village idyll.

In summer the fine beach sand stretches invitingly in a gentle slope under the warm water in the one-armed bay. In autumn the winds swirl bushels of bright multi-coloured leaves into crunchy drifts on the streets and kaleidoscopic armadas on the mill pond. In winter the steep streets are by-times coated with ice, muffled with heavy new-fallen snow or a-trickle with run-off as a sun-warmed south wind freshens.

The village bears the name of its first resident and owner, Colonel Samuel Ryerse, recipient of a 3,000 acre grant for his loyalty to the Crown and service as a Captain in His Majesty's armies during the American Revolutionary Wars. The old Colonel oversaw the construction of the first dam on Young's Creek and the first of a series of grist and saw mills which harnessed the stream's modest power. Later, shipping, lumbering, and milling provided an active village economy although only the most optimistic entertained visions of Port Ryerse as a future hub of commerce. Arduous dredging improved the harbour and schooners and steamers tied up at the great twin piers whose footings plunged to bedrock through the sandy beach. Ship's crews stowed their gear at Cutting's Hotel on King Street and sang mariners' songs in the ale room. Top quality pine, oak and maple rumbled down Commercial Street in huge wagons hauled by snorting draft horses and filled the lumber boats which supplied an Empire. Farmers guided ox-pulled loads of grain from hard-won fields to the five-run stone mill and bought necessities and notions next door at the general store. But in 1872 the Canada Southern Railroad sliced from the much more naturally favoured harbour at rival Port Dover to the county seat of Simcoe and left Port Ryerse to wither on the vine. From then on it was populated by those who lived there because of what the village was or what it had been but not because of what it might become.

The morning of Sunday, February 5, 1888 saw many of the Port's two hundred residents gather at Memorial Church, with its commanding view of both lake and village, for the morning service conducted by the Reverend William Davis. The Port had its share of Baptists, Methodists and Presbyterians but the majority followed the Anglican lead of the still dominant Ryerse family. As well, Memorial was the village's only church and this explained the somewhat unusual ecumenical spirit of the village where the fierce denominational loyalties of the era were put aside. On this particular Sunday morning the focus of attention was on the Brownlee family pew and the young lad who was about to be baptized.

All the old-timers knew old, Edward James Brownlee, one of the better of the village carpenters, who had built, improved or helped furnish many of the homes in the Port. It was his thirty-one year old son, William James Brownlee; a slim, quiet man, who nervously presented his young son this damp and chilly February morning. William was well known to his fellow parishioners as the operator of the village general store. Beside him was his wife, Christina, former village school mistress and daughter of John Shaw, the prosperous miller at nearby Normandale who also now operated the Port's grist mill. Christina, twenty-seven, was a tall young woman whose erect posture and sharp, intent expression gave her a severe countenance. On the following Wednesday, she and William would celebrate six years of marriage. Between them now was their son, now mid-way between his fourth and fifth birthdays, the young lad who carried the names of his two grandfathers -- John Edward Brownlee. Young John had his mother's sober, almost sad expression and her intense gaze so that he looked like a very serious boy indeed, but inside there was much of his father's shyness as well as his mother's serious determination. This sober expression and seriousness of purpose would characterize his life. However, it would also mask the more usual emotions and leave many feeling they did not really know what lurked behind.

John Brownlee was born August 27, 1883[1] in a cottage style frame house built by his grandfather. He was born, in fact in a solid spool bed Edward had crafted from the native woods of the area. However, it was the sometimes quiet, sometimes hectic life of a small village general store which became the first familiar surroundings of John Brownlee.

The Port Ryerse General Store, which the Brownlees operated, was a small boy's stone's throw from the bank of Young's Creek, just below the mill. A squat frame structure on Commercial Street, built in 1835, it was one of the few buildings to survive the fires which destroyed first one and then another of the village establishments. From his bed in the living quarters at the back, young John could hear the heavy clomp of the farmers' boots on the fifteen inch pine plank flooring and the rummaging through the tools, tubs, and nails for a piece of rope or a length of chain. When he could peer over the counter, he could stand beside his mother and watch the housewives eye the bolts of cloth or stock up for the week from the kegs and barrels of oatmeal, dates or beans. He could smell the cheese as it lay on the counter in a huge block wrapped in tissuey brittle cheese cloth. He could hear the sharp rip of the brown wrapping paper as it came off its huge roll and watch the great ball of cord unloop as it draped down from high overhead. He could press his father to leave off his intent peering at his ledgers to draw some of the pictures which he could so quickly and masterfully create.

It was a life of service to the community with occasional unexpected events to enliven the routine. It was this home life that John found much more congenial than the life outside. The only surviving childhood incident, remembered from outside the home concerns sad-eyed, sober-faced little John trudging home alone; his clean, correct clothing soaked because the village urchins, unnerved by his uncongenial presence, threw him in the lake. In contrast were the fond memories of books and magazines his parents read,

---

[1] All the early records including: Baptismal Certificate, Birth Certificate, school and university records, and marriage license, give Brownlee's birthdate as August 27, 1883. All documents from 1921 and later give the birthdate as August 27, 1884. No explanation of this discrepancy presents itself. When Brownlee's age is given in the text, the 1883 date is assumed to be correct even though Brownlee would not have been using it in later years.

of political discussions of his father with neighbours and customers, of the painstaking details of business as his parents struggled to cope with and overcome the social and economic factors which slowly but inexorably were overwhelming their hopes and dreams. It was from such circumstances that John began to arrive at his apprehension that by acquiring knowledge and analyzing problems, adverse circumstances could be overcome.

* * *

On September 12, 1888, just two weeks after his fifth birthday, John's sister, Maude, was born. The family was now complete. At a time when large families were the approved rule, William and Christina's children would remain just two. Christina was determined to avoid her own mother's arduous experience of giving birth nine times in seventeen years.

By the summer of 1890, life in Port Ryerse was no longer very practical for anyone trying to better the life of their family. William could still make the rounds of the local farmers buying meat, dairy products and produce to stock the general store. Christina could still be just as attentive to the customers. They could be as painstaking in their pricing, as frugal in their living and as determined in their saving.

Young John, nearly seven, could even help out around the store. One job which impressed him with its importance was mixing butter. Down the ladder under the trap door that led to the cool storage cellar, it was his task to take the various lots of butter his father had purchased on his rounds and mix them together. In this way the differing colours, consistencies and flavours of butter could be eliminated and a standardized product made available for the housewives of the Port.

However, despite John's pre-school efforts at quality control and the energy and determination of his parents, the facts could not be escaped. Against a background of general business depression, trade in Port Ryerse was dwindling. The age of rail had eliminated the need for its minor port. With the disappearance of the sailors, Cutting's Hotel had become again, as in the early days, the village's only inn. Lumbering was now only something old-timers talked about or young men went elsewhere to do. The young from the well established farms generally moved away to counties north and west, some as far west as Manitoba.

Then, in early August 1890, the mill, the village's only industry, was destroyed by fire. The hastily formed bucket line from the mill pond could not save the mill but through a frantic afternoon of beating back grass fires and dousing flying sparks they were able to save the surrounding buildings including the general store. Yet most of the business base of the village was destroyed in the flames. The crowd who watched the old mill's final collapse sensed the end of any hope of reversing the withering away of their village.

In the month of the mill's destruction, William and Christina Brownlee completed plans to leave Port Ryerse. John's grandparents Edward and Rachel, would go on living in their cottage above the mill pond. William's three sisters would stay behind, each soon marrying. A new proprietor would take over the Port Ryerse General Store, but the Brownlees would catch the train in Simcoe. They were heading west -- west to new opportunities, west to better prospects for their children and themselves, west -- to Lambton County.

* * *

Trees were the first crop harvested in Lambton County but by 1890 the level land was cleared and the spacious fields were filled with crops and herds. Southwestern Ontario was at the zenith of its career as Canada's breadbasket. When the Brownlees arrived in Brigden, about twelve miles southeast of Sarnia, they found a bustling little market town which was both the service centre of the surrounding prosperous farms and the seat of Moore Township. In contrast to Port Ryersee's single general store, there were fully two blocks of businesses including three grocery stores, a hardware, a dry goods, a bank, a hotel with a restaurant and at least three blacksmiths.

However, the Brownlees' ultimate destination was not Brigden but Bradshaw, a typical Ontario "four corners" six miles to the south. Bradshaw consisted of a slightly enlarged version of the little red schoolhouse, a woodframe Methodist Church and attached church hall which was the social centre of the farm community, and a blacksmith shop where horseshoes were shaped to fit the hundreds of horses whose strength powered the entire way of life. The one other structure was the Bradshaw General Store which William, lacking the capital to establish himself in Brigden, would manage as a branch of one of the Brigden stores. At the back of the store were small living quarters where, from the back door, young Brownlee could look out across a creek valley to the farmsteads and fields and see to the northwest the road to Brigden. In sharp contrast to Port Ryerse, the countryside was remarkably open. Nowhere else in Canada, except on the great Western plains themselves, was the eye drawn so easily and naturally to a distant horizon. Nowhere else did the road lie so straight in front, making it seem so natural and compelling to travel to somewhere else.

John Brownlee, just turned seven, began his school career in Bradshaw. He was the only one of the sixty to seventy pupils who did not live on a farm. An older Brownlee would claim that this basically rural childhood gave him an understanding of farmers and their concerns. Certainly his father found the area, the heartland of Ontario Grit strength, a much more congenial climate in which to discuss his interest in and approval of Liberal policies. Christina welcomed the nearby Methodist church and soon was involved in the ladies' church club work. Young John and later Maude were soon regular and attentive members of the Sunday School and in a few years John was participating in the Young People's Club. Like many shy and thoughtful people he found an avenue for social involvement through the highly structured, purposeful activities of church, school and club rather than through the unstructured social skills mastered by the more extroverted.

The year 1896 saw the election of Canada's first Liberal government in eighteen years. This coincided with a perceptible shift from general depression to widespread growth, expansion and progress. Lambton County, no less than any other part of Canada, was alive with the feeling of the dawning of a new chapter in Canadian history - a chapter that would become known as the Laurier Era. In fact, given the victory of a supposedly agrarian-inspired reform party, the general optimism had few equals to that of the previously frustrated Grits of Ontario's south-west. At the same time, the long awaited settlement boom on the Western plains began. Eventually it would take much of Europe and North

America to supply the flood of migrants to the "last best West" but the first waves would come from Ontario.

Of those who came into the general store where John, now in his teens, took his turn behind the counter, there were few without a son,, or a brother, or an uncle who had been "out West". Those who sat round the Franklin heater and traded observations about the weather as they contemplated the dried apricots and the shoe polish were full of stories of sons who after three years in the West had larger farms than their fathers' generations-old acreage. Many were the stories of merchants rising quickly to prosperous and prominent positions in towns with short pasts but unlimited futures. The stories were full of excitement, suspense, even disappointments, but all were infused with a sense of new beginnings, new opportunities and the promise of a better life.

By 1897, John was taking part in the church young people's club speaking programs. This was a painful experience for the shy Brownlee but he discovered that with painstakingly thorough preparation and a serious and important topic he could do creditably well. The community gave encouraging support as the programs featured men and women of all ages speaking on such topics as sailing ships lost in the nearby St. Clair River or new varieties of fruits better adapted to the area. Just as frequently, the topics concerned missionary work or the role Christianity was playing in reforming some individual's life or social ill.

In September, it was time for John to move on to high school. Such instruction was not offered in Bradshaw where only a few went beyond the eighth grade -- nor was it available in Brigden. John, just turned fourteen, must take board and room in Sarnia and be separated from his family except for school holidays and the occasional weekend.

Sarnia, at the end of the nineteenth century, was a thriving little town with a solid core of substantial brick and stone commercial blocks. Docking, warehousing, and transshipping along the banks of the St. Clair nicely complimented the role of supply centre to the prosperous surrounding farms. Canada's first petroleum boom had come and gone. Already North America's earliest commercial oil well at nearby Petrolia was an historical landmark although oil exploration was still one sector of a varied and active economic climate.

Slightly removed from this exciting world of business and industry was Sarnia Collegiate Institute, built in 1890 on London Road. It resembled a small stone fortress with its turret-like corners and Union Jack thrusting high into the air. In fact, all Sarnia's substantial buildings flew Union Jacks, proudly asserting their differentness from their Stars and Stripes neighbours across the river.

Brownlee plunged into his study of grammar, rhetoric, and such literary works as Hiawatha and Evangeline. History was a study of British and European events while Latin, French, Mathematics and Science were required. Bookkeeping and drawing were possible options and a Physical Education program completed the Collegiate offering. His family was proud of his cleverness and his ability as a student but his teachers used the word "diligent" to describe him rather than "brilliant". His dedication to his studies was partly the result of his seriousness about all things, his remarkable capacity for hard work at his studies, and partly from an intense belief that the acquisition of knowledge would provide him with the tools to realize a strong but well concealed ambition. His studiousness and purposefulness still unnerved his peers who made him the butt of pranks -- their unerring hyena-like instincts quickly realizing that the unexpected and absurd would most unnerve Brownlee and reduce him, momentarily, to their level.

Quickly the high school years passed and on August 24, 1900, just three days before his seventeenth birthday, the Sarnia Observer reported the results of the July Departmental Examinations. Among the names of those who passed and received a Junior Leaving Certificate was John Edward Brownlee.

For the next year, John accompanied his father, who sometimes worked as a commercial traveler, on one of his lengthy trips through northern Ontario, and helped out in the general store. His mother believed that at seventeen he was too young to pursue the career which the family now expected him to follow -- teaching school. However, in September 1901 he enrolled, having just turned eighteen, at the Sarnia Model School.

Model schools, a junior version of normal schools since the certificates they issued were good only in the local county, were an attempt to deal with the severe teacher shortage at the turn of the century. Rapid population increase, large families, recent compulsory attendance laws and rising expectations all conspired to put more children in school and keep them there longer than ever before.

Sarnia Model School, like others of its kind, was a full-fledged public school with regular classes in nine grades, together with an additional class of student teachers who received fifteen weeks intensive instruction in the theory and practice of teaching. For the first six weeks, Brownlee and his seven male and twelve female classmates were taught school management, the science of education, school law, reading instruction and hygiene. Three methodology classes provided methods appropriate for instruction at various grade levels. After this instruction and a short period of observation the student teachers were expected to prepare and present twenty minute lessons.

Brownlee's class, "a bright group of students" concluded their "careful training" with a challenging series of examinations. When the Lambton County Board of Examiners met on December 21, 1901, they saw that John Brownlee, eighteen, of Bradshaw had successfully passed all examinations. His marks, while averaging only seventy percent, were good enough to rank him as the highest male and second highest student in the model school class. On the strength of such results it was immediately recommended that John Edward Brownlee be granted a III Class Teachers' Certificate valid for 1902.

Within a month, he was teaching at his home school at Bradshaw. By now he was a slim young man, nearly six feet four inches in height, with slightly wavy dark brown hair and penetrating blue-gray eyes. His size and intent expression, together with his serious and thoughtful demeanor, gave him a "Presence". He did not warm people but he did impress them with aura of competence and sober reflection. This impression was confirmed by his thorough thoughtfulness and hard work. While becoming known as a competent school master, he also enhanced his local reputation as a public speaker in various competitions. With the new prestige of his position, he began to catch the attention of area residents as a handsome young man. John, living at home, had only to walk across the road to school where his sister, Maude, now fourteen, was a senior student. Inside, a centre aisle divided girls from boys with the most junior at the front and progressively more senior pupils toward the back. A large iron box stove stood in one corner, lit each morning by one of the senior boys and fed during the day from a huge annual supply of wood donated by a district farmer. Brownlee shared the teaching duties with John Christian but the school routine was the typical one of collecting autumn leaves, colouring jack-o- lanterns and the anxious excitement of preparing the Christmas program while moving page by page through the reader, the speller, and the arithmetic problems.

By the spring of 1904, after two and one-half years of teaching at $400 per year, Brownlee decided he wanted a career beyond that of a local school master. He was influenced by the era's strong faith in progress and the continual talk of exciting opportunities in the West, but Brownlee was not one to be swept away by the heady optimism of an exciting new century. He was one, though, to analyze current conditions carefully and recognize, after sober reflection, that better opportunities did exist. To take advantage of them and make a larger contribution in the world, greater knowledge and more education were necessary. In short, he decided, he must go to university.

To finance this, he had to augment the meager savings from his teaching salary. His parents, still struggling to provide their own livelihood, could afford only marginal assistance and moral support. The solution came in the form of a summer job, selling door to door a one-volume farm and home encyclopedia. As an important fringe benefit, the job would take him to the West -- to Rapid City, Manitoba.

The first wave of Ontarian settlement some twenty years earlier had covered a large part of southwestern Manitoba. By 1904, this settlement was being overlain with a new, tremendously larger wave sweeping over Manitoba toward the about-to-become provinces of Saskatchewan and Alberta. Rapid City, on the northwest fringe of the first wave, now contained a thorough mix of well established and newly arrived Ontario stock, together with increasing numbers of those from assorted backgrounds among the new arrivals. It was to the people of this area that John Brownlee headed on his first train trip to the West. First, he passed through Winnipeg, self-advertised "Gateway to the West", where commerce was fueled to a white hot heat by the boom of supplying, servicing

10

and (in some quarters) swindling the trainloads of new arrivals. All growth was a geometric progression and no one could avoid the statistical comparisons sure to gladden the hearts of the most boosterish chamber of commerce.

In the farmlands around Rapid City, there was a quieter, more solid type of optimism, less excitement and a lot more hard work. It was here that Brownlee brought his reference book -- the all-in-one volume which hinted of cultural baggage regretfully left behind and yet promised practical advice on life's daily problems where self-reliance often meant success. He was a gangling figure fitting his long body and longer legs to the task of pedaling his bicycle over the dusty roads and trails, learning to keep a wary eye alert for the violent thunderstorms which gathered quietly but ominously in the immense dome of the Western sky. He presented an almost startling aspect as he unfolded his long frame and approached a housewife desperately mopping perspiration from her face as she looked up from her scrub board and wash tub, or as he waited for a farmer in the field to finish a round and bring up his outfit of work horses in that intense swirl of dust, heat and sweat which can only arise, where man and beast work the land. Then he stepped forward with his sample copy, and more often than not took an order. He remembered the experience in later years with pride that he was never thrown off a farm. Whether this was a measure of salesmanship, Western hospitality or a shortage of social contacts might be debated but the spirit of his recollection was correct. He was able to secure at least enough confidence to be given a hearing. With his serious purpose and his reference book in hand, he gained the ear of the working farmer and this was, indeed, symbolic of much of his future career. John Brownlee, not a farmer himself, but ready to put himself and the tools of knowledge at their disposal for the furtherance of their aims, won the confidence of farmers to a degree equaled by few others.

However, all this was in the future as the harvest trains filled with Ontario boys began to arrive. The harvest excursion was a common introduction to the West and a greenhorn field pitcher might get as much as three dollars a day and all he could eat for fourteen hours a day of pitching sheaves. Brownlee did not get involved in this harvest hustle but continued traveling his territory, taking orders for his book, and in early October headed back to Ontario.

In Brigden that summer his parents bought their future home, one and one-half lots and a small two bedroom brick cottage at the north end of the town. It was purchased in Christina's name for $900 in cash and a $500 mortgage from Industrial Mortgage and Trust Company. William continued for a time to manage the store in Bradshaw but the Brownlees now had their home in Brigden. For John though, it was off to Toronto where on October 11, 1904, he enrolled in Victoria College at the University of Toronto.

Chapter 2: Preparing for the Future

The Humber River flows quietly through the rolling hills that wrinkle the landscape at the north-west corner of Lake Ontario. Early in the twentieth century, the Humber and the Don bracketed much of Toronto. The valleys of both provided countryside retreats for the students of the city's university but the Humber, with that mysterious attraction of things westward, was regarded as the superior site for the customary student picnics on the delightfully sun-warmed days that May and September sometimes afforded. However, it was not for picnics on the Humber but to acquire knowledge and develop his mind as an instrument of social and personal advancement that John Brownlee had come to university.

The University of Toronto was a confederation of colleges, a scattered horseshoe of stolid stone buildings arched around Queen's Park above the Legislative Building of Ontario. By 1904, the students were no longer grouped along the strict denominational lines of the college founders but Brownlee, as a Methodist, did register at Victoria College, the "heart of Canadian Methodism". The College provided him with an academic home base and the *esprit de corps* it fostered ensured that it was with his fellow Old Vic' students that he developed the closest ties of his university years.

As was customary, he rented a room in a private home, the first year at 60 Grenville Street. Such rooms did not include meals so several small businesses catered to this need. The most popular was "Tim Healy's" where for $2.50 per week a meager fare was provided. Other places charged $3.00 so most of the Old Vic' Class of '08, facing the same financial necessities as Brownlee, tended to congregate at Tim's. A certain comradeship developed out of the adversity of stretching $25 per month to cover rent, books, meals and laundry tickets. Mcanwhile, the small but noticed minority of female students led a less harried life at the newly opened women's residence, Annesley Hall.

Brownlee chose a challenging academic career, an Honours programme, the route which required the most classes and the highest grades. History and Political Science were his selected specializations but there was a heavy emphasis on languages. English required papers in both Composition and Literature where there were the inevitable Shakespearean plays to study. Latin and two other languages were required. Brownlee, declining to continue his high school French, selected German and Hebrew. There was as well, Ancient History, a full course of Mathematics, and Biology.

Brownlee attacked all these with characteristic purposefulness and application and gradually came to know and be known by his fellow students and the professors. Among the latter he regarded historian George Wrong and Professor Emerson Horning most highly. His regard for Horning stemmed from his involvement in that most prestigious and academic of extra-curricular activities, the Union Literary Society, affectionately known as "The Lit.". The debates, parliamentary discussions and occasional papers of the Lit. appealed strongly to Brownlee. At twenty-one he enjoyed an age advantage over most of his fellows and was confidant that his years of public speaking experience gave him an edge in precisely the skills needed to excel.

Gradually Brownlee began earning a reputation among his fellow students. He was a tall, slender young man, invariably serious, and with an air of analytical detachment about people and events. He was intensely organized and methodical about his studies but disorganized in his personal life. Often his absorption in a problem or text left him late for a lecture and it became common to see "Jack" Brownlee striding across the campus, his remarkably long legs covering ground so quickly that his undergraduate gown snapped smartly out behind him.

At Christmas, he was back in Brigden where the little family celebrated their first Christmas in the brick cottage and basked in the pride, responsibility and achievement of having a son in college. After the holiday, he resumed his round of classes, assignments, Lit. debates and, on Sundays, regular attendance at the Carlton Street Methodist Church. At year's end his hard work and application were rewarded with "A's" in all subjects except Latin, German and Mathematics in which he earned respectable "B's".

Summer meant replenishing financial reserves and Brownlee was fortunate to be included in a group of university students recruited to spend four months in England selling stereoscopic views. It was an ideal combination of a necessary summer job and an extended vacation in the island which even generations old Ontario families referred to as "home". He was back in plenty of time to register for his second year, in Honours Political Science, the usual choice of those with aspirations in the field of law.

How long his ambitions had included law is unclear but as the years passed his course choices pointed increasingly in that direction. The year was a heavy one but in addition to his course load he became much more involved in extra-curricular activities. The first of these was "The Bob".

"The Bob" was one of those initiation rituals with which undergraduates are wont to relieve the real and imagined pressures of their existence. A satiric review caricaturing university life and the incoming freshmen, it required, like most "spontaneous fun events" a lot of behind-the-scenes organization. Brownlee was the president of the nucleus which devised, scripted, cast, costumed and performed a series of skits poking good-natured fun at all aspects of college life. Even his own grave, business-like approach to organizing a frivolous event formed the basis of a sketch but it was the skits based on Brownlee's summer job of selling stereoscopic views to eccentric characters, in England, which won the rave reviews. Acta Victoriana proclaimed the "08 Bob" one of the best ever in "professionalism of drama, quality of writing and avoidance of hurtful stings."

Acta Victoriana, Victoria College's high quality journal, was another area of Brownlee's extra-curricular activity. Each month its sixty-odd pages were filled with articles on College happenings, pictures of clubs and teams, original short stories and poems, and the inevitable jokes, cartoons and snippets of gossip. In his second year, Brownlee was Acta's assistant business manager.

The Old Vic' '08 Class consisted of fewer than sixty students so that by second year everyone knew everyone else. Such intimacy was necessary for the conspiratorial enjoyment of the allusions which occupied the "Personals and Exchanges" page of Acta. The real stories were between the lines, as with a purported comment of Brownlee's at the popular Varsity Rink skating parties, to wit, "I fell like a baby elephant". This small barb scored on both his large size and his lack of athletic aptitude. More intriguing were such cryptic comments as, "Brownlee; 'I had a lovely dream last night. I was on the bottom of a ladder leading up to heaven and all the angels at the top had Annesley Hall faces',", and in the same vein, "Brownlee went to Central Church one Sunday night. The usher smiled a wise smile when he saw him and promptly showed him into the Annesley Hall pew." Was the humour of these jests aimed at embarrassing him as a result of some compromising situation involving the girls' residence or was it based on the sheer improbability of soberly diligent John Brownlee being involved in a college "panty raid"? There were certainly those who doubted that Brownlee was as soberly diligent as he appeared. They were not the last to wonder if they knew the real John Brownlee.

Meanwhile, he remained active in the Lit. earning a reputation as one of the more effective although not the most dramatic of speakers. In debating competitions he was already one of Victoria College's stalwarts and teamed with classmate Fred Albright, almost unbeatable.

Fred Albright, easily the most popular member of his Class, combined striking good looks with a warm magnetic personality. He was one of those who can transform a collection of bored and restless individuals into a warm circle of friends tasting the zest of life. As well, he was idealistic, almost zealous, exemplifying fully the uplifting qualities of a Christian gentleman to which the age aspired.

Brownlee cultivated Albright's friendship, recognizing that he was a perfect foil. His own cool reserve was eclipsed by Albright's magnetic warmth; his sober diligence enlivened by Albright's grace and style. People, attracted to Albright, overlooked Brownlee's own shy aloofness and soon all were warm companions. Through Fred Albright, Brownlee discovered a most fulfilling role: the trusted confidant and counselor of a strong and admirable leader respected for his ability, integrity and high sense of purpose.

Through the following years Brownlee pointed his heavy course load increasingly toward law and maintained his wide range of extra-curricular activities as well. He became a more senior member of the Acta Board, retaining the post of Assistant Business Manager but adding the editorship of the "Personals and Exchanges" page. There would be no more sly barbs about John Brownlee. He was also Assistant Business Manager of the Victoria

College Glee Club which his commercial skills began to put on a firm financial footing. And, of course, his intense involvement in the Lit. continued. Classmates noticed that although he did not appear to be seeking positions, he was certainly acquiring his share of them and more. It was a fine distinction since to actively seek positions was regarded as crass but to serve in them when asked was entirely admirable. Was he as disinterested as he appeared?

As his third year of classes came to an end, Old Vic' students responded to the warm spring days with a week of eager plans for a picnic up the Humber. When the appointed Saturday dawned, wave after wave of low scudding clouds were dampening all beneath them with wind whipped mists of cold drizzle. Undaunted, some wanted to go ahead on the chance the weather would improve. Some even proposed a picnic in the rain as a "lark". Brownlee stood strongly on common sense arguing that the weather would not improve and that a picnic in the rain would be an uncomfortable, ridiculous waste of time. When the majority rejected his good sense, he trudged away ill-naturedly leaving behind the impression that if he did not get his own way he would pick up his marbles and go home. He felt no remorse about a common sense decision. His life was to be crowded with events where his over-riding sense of reasonableness prevented him from joining the crowd.

His examination results that year were impressive. He stood in the top five in all subjects except Economics, where he ranked eighth. Considering the heavy academic load and his numerous extra-curricular activities, the year was very much a success. That summer he spent most of his time selling magazine subscriptions in Toronto, a job in which, as an avid reader of magazines and newspapers, he enjoyed great success. The highlight of the summer, however, was when he and Albright represented Victoria College at the Conference of College Young Men's Associations held in June at Niagara-on-the-Lake.

For nine days, delegates from most Canadian and many American universities attended Bible study sessions and heard various guest speakers appeal for consideration of careers in the mission fields, the Y.M.C.A. or the ministry. These specific appeals were related, as Brownlee wrote in an article in <u>Acta Victoriana</u>, to the larger theme that whatever career one selected, be it profession or trade, "each man is a missionary for through his vocation he exerts an influence over others and has therefore a responsibility to exemplify the higher spiritual values."

> For to us much is given, and from us much will be
> required and if we who are about to become leaders
> among our follow men fail to do our duty, what can
> be expected from those to whom Fortune has not
> been so generous?

* * *

His friendship with Albright, with whom he shared lodgings at 48 Dandonald Street, had grown to the point where they shared most activities. Brownlee was now the salaried Business Manager of <u>Acta</u> and he urged Albright to join its Board. It was a measure of Albright's prestige that almost at once he was chosen President. The recruitment was an interesting measure of Brownlee's insight and management skill. Albright's popularity and idealism would win for <u>Acta</u> the recognition which no one else (and certainly not Brownlee) could achieve. On the other hand, Albright's inexperience and friendship with Brownlee would mean that the actual operation was almost entirely within the latter's control. To Brownlee, the arrangement was entirely satisfactory, taking full advantage of the respective skills of the two seniors. Under his management, <u>Acta</u> enjoyed one of its best years and was left on a solid financial footing.

During Easter break, Brownlee, as Business Manager, accompanied the Glee Club on a ten day tour of the Niagara Peninsula. He made all the bookings and the travel and accommodation arrangements for the thirty-odd singers and pianist A. L. Burt. The Club won complimentary reviews wherever it appeared and Brownlee took satisfaction from having arranged the tour and including several smaller centres where such performances were seldom booked. Because of this successful tour, the Glee Club, too, was left on a solid financial base for years to come.

His involvement in the Union Literary Society culminated in his being named Critic for the spring term, while Albright took the most prestigious position -- Leader of the Government. In this final year, Brownlee even took up athletics, competing for Old Vic' in the inter-college tennis tournament. He concluded his impressive extra-curricular record by being named to the Class Executive.

Academically, his fourth year was less successful. He maintained some of his customary "A"s but in other courses ranked uncharacteristically low. The overall result was a disappointing III Class Honours, indicating a grade average of less than sixty-five percent. Fred Albright was one of fourteen Old Vic' students to graduate with II Class Honours, while four others took I Class Honours with averages over seventy-five percent. Frank Underhill, of University College, won most of the year's major academic awards.

The year book, <u>Torontonensis - 1908</u>, contained the usual photographs and short bits on each of the graduates. Fred Albright, looking youthful and competent, was summed up as "One of Nature's Noblemen" and "on his way to Osgoode Hall." Brownlee, sober as usual, his stylish centre parted hair and rimless glasses giving him a bookish air, was described rather cryptically as "six foot o' man. A 1, Clear grit and human nature." A short account of his achievements concluded: "He hopes to follow law, but whether 'Jack' becomes a lawyer or follows business, one thing we know he will always be, and that is a man."

Given this ambiguous send-off, Brownlee prepared for convocation and the farewell banquet. A warm June sun bathed the verdant campus as the Governors and Faculty in full regalia marched from the East Hall and the graduates from the West Hall to meet and march into Convocation Hall together. The Class of '08 kept its student spirit to the end, breaking into a rousing, "We Will Come Rejoicing, Bringing Home the Sheaves", as the agricultural degrees were conferred. Brownlee was given a parting barb by <u>Acta</u> which supposedly noticed him in a "reminiscent mood during the ceremony of conferring degrees on the sweet girl graduates," and attributed to him the comment: "Say, I wouldn't mind having the Chancellor's job myself" as that worthy put his arms around and kissed each girl on the cheek.

As for his own degree, there was a sense of accomplishment. A long held ambition had been realized. Four years of hard work, both on and off campus, of intense extra-curricular and academic involvement, of meager allowances and deprivations were over. Along with the feeling of accomplishment there was also a sense of release.

Later, as the onslaught of speeches waged on into the night and the keynote speaker, that most ubiquitous notable, Sir William Mulock, waxed eloquent about Champlain's exploration of the Humber almost three centuries earlier, it was noticed that Brownlee was no longer in the hall. Unaware that they were following in the great explorer's wake, he and one of the female graduates, Isabella Govenlock, were paddling up the Humber in a canoe.

Just what transpired between the two that warm summer night became the subject of muted conjecture. Friends of both were surprised by their absence, startled when they returned very late together and shocked when, the next day, they announced their engagement. Even Isabella's best friend had not known of any previous interest of the two in each other. However, at some later time, for some unknown reason, the engagement was broken. It had been an unexpected and uncharacteristically impetuous episode for Brownlee and it raised again the question of whether Brownlee's classmates had really known him. Was he really the reserved and dutiful young man he appeared to be?

* * *

Once the summer was over, Brownlee and Albright were off on a planned trip to the West Coast to survey opportunities for the practice of law. At each major centre along the way they stopped and peddled a line of office supplies and at the same time satisfied themselves as to the current state and future possibilities of the legal profession in the community. The choice was quickly narrowed to Vancouver or Calgary. Brownlee preferred Vancouver but the Alberta city was selected, as he later commented; "for one particular reason, mainly that in Vancouver there were Englishmen, financed from home, in the legal profession and the opportunity for young men without money to start up in law was not as good there as in Calgary."

However, Brownlee, now twenty-five, did not accompany Albright to Calgary but continued his sales job in Toronto for the winter. Perhaps he needed more savings, perhaps there was a lingering doubt about his career choice as he was now quite at home in the commercial world. For whatever reason, he remained for a time one small cog in the large commercial machine of Toronto.

Sometime during the winter he attended a skating party at Varsity Rink where he was struck by the appearance of a tall young lady skating gracefully about. Accustomed to towering above most people, he noticed her relative height and that, although on skates, she was every inch a refined and dignified lady. He looked about frantically for someone to introduce them. Introductions, when finally made, revealed that she was Florence Edy, in the final year of a Bachelor of Arts programme at nearby McMaster College.

Florence was the second youngest of seven daughters of James N. Edy, who, forty years earlier had operated the first photography business in London, Ontario. From there he went on to larger and larger enterprises, moving to Toronto where he died in January 1890. He left his widow Mary, with her own three daughters plus his four daughters from a previous marriage. Florence was only two and one-half years old.

The Edy girls, thrown on their own resources, became a close knit family. They were in frequent contact with their many Canadian and American relatives, one of whom was William Cody, the Buffalo Bill of wild west fame. Mary Edy raised her daughters to lead independent lives and each would pursue, at least briefly, a career. Thus, Florence was at university and planning a professional career. It was an objective she shared with Brownlee and the two were soon "keeping company".

That summer, Mrs. Edy moved herself and her girls to Calgary to take advantage of its bounteous opportunities. The older girls soon found employment, one as a secretary in the newly opened Calgary office of the Grain Growers Grain Company. Florence, turned twenty-two on July 15, 1909, enrolled in Calgary Normal School. Brownlee, now with yet another motive to move to Calgary, ended his Toronto hiatus and joined Albright, already articling with the respected legal firm of Walsh, McCarthy & Carson. The two Old Vic' old boys had rooms at 227 14th Avenue East, only two blocks from where the Edys rented a home.

Calgary, like most western communities, was enjoying boom town growth. The bald prairie of a decade before was now strewn with streets, frame houses, false fronted stores and the energetic bustle of people, animals and machinery. Dollar an acre range land was being hawked by speculators to a ready market at $12 a front foot. Each newcomer was in search of new opportunities and in turn supplied new opportunities for those already there. Brownlee secured a position as law student with Lougheed, Bennett, Allison & McLaws. The two senior partners were widely known but more as politicians and financiers than lawyers. The dapper Senator Sir James Lougheed, one of the last of John A. Macdonald's appointees, was Conservative leader in the Senate, while pugnacious R.B. Bennett, already leader of Alberta's Conservatives, was at the beginning of a career which would see him become a millionaire, Prime Minister of Canada and a member of the British House of Lords. The firm's clientele, a veritable Who's Who of Canadian business, included all the major banks and the Canadian Pacific Railway Company, including its Irrigation and Land Department.

It was an opportune situation for Brownlee. Three years of articling, rather than law school, was then the common preparation for the legal profession. Students performed routine practical work during the day and on their own time prepared for yearly examinations in theory set by the Bar Association. If one of the senior partners took an interest, the student could be excellently prepared. Bennett took such an interest and frequently visited the office after hours when Brownlee was "reading the law". He would ask what facet of the law he was studying and when Brownlee replied, Bennett would launch into an impromptu lecture, pacing energetically back and forth, hooking his thumbs into the vest pockets of one of his expensive suits, illustrating his points by detailed discussion of particular cases and citing volume and page number where the case report might be found. Time and again, the awe-struck Brownlee found the cases recorded exactly as described.

Despite his admiration for Bennett's memory and style, the firm's departmentalization left him little scope to pursue commercial law, the area in which he was most interested. Consequently, he changed his articles to the firm of Muir, Jephson and Adams. Again the choice was fortunate. James Muir, K.C., was one of the province's most respected lawyers. He, too, took an interest in Brownlee and frequently embarrassed the deferential student by spending hours researching points of law he had raised and leaving the case books open and ready for him to find the next morning when he came to work.

That same fall, Florence began her teaching career at a one room school near High River. She was able to visit her family frequently and the relationship with Brownlee "blossomed". A year later they announced their plans to marry as soon as John had been called to the Bar. The following summer, Mrs. Edy, in failing health, returned to Toronto taking most of her family with her. Florence's departure left him to complete his articles without her companionship and encouragement. There was, though, the support of Albright, already practicing with Clarke, McCarthy & Walsh. After intense preparation, Brownlee passed his final examinations and on December 16, 1912 stood before Mr. Justice Stuart to be formally admitted to the Bar of Alberta.

Figure 1

Florence Edy upon her graduation from McMaster University in 1909. On December, 23, 1912, she and John Brownlee were married in Toronto. Their honeymoon trip took them West to their new home in Calgary, where John had just been called to the Bar of Alberta.

(Photo courtesy of the Glenbow Archives NA-2547-8)

Chapter 3: Amalgamation

The Elbow River winds circuitously through the valley which dwarfs its modest stream. Red willow, white poplar and occasional groves of cottonwoods cover the valley floor, in sharp contrast to the sweeping stretches of grassland on the great plains above. By 1912, substantial homes fringed the Elbow's north bank and when the Elboya Bridge opened, it provided access to what a later generation would term, "a new prestige community". Of these new homes, the one nearest the bridge, 4232 - 6th Street West, was the residence of Mr. and Mrs. John Brownlee. It was an idyllic setting with the rippling, tree-shaded stream on the one hand, a sheltering ridge on the other, and the lawns and trees of a park front and centre. In all Western Canada, they could not have found a spot which more closely resembled Port Ryerse.

Florence and John Brownlee were married December 23, 1912, in Toronto, at 119 Balmoral Avenue, the home of Florence's sister, Blanche, and her husband Robert Marshall. The weather was fair and mild, with a high near freezing, as twenty-nine year old Brownlee and his twenty-five year old bride left on a honeymoon trip via Brigden and Chicago, back to Calgary.

In Brigden, William had begun a new career as Editor and Publisher of the local weekly, the Brigden Progress. One of his early issues, proudly proclaiming itself 'Strictly Independent', described Robert Borden's first Cabinet, slow motion photography, a Chinook, and commented on Western farmers decreasing their dependence on banks by storing grain rather than shipping it immediately after harvest. The latter two pieces probably derived from John's correspondence.

Once settled with his new wife in their new home, Brownlee went back to work with Muir, Jephson & Adams. Already the firm did legal work for the fledgling United Farmers of Alberta (U.F.A.). In Alberta, as elsewhere across the West, after a decade of minimal success getting government action to remedy conditions hampering Western agriculture, and after the defeat of promised free trade initiatives in the 1911 election, organized farmers turned to remedial activities over which they could exercise some independent control. The activity attracting the greatest interest in

1913 was "the organized farmer in business" and its most auspicious example, the Grain Growers' Grain Company Limited (G.G.G.). This company was to provide an alternative to the "exploitive, monopolistic private grain corporations" by democratizing business practices. They wished to apply such innovations as the "one man - one vote" principle to shareholders' meetings, eliminate proxy voting, pay patronage dividends, and stress service rather than profit as their guiding principle.

The demand for direct farmer ownership and control of marketing facilities, especially the local elevator, was spreading rapidly across the West. Farmer leaders in Alberta wanted to improve Manitoba's system of numerous small, local companies, and incorporate a province wide farmer owned elevator company. Muir, Jephson & Adams were secured to handle the legal aspects of creating the new company and Brownlee, at first in consultation with Muir, was closely involved in the work. So intense was the demand for the new company that the U.F.A. executive directly undertook its creation, appointing themselves the provisional Board of Directors. Secretary-Treasurer, E.J. Fream, assumed the same role with the new company and in that capacity collaborated closely with Brownlee. That began a relationship which was to play an important role in both men's lives.

Early in 1913, Brownlee was part of the delegation to Edmonton to petition the provincial government to charter the company and provide it with some financial support. The Liberal government, sensitive to requests from the U.F.A., and well aware of the strong farmer demands behind this one, acted quickly to incorporate the Alberta Farmers' Cooperative Elevator Company Limited (A.F.C.E.C.). They also agreed to lend up to eighty-five percent of the original cost of constructing any individual elevator, provided local farmers held a certain minimum equity. This condition was entirely acceptable to the Provisional Board who themselves insisted that local farmers acquire shares (given a par value of $60) representing at least twenty percent of the cost before construction began. The government refused, however, to guarantee any bank loans to the new company. A grain buying company, because of the long delay between payment to farmers and recovery from exporters, needed large financial reserves, usually provided by a line of bank credit. The banks insisted on a guarantee. By prior agreement, the G.G.G. stepped in at this point to provide the guarantees for amounts, during the first year, of up to $300,000. This support was expected since many U.F.A. members were shareholders in the larger company. Indeed, Fream was at the time First Vice-President of the G.G.G. and in charge of its Calgary office. Thus, he was able to introduce Brownlee to farmer leaders in both Alberta and Manitoba.

Brownlee could take considerable satisfaction from his role in the formation of the new farmers' company. Its articles of incorporation, which he had had a major hand in drafting, provided it with a firm basis for relatively trouble free operation. By August 19, 1913 Company officers could report to the first annual meeting that over 3,500 shareholders had subscribed capital in excess of $360,000. The Company had purchased ten elevators and was constructing forty-two others to handle the 1913 crop. Ordinary farmers were completely unaware of the part played in the design of their grain marketing system by the tall, sober lawyer from Ontario but farmer leaders had noticed Brownlee's work and appreciated his talents being enlisted in their enterprises.

He was also gaining acceptance in Calgary business and professional circles. So many graduates from Old Vic' were now in Calgary that an alumni branch was formed with Brownlee as secretary-treasurer. The group met frequently, their activities all informed with a spirit of idealism and optimism. Standards were high and individuals were judged for integrity and the caliber of their ideas. It was in this milieu that Brownlee developed his habit of evaluating opinions on the basis of who uttered them. A comment from someone he respected would be carefully considered, while the same comment from someone who was morally or intellectually suspect would be dismissed out of hand due to its source. Brownlee's peers had similar standards.

These young men took seriously their emerging leadership roles. They sought out and recommended to each other morally educating and inspiring books. Thus, such authors as John Ruskin and Ralph Connor enjoyed immense popularity. Life, though, was not unduly rigorous. Socializing was frequent at dinners or teas. Special efforts were made to guard against cultural isolation and in these early years Brownlee gave a series of talks on the modern poet, Robert Browning. He also taught a Sunday School class in the local Methodist church and, later, joined the Calgary Lodge of the Ancient, Free & Accepted Masons.

In the spring of 1914, Fred Albright returned to Ontario to marry Evelyn Kelly, a 1912 graduate of Old Vic' . They went to England for their honeymoon and were there that fateful first week in August when the progress of mankind suddenly jumped the rails and the horrendous catastrophe, known euphemistically as the Great War, began. They immediately returned to Calgary where Fred, already intending to join the battle, began making provision for his new wife by giving up his private practice and rejoining McCarthy, Carson & McCleod.

Brownlee, for his part, accepted an offer of partnership in the firm which then became Muir, Jephson, Adams & Brownlee. Considering the fervour with which most of his peers committed themselves to the war effort, Brownlee's "business as usual record" again set him apart. Perhaps his eyeglasses explained his complete lack of military involvement but not his absence from the lists of those involved in patriotic fund raising or Red Cross volunteer work. Again there were doubts about whether he completely shared the values and ideals of his generation.

* * *

The volume of legal work for the farmers organization was growing rapidly, in step with their expanding membership and burgeoning businesses. Already a group of disgruntled shareholders were suing E.J. Fream for alleged irregularities and incompetence as general manager of the A.F.C.E.C. Brownlee was able to settle the matter out of court but a more serious case, involving a former Company auditor who had fraudulently certified the statements of an unscrupulous Calgary grain buyer, had to be dealt with dispatch. It was vital for the farmers' own company to preserve a reputation for honesty. The prosecution was vigorous, the funds recovered and the delinquents incarcerated. Brownlee's bill was $200. Considering the sum of such bills, he suggested to Fream that the Company pay his firm an annual retainer rather than continue to be billed on a piece work basis. After investigating, Fream concluded it was an excellent offer and when Brownlee returned from his summer vacation, he was, in fact, the A.F.C.E.C.'s solicitor.

Late in the year, members of the U.F.A. were shocked by the death of their president, James Speakman. The next month, the annual convention chose a new president, Henry Wise Wood. Wood, known throughout Alberta as 'H.W.' , was a tall, lanky farmer who had come to the Carstairs area from Missouri when already in his middle years. The ultimate eclectic, he combined Christian piety with earthy humour, and idealistic theory with down to earth common sense. His casual slouch sometimes caused him to be overlooked as a loafer hanging around a farmers' meeting. However, his deep, gravelly voice and his capacity to articulate the intellectual and emotional concerns of the farmers in plain-spoken, forceful sincerity made him a major figure on the Western Canadian scene for the next twenty years. Wood and Brownlee, so unlike in so many ways, nevertheless quickly came to respect each other. Each learned from the other and Wood was to be a major factor in determining the course of Brownlee's life.

In 1916, though, Brownlee continued to work closely with Fream, and with Cecil Rice-Jones, the new president of the A.F.C.E.C. Rice-Jones was a small, mild mannered man whose rimless glasses and quiet dedication were reminiscent of bank clerks of the day. He was a competent manager of operations with a close eye for detail and a ready fund of common sense. He was increasingly attracted to the possibilities of uniting the various elevator companies into one large corporation with a consequently greater impact on the grain trade and a greater potential for securing the farmers' objectives.

Preliminary discussions revealed that Saskatchewan farmers were not willing to surrender their provincial autonomy. If union was to go ahead, it would be either a federation or amalgamation of the G. G. G. , operating mainly but not entirely in Manitoba, and the Alberta company. It was decided to consult the respective provincial governments to determine their attitude to the unity proposal. Consequently, Brownlee accompanied Rice-Jones to Edmonton where they interviewed the Minister of Public Works, Charles Stewart.

Brownlee initially agreed with Stewart who, while approving the unity proposal in principle, believed that complete amalgamation would not be accepted by the shareholders. Stewart suggested setting up a holding company through which the two companies would actually work but at the same time retain, at least nominally, their independent identities. Rice-Jones rejected this as nothing more than an obvious subterfuge which would create more opposition than it would allay. Brownlee, who had scheduled a side trip to Big Valley where the U.F.A. Local was involved in some legal tangles, agreed to spend all his spare time considering the legal implications of the two proposals. Returning to Edmonton, he telephoned Rice-Jones to announce that he had changed his mind. Amalgamation was best because it was simplest and most straightforward and, while it might be more difficult to put through the annual meetings, the long term benefits would outweigh any initial difficulties. The incident revealed a Brownlee characteristic. He did not make his best decisions quickly. He liked to amass all possible information on a question and then, given sufficient time to weigh all alternatives and assess the implications of each, his decision was usually a sound, far sighted one.

Having accepted amalgamation as the best alternative, he began examining the charters of the two companies to see what legal obstacles might arise and advise his clients accordingly. It was the type of work he most enjoyed. He noticed two possible difficulties. The Grain Growers' charter, an Act of the Federal Parliament, did not grant the power to sell out to another company nor authorize sufficient capitalization to absorb the A.F.C.E.C. The amalgamation could only be accomplished by charter amendments, which meant a referral to Parliament. This was a step G.G.G. directors did not want to take. They were convinced the powerful Eastern business and financial lobby would use this opportunity to remove some of the organized farmers' rights and privileges and arouse public hostility toward their company.

This concern was on everyone's mind when the joint meeting of both Boards convened in the G.G.G. offices in Winnipeg to discuss concrete action. Since the Companies were viewed as only the commercial wing of the organized farmers' movement, the executives of both the Manitoba Grain Growers' Association and the U.F.A. were also present and, for legal advice, solicitors Brownlee for the A.F.C.E.C. and W. Trueman for the G.G.G. Mustachioed T. A. Crerar, looking even more presidential than usual, chaired the meeting which he called "one of the most important that has ever taken place in the history of the organized farmers of Western Canada." He went on to remind the meeting that monetary considerations were not the most important question, that they must consider "all the vital problems affecting the welfare of the country if we are to preserve our forces, conserve our energies and lead the fight which will bring about better conditions. Eastern Canada," he maintained, was "looking to the West for leadership, and the West must look to the rural districts for leaders." It was for this reason that the commercial companies had an added responsibility to work toward union "so that farmers will be provided with a common idea and a common point of view."

Next, Wood voiced his support of amalgamation. Nodding his almost completely bald head and gazing at his intent colleagues through his droopy eyes, he urged them to remember that service, not profits, must be "the foundation stone of our efforts. We must avoid overlapping," he pleaded, "avoid competition, avoid jealousies and remember that we are serving all the people of Western Canada and not one particular section. The only reason that we cannot consider Eastern Canada," he added, presenting a different perspective than Crerar; "is that they are not ready, but we must be prepared to amalgamate with them when they are ready, as they need us."

When the statements of philosophy were over and the discussion turned to the concrete, technical aspects, Brownlee became involved. The alternatives were to obtain from Parliament either a new charter or the necessary amendments to the existing G.G.G. charter. Some thought that the holding company alternative might avoid disclosing such proposals, sure to raise the hackles of Eastern Tories, as abolition of proxy voting or delegate democracy applied to the annual meeting of shareholders. Brownlee pointed out that as soon as any proposal was made to the annual meetings, it would become public knowledge. Later, he cautioned that if the new company wanted to pay patronage dividends, it would have to circumvent the Winnipeg Grain Exchange which had declared the practice unacceptable for its members.

Finally though, the meeting agreed to seek amendments to the G.G.G. charter. It was quickly agreed the company name should become the United Grain Growers Limited. Much more controversial was the question of shareholder voting at the annual meeting. The older company followed the more traditional practice of allowing only personal or limited proxy voting. The Alberta group were adamantly opposed to proxy voting and insisted upon the system they had developed of organizing shareholders into Locals which, in turn, elected delegates to the annual meeting. There was a threat of division along provincial lines but at length the Alberta practice was adopted. Later, another of Brownlee's concerns was met by agreeing to seek an amendment to increase authorized stock from two to five million dollars. On the most sensitive question, which Brownlee next raised, of how the exchange of stock would take place, an eight man subcommittee was appointed to appraise the assets and arrive at a valuation of each company's stock. They were to employ accountants and legal advisors and Brownlee was thus closely involved.

He had attracted favourable notice at the important Winnipeg meeting. His sympathetic attitude to the farmer leaders and his moderate yet informed advice, counseling them as to how they could achieve their objectives rather than stressing how the law might thwart them, as many lawyers were wont to do, earned him respect and confidence. In future discussions, there was an almost complete reliance on Brownlee's legal opinions.

By December 1916, the sub-committee completed its appraisal and recommended that each G.G.G. share be converted to one share in the new company while each share in the Alberta company be exchanged for two shares in United Grain Growers Limited (U.G.G.). Brownlee prepared and presented the sub-committee's report to the annual meetings. He also determined what amendments the A.F.C.E.C. would have to obtain in its charter to expedite the amalgamation. Personally he feared there might be stiff opposition to amalgamation at the annual meetings so he also began preparing contingency plans for such possible developments as an injunction being sought by dissatisfied shareholders trying to block the transfer of shares.

Everyone was surprised, when the annual meetings took place, to find a ready acceptance of the proposals. Shareholders, though, had a lot of questions and Brownlee was frequently called to the podium to answer them. His thorough preparation and detailed study of the issue for two years was apparent. He was able to give thorough answers showing, in his moderate way, that the recommended procedure was the wisest and most promising alternative. Because of his thorough grasp of the situation, he was able to assume the style by which he would later be characterized -- an expert, authoritative voice, able to convince farmers as to what was in their best interest despite their actual or potential reservations.

With approval in principle of amalgamation, he set about preparing the necessary forms, agreements and other papers for the companies to wind up their operations. Later, he drew up the by-laws, stock certificates and other instruments necessary for the creation of the new company. It was a major task, complicated by the size and diversity of the business and by the very real possibility of controversy or division between various personalities or groups. During June, despite a growing volume of other legal work he had to deal with, he shuttled back and forth between Calgary and Winnipeg ironing out the many wrinkles that disturbed the tailoring of amalgamation. Almost every question required a legal opinion. How should delegates be elected? Should the schedule of dividend payments be in the bylaws? What powers did the Alberta government have as a mortgage holder of much of the company's assets? Brownlee was continually being asked for opinions, for reports to the Boards, or being commandeered to serve on special committees to examine the more sensitive matters.

At one point the concerns became so serious that a special sub-committee of Crerar, Trueman, Rice-Jones and Brownlee was asked to completely re-examine the entire amalgamation proposal. Trueman argued that each Local would have to approve the terms of amalgamation just as they had voted on the principle earlier.

Even Brownlee thought this was excessively cautious and recommended that approval at the annual meetings be considered sufficient. His suggestion was accepted and it was decided to proceed, with the new company officially coming into existence on September 1, 1917. All the steps taken would be submitted to an annual meeting in November which would wind up the affairs of the old companies and be the first annual meeting of the new one. Brownlee advised all the officers to be thoroughly prepared to explain and defend their actions and took his own advice very seriously.

Meanwhile, the Brownlees were comfortably settled into their beautiful new home. A first born, John Edy Brownlee, had arrived in December of 1915 and now a second son, Alan Marshall Brownlee, was born in September, 1917. Yet even before Alan's birth, the early glow of happiness was muted. Florence had been debilitated by a severe cough, and a general lassitude which raised the spectre of tuberculosis. The pregnancy and delivery had been difficult and for months afterward she was virtually an invalid. The home life was quieted by illness, anxiety and concern. The network of acquaintances which had increased along with John's rapid rise in business and professional circles, the visits of Florence's relatives and the college friends of both, were all entertained less frequently. Now, although they would always remain the gracious host and hostess with impeccable manners, it was only the closest of friends who visited. Among these friends was Evelyn Albright. She was now a second year law student as she tried to busy herself in activity to escape the anxiety and uncertainty while Fred served overseas. As it would happen, her efforts to establish the basis for her own career would soon take on an even more poignant significance.

Albright had grown impatient with his inactivity in England and, in a desperate bid to get to the battlefront, resigned his non-commissioned officer status and, as a private, transferred to the 50th Battalion of the Canadian contingent in France. There, on October 26, 1917, warm, magnetic, idealistic Fred Albright, one of nature's noblemen, as his classmates had described him, became another rotting carcass among the thousands in the blood soaked quagmire. War propagandists tried to turn the battle at Passchendaele into an Allied victory but the men there sensed what the historians confirmed: over 700,000 dead and maimed in a net advance of two square miles of mud. During the World War I, more than 60,000 other Canadians died in an obscene slaughter which an intellectually deficient and morally bankrupt high command termed a war of attrition. Calgary mourned Albright's death. So many died but there was a special poignancy about the loss of one whose life had promised so much, who had been, as had so many who fell, a leader. It was the moral dimension of their loss which was the most difficult to fathom. Optimism, altruism, idealism, the application of Christian principles to social institutions, all received a mortal wound with the loss of so many who had embodied those qualities. Nevertheless, the ideals to which an age had once aspired did linger on and those in the farmers' movements and other reform groups redoubled their efforts in an almost frantic attempt to convince themselves and other survivors that the slaughter had not been in vain, that a just world might still be built.

Brownlee was shocked, saddened and perhaps more than a little disillusioned by his best friend's death. However, three weeks later, he was defending his report on the details of amalgamation before the first annual meeting of shareholder delegates of the U.G.G. He carefully pointed out that the directors had been guided by legal advice throughout so that everything was in order. The directors were relieved and impressed by those assurances, by his sober, detailed statements and assistance in answering the numerous questions. It would not be the last time they were indebted to him for the expertise which enabled them to defuse a potential controversy. Earlier they had expressed their regard in concrete terms naming Muir, Jephson, Adams & Brownlee as solicitors for the U.G.G.

Following final approval of amalgamation and the draft by-laws of the new company, the U.G.G. was at last approved by its creators as a fully established entity. Brownlee had played a major role in its creation, designing the instruments which produced it and through which it would operate in subsequent years. It was, in fact, one of Western Canada's largest and most diversified commercial concerns with assets well over $6,000,000. In addition to handling grain, it supplied a wide range of services and materials to farmers through such subsidiary companies as United Livestock Growers Limited and the Public Press Limited. Early in 1918, partly at Brownlee's urging, it expanded into yet another area of business with the creation of United Grain Growers Securities Limited.

Figure 2

The men who created the United Grain Growers Limited (U.G.G.) photographed in October 1916. Seated in the chair in the centre is T. A. Crerar. Seated on Crerar's left is Cecil Rice-Jones and to Crerar's right is Henry Wise Wood. Immediately behind Crerar is E. J. Fream and behind Wood is W.H. Trueman, the Winnipeg lawyer Brownlee supplanted as the legal advisor to the organization. Brownlee is in the back row on the extreme left, but his performance soon moved him to the forefront of farmers' organizations in Western Canada.

(Photo courtesy of the Glenbow Archives
NA-2663-3)

Chapter 4: Behind the Scenes

In the immediate post-war period, Brownlee, like so many others in the West, began applying his thoughts, as shaped by his training, experience and personality, to the problems of Western agriculture and Western development generally. Some were led to advocate political solutions such as the Non-Partisan League or the low-tariff element of the Liberals. Others were attracted to such monetary reforms as inflating the money supply or having government become a commercial lender. Brownlee kept himself informed about the turbulent ideas for reform but his own proposals were definitely not radical.

He suggested the U.G.G. expand into insurance, investment and real estate and Rice-Jones, now Vice-President and General Manager, gave him ready encouragement. The support for such an initiative resulted from the continuing hostility of the business community, particularly Eastern Canadian manufacturers, to the farmers' companies. When they attempted to sell binder twine, no Canadian manufacturer would supply them, when they opened a farm machinery sales division, customs regulations were juggled to force their costs above competitors' prices, when the U.G.G. proposed selling hail and other insurance, no Canadian underwriters would cooperate but instead lobbied all levels of government to refuse to license the U.G.G. or its employees. Insurance regulations, the Hail Underwriters' Association claimed, prevented the U.G.G. from offering their planned Local rebates on the sale of hail insurance to members because each member was, by definition, a shareholder in the Company.

This position irked Brownlee, who was firmly committed to the principle of reasonableness in business, and began to give him some insight into the grievances of farmers. However, he ascribed exploitive, manipulative and hostile practices to the moral and intellectual shortcomings of particular individuals rather than to any systemic practice. He took the battle directly to the opposition.

"When in Regina, I had occasion to meet Mr. Smart ... vice-president of the Hail Underwriters' Association," he wrote to Rice-Jones, going on to explain how he had pointed out that the status of U.G.G. Securities Company, as a subsidiary, negated the underwriters' objection since the junior company was at arm's length from a shareholder in the parent company. He was confident that he had forced "them into a very awkward position" as "in order to refuse our position they must necessarily take the stand that no company whose shareholders are farmers can write insurance." He was confident that the underwriters would "hesitate a long while before taking such an extreme stand." He concluded, with his characteristic faith in reasonableness, that once the "real misunderstanding" had been cleared away, there was no reason why "a friendly relationship could not exist."

Meanwhile, the U.G.G. Securities' business was slow to develop, due to the hostility of the financial establishment. For example, early in 1919, the Company attempted to place a series of debentures. Winnipeg brokers insisted on a "floating charge" on the trust mortgage securing the debentures. F. M. Black, Company treasurer, was experienced in financial circles and knew that a "floating charge" was not normal practice. The Board decided to by-pass the brokers and try to secure the funds directly from private interests. Black and Brownlee were chosen to go East and "take up the matter with private parties." Accompanied by Rice-Jones they made the rounds of Toronto financial houses but could find no one prepared to deal with them directly. Rice-Jones made a side trip to Ottawa to confer with Crerar, in the throes of resigning from the Union Cabinet which he had joined two years earlier. Black went on to Montreal where he met the same uncooperative attitude as in Toronto. Eventually, facing time pressure for the funds, he was forced to begin negotiating with a broker, J.M. Mackie of United Financial Corporation. Mackie insisted the debentures would be hard to place and that a special "floating charge" would be necessary. Black countered with a draft contract, prepared by Brownlee, which specifically rejected the "floating charge". The negotiations broke off and in the interlude, Black, entirely by chance, met an old friend, T. B. Macaulay, who had become General Manager of Sun Life Assurance Company. He told Black that his company had already agreed to purchase the entire U.G.G. series from United Financial at the price asked. When Black returned to find Mackie still pleading that the issue would be difficult to place, his disgust with Mackie and his ilk, a disgust all too common across the West in relations with Eastern financiers, was hard to conceal. He was unable to breach the confidentiality of his information but used it, nevertheless, to take a strong stand and eventually the contract, as Brownlee had drafted it, was signed.

Meanwhile, in Toronto, Brownlee was involved in an even more delicate transaction being carried on by J.R. Murray, the Assistant General Manager. Murray was one of the shrewdest business heads with the U.G.G. but that shrewdness would, in a few years, take him out of the Company and back to the private grain trade, leaving many bitter former associates behind. However, in June, 1919, Murray's task was to dispose of the Company's shares in the Home Bank. Home had become the banker for the G.G.G. in its early years when the other chartered banks refused it a line of credit. For a time, Home Bank had attracted the attention of reformers interested in democratizing a bank by creating a broadly based group of shareholders. The G.G.G., in its own right, and most of its directors, particularly Crerar, had purchased the Bank's stock to give the lead in cementing a union between organized farmers and at least one financial institution. By 1919, though, Crerar had serious doubts about the Bank's management and its financial strength. He and other U.G.G. officers faced a dilemma, however. If they made their doubts public, they might precipitate the very collapse of Home Bank stock they had begun to fear. On the other hand, if they took no action and the Bank failed, they would have failed to protect their own shareholders and other stock holders and depositors.

The first step, then, was to dispose of the stock the U.G.G. held, as quietly as possible, so as not to damage the market. Murray discovered the Toronto financial community was completely unconcerned about Home's condition and quickly found a buyer, one Daly, who wanted stock as part of his own scheme to gain control of the Bank. Black returned to finalize the sale. Murray, anxious to dispose of the stock yet fearful that at any moment the market might falter, urged Black to have Brownlee draft a sales agreement to insure the terms of payment were honoured. He was afraid that if the market for the shares collapsed before the payments were completed, the U.G.G. might be caught by the double liability clause of the Bank Act. Black thought the less said the better, and refused to risk creating suspicion by insisting on a strictly prepared document. Brownlee inquired about

Daly's financial condition, and, finding it good, agreed with Black that Daly was likely to honour the terms of payment. The stock was held in trust until payment was completed, on December 29, 1919. The next U.G.G. Annual Report mentioned the sale of 1,028 shares of Home Bank stock at its par value of $100 per share. The management breathed a large, collective sigh of relief.

The young knights of the U.G.G. had acquitted themselves well against the dragons of Eastern finance. Brownlee was confidant, perhaps over-confidant, that approached skillfully they could be dealt with reasonably. He was to learn that these dragons were much less "reasonable" when they were not as well fed.

Brownlee took advantage of his stint in the East to visit his parents. Their financial position was not good. The Progress while fulfilling for William, was not supporting them and they were being hard pressed by their mortgage holder. To supplement their income, William had taken the position of Treasurer for Moore Township. Then, the Progress building burned to the ground and while William salvaged some of his equipment, his days as a newspaper publisher were over. Obligingly, the Township Clerk soon retired and William embarked on a new career as Clerk-Treasurer of Moore Township.

When John returned to Calgary, he was accompanied by his sister, Maude, who would now live with the family and help care for the two young boys as Florence prepared for the birth of her third child. That experience was even more difficult and the outcome tragic, as the baby daughter died. The physical and psychological effects of the episode were traumatic and subsequent complications of a tubercular infection left Florence a near invalid for several years. Maude befriended Florence and looked after her and the rest of the family. Shortly she was assisted by a full-time maid. The Brownlees were to employ one, more or less continuously, for the next sixteen years.

While events at home had taken a tragic turn, Brownlee's professional career was rapidly progressing. In July, 1919, the U.G.G. recognized the growing volume and value of his services by offering him the general solicitorship of the Company at a salary of $6,000 per year. The offer was an attractive one and he accepted immediately, leaving his partners Muir, Jephson and Adams. The variety of his legal work was now immense. There were individual actions against the Company to defend, large financial dealings to supervise and wrangles with various associations and off-shoots of government to superintend. There were even times when his opinion was sought on matters of state, particularly when Crerar began to figure again in the political headlines of the day.

Besides his legal work, Brownlee also pursued his commercial interests by developing U.G.G. Securities. When the business volume of the subsidiary merited it having its own general manager, he was the prime candidate. After some delay, on September 29, 1919, he was appointed with a salary adjustment to $7,500 to reflect his increased responsibilities. He moved into Suite 320 of the Lougheed Building, the one-quarter square block, six story commercial bloc which was the pride of Calgary.

That winter, as part of senior management, he took part in the week long training seminar for department heads and junior management. He led a session on, "The Company and the Public" and, in characteristic fashion, proceeded to divide his topic systematically under various headings. There was an echo of his college report on the Young Men's Christian Association conference when he cautioned that there was an onus on all of them "to correctly interpret the spirit and ideal of the Company. ... every man has a certain amount of influence ... and it will never be known when a small courtesy will bring big returns for the Company." It was an interesting shift. Where once the ultimate concern he had said was "the higher spiritual values" it was now "big returns for the Company". When society drifted in a secular, materialist direction, he would not be left behind.

Despite Brownlee's promotion to senior management, events were now to reveal that his place within the U.G.G. was less important to his immediate future than his associations, formed as a sideline, with the occupants of the second floor of the Lougheed Building -- the officers and staff of the United Farmers of Alberta. In 1920, the U.F.A. was nearing the crest of its immense wave of popular support. Membership had doubled within three years to more than 30,000 farmers with 4,000 farm women enrolled in the United Farm Women of Alberta (U.F.W.A.). The U.F.A. Annual Convention had eclipsed the provincial legislature as the most significant and exciting policy making body in the province. U.F.A. ranks were glutted with individuals with urgent concerns for social reform: from prohibition to pest control, from communal property to consumer cooperatives. With the zeal of those who have applied an ethical critique to society and found it wanting, the optimism of those who believe that education and legislation can create a more just society, and with rhetoric super-charged with the slogans and sacrifices of the War; the members of the U.F.A. sought, with the intensity of those swept up in a religious revival, to use their association as an instrument to usher in a millennial-like age.

Brownlee, baffled and embarrassed by their emotional intensity could not help but observe that "the U.F.A. and its policies became almost a religion with many of its supporters and it is not without significance that one Sunday each year was designated U.F.A. Sunday and was ... observed as such throughout the whole of Alberta."

The enthusiasm for reform spread quickly. At the Annual Convention of January, 1919, it completely overwhelmed Wood's rear-guard action against direct U.F.A. involvement in politics. The momentum obliterated distinctions between federal and provincial politics and Alberta farmers suddenly found themselves in their first election foray -- a provincial by-election at Cochrane. Wood was the key-note speaker at the nominating meeting which chose Alex Moore as the Farmer candidate. A Calgary Herald reporter covering the meeting was struck by H. W.'s analysis of society as "we versus they". The report, distributed across the country on the wire service, catapulted Wood, the U.F.A. and their ideas into the limelight of national controversy. The sharp criticism of Wood's philosophy by the daily press, traditional antagonist of the organized farmers, rallied even greater grassroots support behind the farmers' movement.

Brownlee's work for the U.F.A. was varied. For a time he wrote a legal advice column in the short lived Western Independent. Farmers from across the province wrote in with questions of law and, for a dollar, received a general, preliminary opinion. He also advised the Executive frequently, sometimes about dealings with the provincial or federal governments, more often as to the legal implications of one or more of the vast welter of resolutions which surfaced each year. In the course of such work he encountered the leading figures of the U.F.A., individuals with whom his life would soon be inextricably bound.

There was William Irvine, a defrocked Unitarian minister whose editorship of The Nutcracker and fiery platform eloquence had led the Non-Partisan League to a bold challenge of the U.F.A. He was now editing the Western Independent and continuing his exhausting speaking schedule in an effort to secure a leading role in the movement. His publication, in 1920, of The Farmers in Politics was an important event in the farmers' political crusade. Brownlee regarded it as vastly over-written. He eyed Irvine, as he did all emotional and dramatic public figures, skeptically. He assumed his rhetorical flourishes disguised from most what was at bottom a rash and irresponsible approach to public issues. Irvine, for his part, regarded Brownlee as a cold fish whose much vaunted prudence and moderation resulted merely from his lack of any real support of the farmers.

Another contact was Irene Parlby, founder of the first U.F.W.A. Local and a leader of the farm women. Along with her Oxford educated husband, Walter, she was more at home with Shakespeare than with The Farmers in Politics. Nevertheless, her air of refined gentility did not diminish her fierce advocacy of social reforms, particularly legal protection for women and children. She relied on Brownlee for advice about the legal technicalities of reform. He overestimated her naiveté but she tolerated his slightly patronizing approach in deference to his expertise.

Yet another contact was Herbert Greenfield, a hale-fellow-well-met farmer from Westlock who chaired the 1920 and 1921 annual conventions and was the chief organizer of the dramatically successful membership drive of November 1 and 2, 1920, in which literally every farm in Alberta was canvassed. Greenfield's buoyant personality and fund of humourous stories made him an engaging character. To Brownlee, he was a warm hearted soul who typified the best qualities of the well-meaning, down to earth farmers. Greenfield, not a penetrating thinker, accepted Brownlee as an important adjunct to the U.F.A. and was suitably impressed with his legal talents without troubling himself with trying to understand them.

Brownlee's most significant and closest association remained, however, with Henry Wise Wood. Wood enjoyed having Brownlee to act as a sounding board for his fertile fund of ideas. He could bring the background and point of view of those Wood usually found arrayed against him, yet be a trusted and sympathetic friend. Brownlee felt privileged to be exposed to the insight and experience of "H.W".

Wood might strongly eschew party politics but no one in Alberta could better capture a farmers' meeting or guide a controversial resolution through a stormy convention. His strength of leadership was based on his sincerity, his integrity and his unquestioned ability to articulate to farmers and for farmers their concerns and aspirations. Brownlee was too pragmatic to adopt Wood's vision but there was a great deal one might learn from Wood about the farm movement and how to lead it. Brownlee was an observant student.

Throughout 1919 and 1920, Wood was called, increasingly, to address U.F.A. meetings across the province, particularly in the southern and eastern grain belt. As often as not, he was accompanied by Brownlee. Usually they traveled by train but in the summer, if the roads were good, they set out by automobile. Brownlee was a "motor" enthusiast and while he took no interest in the mechanical side of things, he was to enjoy driving for the rest of his life. What a picture they were, jolting along a dusty road, Wood, his black bowler hat perched on the back of his bald head, draping his lanky frame casually against the door, one frayed elbow of his dark brown striped suit stuck out into the hot wind, eyeing the passing crops while he threw out a mixture of speculations about the nature of God, the deviousness of the Canadian Manufacturer's Association and the incidence of grasshoppers, all within the same sentence. Beside him, Brownlee, upright behind the steering wheel, his long legs working the pedals, replying to Wood in his dry measured voice with its curious rising inflection at the end of each sentence. Then they would come bumping into a country school yard where a few cars and a larger number of wagons, buggies and teams were drawn up before the school house. There would be an eager rush to greet "H.W." and, as an afterthought, Brownlee too. Then they would be inside the schoolhouse where farmers and their wives squeezed uncomfortably into their children's ink stained desks or perched on the few extra wooden benches brought in for the occasion. A short business meeting of the Local would follow and, with the crowd still a little restless, Brownlee would give some statistics about growing membership, review the services offered by the U.F.A. central office in Calgary, and answer a question about a farmer's legal protection in dealing with a machinery company. Then, the highlight of the evening -- the President himself. Brownlee would settle back and watch Wood present his characteristic mix of salty humour, rural idiom and religious inspiration. The weathered, care-ridden faces would drink in how they, through their farm movement, were part of a vast plan of God's in which conflict, competition and injustice were going to be replaced by harmony, cooperation and equity for all. History was unfolding according to immutable laws designed by God and they, the farmers of Alberta, were in the forefront. Electing other farmers to represent them was one step but more important was the strength of the U.F.A. which must educate and lead by exemplifying the democratic, social justice they wished to bring to society at large.

At the end of the evening there would be hot tea and coffee, some hearty sandwiches, and a buzz of conversation about crops and old party corruption, fund raising and the tariff. Finally, Wood and Brownlee would climb back in their car and putt off into the night, leaving behind another knot of farm people with renewed pride in their weighty role in reforming the world and renewed hope that through the U.F.A. they could help create a new and more just society.

As U.F.A. political activity increased, Brownlee launched his own personal study of the "Political side of the Organized Farmers' work." He set about in his characteristic way -- collecting,, as much information as possible. In October, 1920, he had a long discussion with Thomas Crerar who, since resigning from the Cabinet, was part of a small group occupying the cross-benches of the House of Commons. Through Crerar, Brownlee obtained an introduction to E. C. Drury, Ontario's new premier, following the startling election victory of the United Farmers of Ontario. Crerar also alerted Charles Stewart, the Liberal premier of Alberta, to Brownlee's interest in politics and arranged a meeting between the two.

Brownlee, recommended by Crerar and trusted counselor of the most influential and potentially the most powerful group in Alberta, received a more attentive audience from Stewart than he had years earlier as a neophyte lawyer representing the A.F.C.E.C.

Brownlee, too, adopted a different tone and described quite frankly the momentum carrying the U.F.A. into provincial as well as federal politics. Wood and most U.F.A. executives, he advised, were opposed to provincial involvement but the pressure from the membership was so strong it could not be diverted without some changes in the government. He assured Stewart that he, personally, was well regarded and there were no serious complaints against his administration. "With some changes in the Cabinet," he confided, "there was a possibility that he would have no opposition from the farm organization." But, he cautioned Stewart, "under no circumstances should he call a snap election as that would be taken as a challenge." Stewart was a veteran politician and he took this gratuitous advice as a thinly veiled threat. He reacted with outward calm but inside he raged. Brownlee remained unaware that he had sown the seeds of a vicious enmity. Charles Stewart would devote much of his future career to thwarting Brownlee whenever possible.

Brownlee's experiences had made him one of the best informed people in Canada on the political aspects of the farmers' movement but it was an academic kind of knowledge. He would never fully understand the emotional depths and undercurrents on both sides of the controversies ahead.

* * *

Brownlee was shortly to make strong claims for his political virginity but his study of political issues and his rising place in the farmers' councils were enough to propel him into the political gossip of the day as a possible federal candidate. Indeed, his status within the city of Calgary was growing. He was still an active Mason and had taken an interest in golf, both on the links and on the Board of Directors of St. Andrew's Golf and Country Club. He had joined the Kiwanis Club and was still secretary of what was now an all-Alberta chapter of Victoria College alumni. Finally, he was one of the most successful and promising lawyers in the province and, when the U.G.G. increased his salary to $9,000 as of January 1, 1921, he was one of the best paid.

His salary reflected his growing stature within the U.G.G. He circumvented the ostracism of Canadian insurance companies by concluding an agreement with Car and General Corporation of

England and got the insurance branch growing rapidly, first in hail and later in fire and accident insurance. As well, insuring the Company's hundreds of elevators, coal sheds and agents' houses, as well as the thousands of carloads of grain, was a major item. Other dimensions of U.G.G. Securities' business were hard hit by the impact of the sharp, post-war agricultural depression. U.G.G. shares moved slowly. Floating debentures continued to face obstacles thrown up by Eastern financial interests. Administering farmer estates proved more complex than first believed and Brownlee had to make several trips to Eastern Canada to study the operations of trust companies there. Most disappointingly, the post-war settlement boom, which he and others had expected, did not materialize. Indeed, with the economic decline some regions lost population. By early 1921, both the Calgary and Winnipeg offices of the Land Department (opened in 1919) were closed, having lost $5,000 each the previous year. Brownlee put the best possible face on this disappointing showing in the annual report, explaining to shareholders that the losses resulted mainly from failure to recover capital costs. Once these were covered, he argued, the lower overhead would mean operations in the black. Crerar was less optimistic and insisted that each subsidiary be self-supporting. The activities of U.G.G. Securities were cut back sharply pending the return of better days.

Brownlee and Crerar maintained, however, a close relationship. Crerar thought Brownlee was well-informed and the most discreet and discerning person attached to the U.F.A. He used him frequently as a source of information or as a reliable channel of communication with Alberta leaders whose attitudes Crerar never adequately grasped. Sometimes he asked Brownlee's advice on how to approach them and in his replies it became clear that Brownlee had come to think of himself as both a part of the farmers' movement and as a Westerner. He had been in the West over a decade and was deeply stirred by its potential. He had become an able and ready defender of its people. Not an emotional man, John Brownlee came to love the West.

Brownlee's special relationship with Crerar, at this time, and his interest in politics came together to play an important role in the famous Medicine Hat federal by-election. This campaign was rightly regarded as a pivotal battle in Canadian political history.

Crerar, was capturing attention as at least the nominal leader of a new third element in Canadian politics, beginning to be dubbed "the Progressives" by the press. Crerar, himself, recognized the importance of the contest and wrote to Brownlee even before the by-election was called urging him to advise Wood and Greenfield (now Vice-President of the U.F.A.) to take steps "to secure some sort of organization in the City" of Medicine Hat and to make a definite attempt to cooperate with "the Labour men."

It soon became apparent that the future of the Dominion government was directly related to the by-election results. It was now obvious that Farmer candidates would play a major, perhaps a determining role in the impending general election. All sides agreed the Medicine Hat contest was a bell-weather, the first real measure of the effectiveness of organized farmers in politics. The U.G.G. was the country's leading farmer organization and its president touted by some as the next Prime Minister. It is not surprising then that U.G.G. officials suspected political motives behind the disclosures, beginning in April, of irregularities at the U.G.G.'s Lakehead terminal elevators. A Royal Commission was quickly impaneled and Brownlee, as the Company's solicitor, appeared at a series of erratically scheduled hearings across the West. All through May, 1921, the charges dribbled forth but the most serious ones emerged at a surprise hearing in Fort William on Saturday, June 4. Former employees at the terminal were produced who testified about bins with false bottoms, bribes of railway employees and gross overages sold at large profits. The fact that these allegations concerned the period 1912 to 1914, confirmed the suspicion that they were timed to maximize their political impact. Brownlee was called to an emergency meeting of U.G.G. directors and senior management to discuss the Company's reaction to the charges. The confidence of the farmers had to be maintained and while the main concern was the future of the business, the political implications of the farmers' confidence were not far from their minds.

They decided to launch their own investigation and on that basis, Brownlee obtained an injunction halting the hearings on the ground that the Company needed time to collect information before it could reply to the charges. This move prevented further formal disclosures until after the Medicine Hat vote. Crerar then tried to calm farmers by announcing there would be the "fullest possible investigation", by outside parties if necessary, and that all information would be divulged to farmers in the frankest manner.

Voting in Medicine Hat was now only days away. Crerar urged Brownlee to use all his channels to insure that U.F.A. Candidate, Robert Gardiner, was alert for any attempt by his opponents to pit town voters against the rural, or the northern part of the constituency, against the south. He declared, revealing his own concerns, that the government forces would focus their attack on "Wood's economic class group theory. . . . This should be clearly avoided and the Government's record attacked and attacked vigorously." Crerar was obviously anxious about the result but when the votes were tallied, Gardiner had scored one of the largest electoral victories in Canadian history. The Farmers' movement across the country, and especially in Alberta, was exultant. For many U.F.A. members, winning the urban polls in Medicine Hat was an amazing and unexpected confirmation of the tremendous momentum of their ideals. Almost all were unaware of the small, behind-the-scenes, but not insignificant role John Brownlee had played in that victory.

The Medicine Hat triumph was a tremendous, though somewhat superfluous, boost to the enthusiasm of the U.F.A., now in a frenzy of preparation for a provincial election. Premier Stewart had ignored Brownlee's warning and called a snap election, for July 18, 1921. If it was an attempt to catch the U.F.A. unprepared, it was a gross misjudgment. Although not formally structured for a provincial campaign, the 35,000 U.F.A. members were the most intensely organized group in the province. Within two weeks, forty-four constituency associations, on their own initiative, had nominated candidates.

At this point, with the Medicine Hat by-election over, the Royal Grain Inquiry set over until the fall, and the U.F.A. fully preoccupied with an election campaign, Brownlee left for a month's holidays in Victoria. Before leaving Calgary, he chatted with Wood about the upcoming vote. H.W. believed the U.F.A. might elect as many as twenty; he hoped for no more as he thought farmers should merely have a strong voice in the legislature, not form the government. Soon Wood knew his prediction was wrong. What he feared was, it appeared, about to happen. He sent a telegram to

Brownlee reading simply, "The tide is running high. Your services will be required. Be ready." Somewhat startled by the wire, Brownlee was on hand at the office of the Victoria Colonist as the election results from Alberta came in. These were even more unexpected. The U.F.A. won 38 of the 61 legislative seats.

Soon there was another wire from Wood, urging him to return. Feeling the need of his holiday after a demanding year and thinking there was little he could do, he declined. However, another telegram, even more urgent, prompted his reluctant return. When he arrived in Calgary he was amazed to find that Wood wanted him to take on a new job -- the Premier of Alberta. Wood was, of course, the obvious candidate but he declined for three reasons. First, he felt he was not qualified; secondly, that he was too old; and thirdly, and more positively, he believed the presidency of the U.F.A. was a more important job. To many, proposing Brownlee, after they had just finished campaigning so strongly for authentic farmer representation in government, was inexplicable. To Wood the choice was obvious. Leading the government required someone skilled in the law, competent in administrative technicalities and confident in dealing with the other, non-farmer groups in society. Brownlee met all those qualifications. The 38 elected members could represent the farmers' viewpoint strongly and accurately but, to Wood, none of them was as qualified to lead the government as was their solicitor - John Brownlee.

What most critics failed to understand was that Wood saw the provincial government as becoming one more department of a much larger and potentially more influential and significant farmers' movement. He could not convince Brownlee to accept his nomination. As it emerged, Brownlee's pragmatic assessment was correct. Many farmer members-elect would not have accepted a lawyer for leader. The few who knew Brownlee respected his abilities but they all reflected grassroots attitudes which confirmed the shrewdness of his decision.

Other possibilities were considered, including George Hoadley, the only one with significant legislative experience. However, Hoadley had sat as a Conservative and was thus unacceptable for a group which had campaigned so strongly against the old line parties and the party system. Finally, the only choice appeared to be Herbert Greenfield. He reluctantly accepted and began consulting the members-elect about a possible Cabinet slate.

Brownlee seemed the logical choice for Attorney General but some of the more radical questioned the need for any lawyer to be in the government. As a measure of his necessity, they called him in to provide an accurate answer to the question of whether the Attorney General had to be a lawyer. He replied in his usual dry, measured way that there was nothing constitutionally forcing such a choice but, he went on, if the Attorney General were not a lawyer he would be "dependent almost entirely on the advice of his deputy minister or other members of his staff since his duties consist almost entirely of matters of law." They were all to discover that the Attorney General's duties could go far beyond mere "matters of law" but his answer convinced even the most radical that he should be named. As soon as the meeting adjourned, Greenfield asked Brownlee to accept the Attorney General's portfolio. He asked for time and, indeed, there was much to consider.

For one of the leading lawyers in Calgary, accepting a Cabinet post would mean a substantial reduction in income. He would have to leave his beautifully situated home and move his near invalid wife, and two sons almost ready to start school, to Edmonton. He would have to leave his associates and his career with the U.G.G. In return, he would accept an uncertain future. No Farmer government had yet survived a second election. The almost complete lack of legislative experience in the U.F.A. would mean that the Ministers, and especially Brownlee, would have a heavy load. There were extremely high expectations among the rank-and-file about what the new government could and should accomplish. Friends, including Crerar, counseled caution.

On the affirmative side of the debate, which Brownlee quite formally went through, in his mind, was the sense of duty to society which he had been taught since infancy. As well, there was his loyalty to the U.F.A. and to his friend, Wood, and, although he would not admit it, the sense of achievement at being the King's advisor on matters of law for the Province of Alberta, before his thirty-eighth birthday. He decided to accept.

Figure 3

Typical crowd of rural Albertans waiting to meet Henry Wise
Wood and John Brownlee.
United Farmers of Alberta members listened spell-bound as "H.W."
explained to them their role in the divinely inspired reform
movements which were ushering in a new age of co-operation and
social justice for all.
Brownlee answered legal questions and reported membership
statistics..

(Photo courtesy of the Glenbow Archives
NA-3657-6)

Chapter 5: Attorney General of Alberta

The North Saskatchewan River sweeps languorously through the city of Edmonton. In August, the pebbled sand bars emerge and on them gather the Franklin's gulls and killdeer for rest and recreation and to probe the mysteries of the insect world. From time to time their investigations are interrupted by such clamourous goings and comings as was the train bringing Brownlee to the capital, which wheezed and rumbled and squeaked its way across the top of the High Level Bridge. He saw the explosion of white dots on the sand bars far below him but his eye was drawn to the imposing sandstone columns and dome of the Legislative Building, soon to be his new workplace.

The next morning,, August 11, 1921, Greenfield met the U.F.A. members-elect to inform them of the arrangements for the change of government and to present his "nominations" for the Cabinet. The first priorities of the new government, he declared to applause, would be to prepare "a complete financial statement of all the affairs of this province, so that we may know exactly what conditions were financially at the date we took over," and to devise "some scheme" to assist those in the dried out areas of Southern Alberta which was not a "dole" or "relief" but "actual Employment to carry them over the difficult period."

He was about to move on to the announcement of his Cabinet selections when he was interrupted by Lorne Proudfoot, a lean, hawk-faced veteran of Independent Farmers' political action. He asked Greenfield to explain the principles which had guided the selection. The press had reported that the Labour group was to be represented but, he asked, would any of the fourteen Liberals elected be invited "to represent their group" in the Cabinet. Greenfield ventured his opinion that none of them would accept such an invitation but, he hastened to add, the point should be discussed. Proudfoot declared:

> We are starting out much after the manner of the old parties. I think if we could do away with the Official Opposition and instead get all parties to cooperate in carrying on the government, it might be better. I would like

to see an invitation sent to the Liberal group asking them to fill at least one or two positions in the Cabinet. If they ... carried on a policy of obstruction, they could be removed.

In this halting, homey yet extremely earnest way, just as one farmer might suggest to his fellows how a threshing crew might better be deployed or a ditch widened to end spring flooding; Proudfoot delivered his challenge to decades of British parliamentary practice. What he, and those who thought like him, had in mind was a model of government comparable to the board of directors of a company. In fact, they had campaigned for what they termed a "business administration". No company was managed, they believed, by one party of the directors proposing policies and another party constantly criticizing, condemning and advocating different policies. No board meeting was characterized by staged debate punctuated by heckles, catcalls and votes of non-confidence in the executive committee. Differences there might be but these were worked out in over-the-table discussions on a man to man basis, in an atmosphere of reasoned persuasion and hard nosed bargaining; not amidst juvenile theatrics and intentionally perverse negativism. The business model, used on local school boards and municipal councils on which Proudfoot and several others had experience, would serve them better than the old, apparently artificial parliamentary system. What worked for a company as large and diverse as the U.G.G., they believed, should also work for the province whose business, the competent administration of the joint projects of the citizenry, was as vital to its citizens as was the success of any company to its shareholders.

Irene Parlby pointed out to Proudfoot that the Liberal Party was neither an economic group nor democratically organized. Thus, only Farmers and Labour qualified under the U.F.A.'s definition of a "group". Her observation led to an apparent consensus that since they had been elected in the majority, it was their responsibility to form a government.

Greenfield then announced his Cabinet nominations: Vernor Smith, Minister of Railways and Telephones; George Hoadley, Minister of Agriculture; Richard Reid, Minister of Municipal Affairs and Public Health; Perren Baker, Minister of Education; Alex Ross, Minister of Public Works, and John

Brownlee, Attorney General. Greenfield himself would be Provincial Treasurer, temporarily he indicated, as the new Government hoped "to go outside and get a real financial expert to take over this portfolio, which at this time is the most important part of the Government's work." The "outside expert" they had in mind was the U.G.G.'s F. M. Black but they were unable to persuade him to leave Winnipeg.

Greenfield spoke briefly in support of each of his nominations. Of his choice for Attorney General he said simply, "I felt that I would have in Mr. Brownlee a man that I knew from personal experience, and a man whose judgment the Executive Officers of the United Grain Growers both here and in Winnipeg, had leaned heavily upon during the last few years." He concluded with a comment about his belief in the equality of the sexes and his view that the Cabinet would not have the advantage of all the important viewpoints if it did not contain a woman. With that he announced, to hearty applause, that Irene Parlby had accepted his nomination for Minister Without Portfolio.

After the noon adjournment Brownlee was at last invited to join the meeting which resumed on a note indicating that Proudfoot had been doing more than eating lunch. He returned more confidently to his earlier theme, moving formally that "the elected members of the U.F.A. group ... deem it advisable that our leader ... offer a part of the portfolios to the Liberal group." An attempt to table this motion passed by a majority of only two votes so Greenfield urged that the whole matter be reconsidered. As the same ground was covered again it was apparent that a slight majority supported the traditional course Greenfield was following while a stubborn minority held out for the U.F.A.'s pledged objective of "group" representation. Finally, an apparent compromise was agreed to by affirming that the U.F.A. would continue seeking group representation while recognizing that much of society was not yet organized into democratically structured economic groups.

Proudfoot and his supporters had lost the battle. They were handicapped, as the less traditionalist members would continue to be, by their lack of influence, their relative lack of articulateness and a sense of insecurity and deference in the face of institutions they believed in their hearts needed to be reformed.

They were in the main actual "dirt farmers" and they represented what some would term the "radical element" of the U.F.A. They were held in check, with few exceptions, by the "conservative" element of the group which quickly came to be led and dominated by those such as Hoadley, the Conservative, and Brownlee, the lawyer, who were, in fact, additions to the U.F.A.

The members-elect were unaware of that future, though, and proceeded to discuss and vote upon Greenfield's "nominations". In true grass-roots-democracy fashion, each proposed Minister was asked to leave the meeting room in the MacDonald Hotel and wander in the hallway while the merits of his or her choice were considered and voted upon. From there it was an easy matter to fall into their accustomed practice at U.F.A. conventions of passing resolutions urging the Government to specific action. A motion favouring a government guarantee of a $600,000 bond issue by the United Irrigation District was well under consideration before Hoadley declared the meeting had no power to pledge the Legislature or the Government. Later, Brownlee intervened sharply in a debate about whether nominations of Justices of the Peace should come from U.F.A. Locals or the Provincial Political Association of the U.F.A. "The whole matter," he advised coolly, "is entirely under the Department of the Attorney General."

Such ideas for the increased democratization of political institutions were not that easily quashed, though, and as Brownlee was to discover, they would continue to re-surface in the years ahead. These first few meetings had revealed most of the various currents of opinion and the differing basic assumptions within the U.F.A. Brownlee never supported any of the so-called radical proposals. He was to have his hands full at times defending what he judged to be the "sane" approach but by his commanding presence, unquestioned superior expertise and knowledge of issues, he was able, to a remarkable degree, to hold the lid on the pressure for substantive reform.

* * *

Almost immediately after being sworn in, on August 13, 1921, the Cabinet met to consider the plight of the victims of depression and drought in the dry areas of the south. Some families, especially those in areas experiencing a third successive year of almost total crop failure, required immediate relief. Brownlee suggested the Alberta Provincial Police identify cases of destitution and starvation. He also thought the new government "might hold a Conference with the Judges and Masters-in-Chambers ... to see how far the courts were prepared to go" to avoid the added hardships of mortgage foreclosures.

Beyond these immediate needs, however, there remained the larger problem of those who, more because of low prices than low yields, were unable to support themselves and their farming operations. Particularly troublesome were the debt charges, most contracted at the high prices and high interest rates of the war years and many contracted at the urging of the national government's call for large scale increases in agricultural production as part of the war effort. Now over-extended farmers were trapped paying high prices for financing while the prices of their own commodities had taken a serious drop. Brownlee was one of those who began looking for long term solutions. The first step in such a search, for him, was to collect all possible information bearing on the problem. As part of this study, he immediately began to familiarize himself with his new Department.

Early Monday morning, August 15, 1921, Brownlee strode up the steps of the Legislative Building, across the Italian marble floor of the great rotunda where the splashing hiss of the fountain echoed through the giant stairwell to the dome high above. On the second floor he followed the dark mahogany paneled hallway to the East Wing where he met his Deputy Minister, A.G. Browning and the rest of the legal and clerical staff. Browning had already served two years under the Liberals but Brownlee firmly supported the U.F.A.'s commitment to a civil service based on merit rather than political affiliation. There were to be few changes in senior personnel. Beyond the Buildings, a large network of people were also now under his jurisdiction: Crown prosecutors and Crown agents across the province, the staff of the two land titles offices and of the provincial jails and mental asylums, and the 200 officers and men of the Alberta Provincial Police (A.P.P.). The Courts were, of course, independent but Brownlee was the Minister responsible for providing them with the means of carrying out their duties.

Extensive as were these strictly departmental responsibilities, the major demand on his time and energy was as legal counsel to the Cabinet. Virtually every issue seemed to require his expertise, from drafting legislation to advising on a certain policy's legal and constitutional implications. It soon became apparent that all his Cabinet colleagues would rely on him heavily, not only for advice on "matters of law" but also for such routine guidance as how to frame a letter or what position to take when being interviewed by a certain group. Far from the least dependent was Greenfield. Within days of taking office, Brownlee was providing, the Premier with the most detailed advice. For example, he asked Brownlee if he should accept the presidency of a "league for better citizenry". Brownlee firmly lectured his naive Premier on the political facts of life telling him he should give only a "general expression of sympathy" and avoid any further commitment as: "In the first place you have no time. In the second place, if the public displays no interest it would be better if you were not associated with it ... In the third place, you can very reasonably take the position that this movement will gain strength and have more effect if it is entirely a movement of the electors." Such sage advice was only the beginning of a constant flow of advice to Greenfield. Soon almost every piece of significant or controversial correspondence was being referred to him and he obligingly provided suggested draft replies. Increasingly, these suggestions went out over Greenfield's signature unchanged.

Greenfield and the other Ministers also delegated to Brownlee the responsibility of making statements on such controversial issues as Prohibition. Alberta had had Prohibition of a sort for over five years but the Liberals' Act was full of loopholes and the U.F.A. were pledged to tighten the legislation and implement the will of the people. Especially in rural areas, this heavily favoured more stringent liquor control. Brownlee, on one of his weekend visits to his family, still in Calgary, was button-holed by the press, anxious for some controversy about new liquor legislation. He handled it smoothly, declaring: "I do not propose to make any hurried or ill-considered move, either in legislation or in the administration of the present Act. The Department is at work compiling information and analyzing and comparing the liquor laws of the other provinces". Concluding that he had met with such interest groups as the "medical and druggists' associations" he firmly declined to recommend any policy until "this investigation is completed."

While he was busy becoming an expert on literally every major issue facing the government, it was necessary to tidy up the loose ends of his previous career. The U.G.G. Board agreed to relieve him of his duties as general manager of U.G.G. Securities but he would retain the position of Company solicitor, although not for long as salaried counsel. He soon organized his own firm, John E. Brownlee & Company, which acted under retainer for both the U.G.G. and the U.F.A. He secured the services of his former tutor, James Muir, K.C., now retired from his own practice, as advisory counsel. Soon he added T.C. Rankine and, later, William Hall as staff and then partners. The Alberta Bar Association recommended Brownlee for King's Counsel and thus he, himself became a "K.C."

On the personal side of things, he was living in a suite at the MacDonald and commuting by train to Calgary each weekend. Maude was still living with the family and helping to care for Florence and the boys although she also was employed as a stenographer by the U.G.G. Florence was often confined to bed and was subject to colds and viral infections. She missed her family and the social life in the East and, unlike her husband, would have gladly returned there. The boys, too, seemed to have more than the normal childhood complaints. Young John was a nervous and restless child, while Alan was described as both "high-strung" and "sickly". He was taken to a number of doctors who ventured such diagnoses as "weak blood" and "bad nerves". Florence worried a good deal about the health of her sons and this, in turn, seemed to exacerbate her own condition. Brownlee was anxious to find a home in Edmonton so he could spend more time with his family, while Florence was reluctant to leave her friends and the familiar surroundings of her home. Brownlee, with all his commitments, had little enough time for house hunting.

Back in Edmonton, Brownlee faced a vast array of demands. Letters poured in, several misspelling his name, requesting positions or favours or advice. It was still an age when citizens could write directly to a Minister and expected, and got, a personal reply, usually within a week. There were numerous interviews with those anxious to present their views to the Cabinet. The province's brewers, for example, presented a detailed brief pointing out the contribution of their industry in terms of capital investment, payroll, taxes and freight paid, and (farmers' government take note) the market provided for up to a million bushels of malting barley per year.

The things he had to attend to ranged from the mind-bogglingly complex to the absurdly minuscule. An example of the former was the problems in the southern dry areas. The Cabinet, reflecting his approach, opted for further study and was able to borrow the services of southern Alberta veteran, C.A. Magrath, from the federal government to chair a three man investigation. As for the minuscule, Brownlee found himself issuing formal fiats to prosecute individuals breaching the Lord's Day Act "by selling one ice cream soda drink." Administering the Lord's Day Act required the wisdom of Solomon. To one complainant he pointed out that the Act did allow the performance of essential duties and the sale of essential foods, such as milk, on Sundays. Ice cream was usually not an essential food, he remarked, but, he went on, perhaps with his own two small boys in mind, in the midst of a summer heat wave perhaps it could be considered a necessity. He instructed police commissioners not to ask for fiats to prosecute such sales.

However, the Lord's Day Act was to supply no end of controversy. One tempest raged around the Sunday concerts of the Edmonton Symphony. Reverend Charles Huestis, head of the Lord's Day Alliance, led a spirited attack against these concerts on behalf of those from across the province who were disturbed that sophisticated "long hairs" were being allowed to breach the law. Huestis contended that restricting the concerts to subscription holders amounted to charging admission, and that paying the musicians an honorarium meant that they were gainfully employed in their regular profession on Sunday, both points which the Act forbade. Brownlee countered that the courts had already held that the two practices were not breaches of the Act. He might admit, if not pressed, that the practices had avoided breaching the Act by some rather involved legal technicalities but to Brownlee, the law was a very technical body of rules and, however unfair the practices might seem, they were not illegal. He was to be continually frustrated in his numerous attempts to explain to people that "the law" was something quite different than what a particular group might consider in their hearts to be "right". Huestis retorted that if the practices were not illegal they should be and that it was up to the Attorney General to see that they were. Brownlee pointedly declared he did not wish to debate the matter any further and concluded testily that: "I believe I fully appreciate the place of the Sabbath in the moral life of the community."

While this controversy was ranging rural against urban residents, many rural districts were being split over the question of farm work on Sunday. Brownlee was convinced, from police reports, that many complaints resulted more from neighbourhood factionalism than from a sincere desire to uphold the Lord's Day Act. Such complaints became even more troublesome during harvest. Brownlee was sympathetic toward the farmer who, having been subjected to previous crop failures, frosts or early snows, was so anxious to get his grain in the bin that he worked on Sunday. Over the next two years he developed a policy of considering each case strictly on its individual merits. He considered the previous years crop successes, the general economic condition in the district, the reputation of the person complained against, the weather conditions and the time of year. Prosecution occurred only when Sunday work seemed an unnecessary and blatant breach of the Act although even this had to be modified when Seventh Day Adventists complained of the religious persecution of being forced to observe a day that was not the true Sabbath.

Meanwhile, the mass and variety of correspondence continued. One letter, from Robert McCool, secretary-treasurer of the Crossfield Cooperative Association, asked Brownlee to withhold final payment to a government road gang foreman who had a sizable account at the Association's store for groceries he had purchased for the road crew. The local community knew that the foreman was "boozing, away" his pay cheques. It appeared likely the Association would be left with a bad debt. McCool suggested that the final pay cheque be attached as against the account receivable. Brownlee forwarded the matter to Alex Ross, the Minister concerned, pointing out that he was aware such attachments were contrary to policy "but there seems to be considerable merit to the position taken by this Association and as

I know the men connected with it personally I will be glad to render any assistance which we fairly reasonably could provide." Such consideration of the merits of the facts and individuals involved was typical of his handling of requests. He insisted on having the facts themselves rather than someone else's summary. Whenever possible he preferred to meet people face to face rather than indulge in controversy through the mails.

Another letter, from a law firm in southern Alberta, complained of malicious prosecution of their client, one G.F. Clark. Brownlee had both friends and the A.P.P. make inquiries as to Clark's character. The reports came back that "Nobby" Clark was a "gun man and general nuisance" who had threatened people and killed cattle. Brownlee promptly informed the lawyers, "I am of the opinion that your client is an irresponsible and dangerous person and have instructed the Department to proceed with any charges now pending against him. If you wish to know the reasons for my decision, I will be pleased to meet you at any time."

By now, Brownlee was firmly in charge of his Department but a seat in the Legislative Assembly had still to be secured. Neither he nor Greenfield had been a candidate in the general election. The riding of Ponoka was open as the successful U.F.A. candidate, Percival Baker, had died on election day from injuries received when struck by a falling tree. The decision as to who should assume the seat depended on where a second seat might be secured. This was solved when the member for Peace River, D. M. Kennedy , resigned to contest the December 6, federal election. Greenfield seemed a more likely candidate to represent the rugged northern frontier and both he and Brownlee were acclaimed on December 9, 1921.

Brownlee became an attentive and well-regarded M.L.A. Ponoka riding was in the heart of the lush, fertile farmland of central Alberta. Its principal towns, including Ponoka itself, were strung, conveniently along the Edmonton to Calgary railway. Ponoka was the site of the province's mental hospital and asylum, a source of several controversies about persons improperly confined or treated. He gave close attention to these complaints, as well as to all correspondence from his constituents. Before addressing any meeting in the riding, he took even more than his usual assiduous care in preparing thoroughly for any question he might be asked.

Such care was typical of his approach to all questions but it was also wise politics.

By the time Brownlee secured his seat, Alberta had been swept by another paroxysm of political excitement during the campaign for the federal general election. The U.F.A. were even more transcendently victorious, sweeping all twelve of Alberta's seats. The national results were, however, inconclusive. The Liberals won 117 seats while the Conservatives sunk to an all time low of 50. A total of 65 assorted "Progressives" were also elected; entirely from the West and rural Ontario. Clearly some type of alliance between the "Progressives" and the Liberals would transform the latter's shaky claim to power into an overwhelming majority. Crerar was most anxious to take advantage of what seemed a glorious opportunity to transform the Liberal Party into a low tariff and truly liberal reform group. William Lyon Mackenzie King, the new Liberal leader, had ideas as well about a possible "fusion" and sent a secret emissary to meet with Crerar in Winnipeg. Crerar had two objectives: first, to wrest enough concessions from King that most "Progressives" would support the merger and, second, to take three or four strong men with him into the Dominion Cabinet. He told King's messenger that he must have: a "satisfactory understanding" on the tariff, an agreement to give "public ownership of railways a full and fair trial", a "reduction in freight rates", a commitment to attempt to "secure a reciprocity agreement if possible", and an agreement to "transfer the natural resources to Western Canada" with a suitable financial adjustment.

As for Cabinet colleagues, Crerar quickly sent a confidential telegram, in code, to Brownlee, inviting both him and Greenfield to a "highly important" consultation in Winnipeg. When Brownlee replied that he could not go to Winnipeg on such short notice, Crerar sent off his own emissary, J.R. Murray, to meet secretly with Brownlee and Greenfield at the Palliser Hotel in Calgary. Brownlee asked T.C. Rankine, of his private law office, to reserve a meeting room and Rankine naively wired Crerar to ask if he should reserve a room for Murray as well. This brought a prompt reply:

No need reserve room. Murray not going. Another wire following immediately. Do nothing until you get it.

The second telegram, in code, explained:

Reserve room but in your own name. Also be sure let nobody except Greenfield Brownlee know Murray going up. This important. Use code when sending wire. This cancels previous wire which only sent so operators will not know.

The stakes in this amateur intrigue were high. Crerar wanted Greenfield or Brownlee to come into the Cabinet with him as an Alberta representative. Such an approach was necessary because of the lack of cabinet material among the elected "Progressive" members. The best of the farmer leaders were already in the provincial association executives, the farmer owned businesses or the provincial Cabinets. Crerar would have nothing to do with Wood but Greenfield and, especially, Brownlee must have seemed likely possibilities. Like most outsiders, he still overestimated Greenfield's ability. From Crerar's point of view, if he could take either into the Cabinet, that might allay U.F.A. opposition to "fusion" at least long enough for some positive results to be produced.

Brownlee was politically astute enough to realize, and advised Greenfield accordingly, that if either was foolish enough to accept, it would be taken by U.F.A. members as an outrageous betrayal and they would certainly suffer the ignominy of not being able to win a seat in their own province. That Crerar would consider such an alternative underlines his serious lack of understanding of the U.F.A. The U.F.A. participated in the loose confederation of provincial farmer organizations, to the extent of endorsing the New National Policy of the Canadian Council of Agriculture. This document called for lower tariffs, lower freight rates and progressive income tax. For most Manitoba and Ontario "Progressives", such policy revisions were what the Progressive Movement was about. Such limited aims did not reflect the U.F.A.'s philosophy. The U.F.A. sought fundamental democratic political, economic and social reforms, not simply for the sake of revising certain policies but for the realization of justice and social harmony. They had just overwhelmingly rejected a provincial administration which had been entirely adequate to their needs on the policy level. Their participation in politics was a quest on the basis of principles, not policies. Crerar, content to dismiss such effusions on principle as the "crank notions" of Wood, missed the point.

With Brownlee and Greenfield declining his offer, Crerar set up a meeting with the only other credible alternative, Charles Stewart, the recent Liberal premier. Stewart, however, had no need or desire to ride the coattails of Crerar. He was on his way to Ottawa where he would enter the Cabinet in his own right, an unhyphenated Liberal, and become Minister of the Interior, a position from which, not incidentally, he was able to out-maneuver and balk many of Brownlee's plans in the years ahead. Crerar met the Western "Progressives" in Saskatoon on December 20, 1921, but with no concrete commitments from King and no effective Western supporters, his idea of reforming the Liberal party by means of a "progressive" transplant had failed. The Members-elect voted to retain their independence but to support any "progressive" legislation King might introduce and Crerar's entry into the Cabinet if he wished, on his own. A meeting of Ontario Progressives in Toronto produced a similar result and, with the collapse of negotiations to take Premier Drury into the Cabinet, the scheme of Liberal-Progressive "fusion" came to nothing

For Brownlee, it had all been a rather heady experience. Only six months before he had been simply another rising corporation lawyer and already he was a provincial Minister and had just received a serious offer of a federal cabinet post, all before contesting an election or even making a single political speech. However, the excitement soon passed and it was back to what was now becoming the routine of complaints about conditions at Ponoka Mental Hospital, requests that the amount of liquor dispensed by prescriptions be reduced, briefs from brewers pointing out their product used all Canadian ingredients, demands for more rigorous enforcement of the Lord's Day Act, charges that lawyers fees were exorbitant, legislation to revise, reports to prepare, and, through it all a steady trickle of correspondence sent down from the Premier to which was attached the simple memorandum, "Kindly let Mr. Greenfield know what to reply to this."

Chapter 6: Problem Solving

The coming of 1922 meant two major events: the annual U.F.A. convention in late January and the first session of the new Legislative Assembly, scheduled for early February. The Convention would be a boisterous affair celebrating the two stunning election victories. Members were alive with expectations, and even more resolutions, directing their new government to a vast array of reforms, from working for world peace through the League of Nations to supporting the construction of ladies' rest rooms in small country towns. Just before the Convention opened, the entrance of Charles Stewart into the Dominion Cabinet prompted an emergency meeting of the U.F.A. Political Association. Joseph Shaw, a slim victor over R.B. Bennett (briefly Minister of Justice under Prime Minister Meighen) in Calgary West, reported that he had been approached about resigning in Stewart's favour. As Brownlee had expected, such news provoked a storm of outrage. Wood lashed out fiercely saying, "farmers are sending twelve disciples to Ottawa who can spread the gospel of democracy in a particular and peculiar way more than any other set of people ... there has been a resurrection in Alberta. There is not going to be a Judas Iscariot among these twelve men."

Shortly, U.F.A. ranks were given another shock by the sudden death, after a short illness, of the premier's wife. The news muted the tone of the Convention, and when Brownlee, giving his scheduled talk to the U.F.W.A. on 'Legal Information All Women Should Have' stressed the importance of everyone having a will, thoughts of Mrs. Greenfield's untimely demise were not far away. The impact of the loss seemed to carry on into the opening session of the Assembly where Greenfield's preoccupied manner and lack-lustre performance were attributed to his continuing grief.

Brownlee had prepared carefully for the session. He was to be unusually sensitive about possible embarrassment in the face of Opposition questions or attacks. Therefore. he tried to anticipate their strategy, and be thoroughly prepared to deal with it. His Cabinet colleagues also prepared in their way but none had the legal training or the depth of debating experience. At thirty-eight, he was the youngest Minister, yet he would soon be recognized as the Government's most competent member both within and outside the Assembly. The backbenchers, for their part, had their ideas about changing the rules of the parliamentary game. They wanted to dispense with the institutionalized contentiousness of the Official Opposition and debate proposals on their merits, rather than along strict party lines. Rather surprisingly, these more radical U.F.A. M.L.A.'s found themselves in the same position as their brothers in the House of Commons; a minority who wanted to change the rules but who were unable to do so because to introduce new rules, they would first have to win under the old ones.

Following the Speech from the Throne, the Liberals launched the traditional attacks. Their ranks had been thinned since the election by the departure of Stewart and Duncan Marshall, the former Minister of Agriculture, who was beating the hallways of Ottawa in hopes of raising a sinecure. The Liberal leadership devolved upon John R. Boyle, the former Attorney General, who showed vigour in the Assembly but whose letters to King were a mixture of useless information and pleas to be rescued by an appointment to the bench.

This was, of course, unknown to the U.F.A. members who found themselves being interrupted on technical points, asked detailed questions based on documents the Liberals had taken with them in their exit from office, or listened to their proposals being ridiculed as constitutionally impossible. Brownlee waited some time before rising in his place. Even to some U.F.A. members, he was still an unknown quantity. They saw him standing, his face and body carrying more flesh than in previous years, resting his imposing six foot four inch frame lightly against the desk behind him. His hair was less severely parted in the centre than in his college days but his rimless glasses, high tight winged collar, and dark, bulky suit made him look very much the part of the bookish, corporate lawyer. He spoke firmly and deliberately, pacing his remarks carefully, as an experienced platform speaker. He had prepared carefully, more carefully than most could imagine, but he spoke easily, without notes, looking squarely at the Liberal benches. He began with a thin smile and a rather forced good humour to emphasize the tone of his remarks.

"I came into this House with considerable trepidation," he said, "because I knew that sitting opposite would be the former giants of this House, men with ability, experience and skill. Since coming in I've listened to all these men - giving their best - and now I blush at my own modesty."

Behind him the U.F.A. ranks heaved a collective sigh of relief. Here at last was their champion, someone who could match, even dominate, the Liberals on the other side. Despite their theories about cooperative government, they settled back with relish to watch Brownlee defend their proposals, attack Opposition assertions and tear the Liberal contentions to shreds. Yet all was done with an air of gentlemanly reserve and detachment. Brownlee operated as the well-mannered yet firm school master pointing out errors in the Liberal boys' sums, not as a fiery orator or partisan political in-fighter.

Brownlee easily outclassed the majority of the members and it was soon evident he was the strong man of the Cabinet as well. Increasingly Greenfield, when faced with a difficult question, would lean over and consult with his seatmate, Brownlee, before rising to answer. He could then give the answer quite capably but it was obvious to all that Brownlee had supplied it. The backbenchers soon found this, despite the return of Greenfield's buoyant personality and hearty manner, rather humiliating.

The session did not run smoothly for the new Ministry despite their supporters being in a comfortable majority. Alex Moore (U.F.A. - Cochrane) was one of those out to destroy the old conventions of partyism. He chose to do this at the outset by countering Greenfield's nomination of O.L. McPherson as Speaker with one of his own -- Dr. J. S. Stewart (Independent Conservative -Lethbridge). Dr. Stewart saved the Government embarrassment by declining this unexpected nomination.

A more serious incident involved the fate of a Bill to amend the Dairyman's Act, fondly known as the Cow Bill. The Act had been introduced by the Liberals to provide low interest loans to farmers to diversify by buying cows to build up a herd. When the time came to market the cattle produced, and to repay the loans, prices had fallen so sharply that all who had ventured into the programme lost heavily. Thus, many U.F.A. members wanted the measure scrapped, not merely amended. The Ministers were unaware of this since these same backbenchers were the ones who most strongly supported the U.F.A. contention that the caucus was one of the most glaringly anti-democratic features of partyism. A Member's duty, they believed, was to express the views of his constituents on the floor of the Assembly. To be muzzled by caucus discipline was to supplant the voice of the people by the interests of the party bosses.

Thus the Bill passed through first and second reading, then through Committee of the Whole, and finally third reading with the U.F.A. back rows ominously quiet. The Ministers could change it all they liked, they were waiting to quash it completely. When third reading had passed, one of them rose to ask if it was now time to speak against the Bill. Brownlee, assuming the Member was simply unfamiliar with the rules, suggested to the Speaker that "since the House has charge of its own rules and procedure, Mr. Speaker consider the previous motion as not having been put." This suggestion was accepted and the backbenchers then followed one another in attacking the Act, citing losses that farmers had sustained, and questioning the Government's wisdom in interfering, in the supply-demand quotient of cattle stocks. The Liberals, almost asleep previously, suddenly came alive and after hurried consultation, Boyle launched into a spirited attack of the Act, which he had helped to draft. The upshot was that when the vote was taken, only the support of the Labour group saved the Government from defeat at the hands of its own backbenchers. As the latter tolled off their votes against their Government, Brownlee shook his head and said to Greenfield wryly, "Why in the world did I ever come up to this place anyway?"

This experience taught the U.F.A. group two lessons. First, it was obvious the Liberals would attempt to capitalize on any divisions within the farmers' group. Secondly, a meeting of members was necessary to discuss proceedings. At that meeting, Brownlee won acceptance of his view that such meetings should be held regularly so that the Government could be fully aware of the opinions of its supporters. Changes could then be made before taking the matter into the Assembly where the Liberals were always waiting to defeat them. When some Members objected that defeat on a particular measure should not require the Government to resign, Brownlee warned that there was "one other very important person in the Government of Alberta and that is the representative of the Crown in the person of Lieutenant-Governor Brett." He pointed out it was the Lieutenant-Governor's prerogative to ask for the resignation of the Ministry at any time he believed it did not have or did not merit the confidence of the Assembly. The U.F.A. might not consider a defeat a vote of non-confidence but if the Lieutenant-Governor did, he could ask for their resignation and they would have to give it.

Some Members were not yet mollified. The U.F.A. had a firm commitment to end the muzzling of the people's representatives by the threat of the Government resigning if any measure was defeated. They wanted measures to be debated fully and strictly on their merits alone. Alex Moore and Russell Love (U.F.A. - Wainwright) therefore introduced a resolution that the House adopt, as its practice, that the Government only be required to resign if defeated on a specific vote of non-confidence.

The Moore-Love resolution prompted dire warnings from across Canada about the far-reaching constitutional implications of these wild Albertan innovations. R.B. Bennett urged his former student to advise his colleagues of the unconstitutionality of the proposal "with ample references to the authorities which you will find in Todd and Bourinot, and then ask that the resolution be withdrawn." Brownlee had an even more adroit way of handling the difficulty. As he explained to Bennett, "a clause in the U.F.A. Platform advocated action along the lines of the Moore-Love resolution and all the Members on the Government side ... felt themselves obligated to take some action." Therefore, he moved an amendment which changed the resolution from a commitment to specific policy to a general, almost ambiguous statement of intent. He concluded, "I think the whole matter can be considered as a minor incident which will have no effect whatever."

Thus, the "radical element" lost another battle. By similar adroit moves, the entire "group government" theory, of which so much had been made (and would continue to be made) by the critics of the U. F. A., was defused. H.W. Wood, the only one who might have forced some action on these ideas, took an attitude of non-interference in the conduct of the government. Brownlee was as close to Wood as anyone and had discussed the theory with him. However, he was never convinced that Wood had seen "his way through it completely. In his thinking he always came up against practical problems for which he did not readily have the answer."

With Wood not prepared to force his theories, and no one in the Cabinet, least of all the practical Brownlee, to take them up, after the earliest days little or no attention was paid by the U.F.A. government itself to "group government". The only significant impact was the inclusion of Labour member, Alex Ross, in the Greenfield Cabinet. The other four Labour Members, though, sat on the Opposition benches.

The gradual disappearance of uniquely U.F.A. ideas about the approach to governing coincided with the adoption of traditional Assembly practices. Tiring of Liberal jibes and attacks, the U.F.A. Members came up with discomfiting ammunition of their own. The Liberals, it appeared, had made very liberal use of the Land Titles Offices as a source of sinecures and patronage positions. Fifteen employees there had been on paid leave during the election campaign. One leading Edmonton Liberal had been on full salary at the Calgary office despite having visited the southern city for only two days during the previous year. Even more glaring had been the Liberal largesse in supplying telephone poles to the provincially operated telephone system. Well over $100,000 worth of contracts had been awarded, it was charged, largely in Liberal ridings, in the few weeks prior to the election. U.F.A. Members described veritable mountains of stockpiled poles, enough they claimed to supply the province for nine years. When Liberal attacks on government spending became too pointed, murmurs about Liberal telephone poles rumbled out of the U.F.A. back benches.

The most important legislation of the Session was the Drought Area Relief Act. Essentially it incorporated Brownlee's solution to the problem. It had soon become clear that the drought, while a serious short term problem, merely threw into sharper relief the much larger problem of the inadequacy of farm incomes, particularly in relation to the credit facilities available. Most farm mortgages, for example, were being written for a five year amortization, a length of time which, given the capital amounts involved, provided no opportunity to retire the mortgage at the end of the term. If the renewal corresponded with depressed agricultural commodity prices, making it impossible to pay even the interest, wholesale foreclosures might ensue. Even if they did not, the anxiety over large scale, irredeemable debt, demoralized those who had done their best but were still unable to honour their commitments. Brownlee, still with great faith in reasonableness, thought that the people concerned should be able to work out such problems through direct negotiation. Consequently, he proposed a solution which, characteristically for him, called for only moderate change in existing institutions.

A commissioner was to be appointed to whom farmers in a defined area could voluntarily submit both their financial problems and the administration of their assets for the payment of creditors. It was hoped the plan would have two main advantages: first, allow the hard pressed farmer to avail himself of some skilled, objective counseling to relieve his beleaguered feeling and second, introduce a neutral party to apportion fairly any available funds among the creditors. Brownlee believed this would encourage creditor reasonableness by assuring them that no other creditors could strip the farmer of all his available funds. Such every-man-for-himself bill collecting had resulted in frequent use of the courts as creditors jostled for position. These frantic efforts accumulated more costs which the farmer could not afford to bear. Court costs of twenty or thirty dollars were a sizable item when the net disposable income of many farmers was under $200 per year.

As Drought Area Commissioner, Brownlee chose a man known to farmers as a capable administrator, his friend and former mentor - E.J. Fream. Fream established an office, recruited a small clerical staff and was ready by August to receive requests from farmers for assistance.

By this time, farmers all across the West were intensely concerned about the coming harvest -- not because of drought, which affected a relatively small area, but because of low prices. During the War, at a time of rapidly rising grain prices, the federal government closed the Winnipeg Grain Exchange and placed the buying and selling of wheat under an appointed Board of Grain Supervisors. This system, at first viewed skeptically, proved to be an orderly marketing method and most farmers were convinced that the subsequent high prices were due largely to the removal of private grain traders and speculators from the market. It was charged that these speculators manipulated the price of grain to the disadvantage of the farmer and sinfully "gambled" with the hard won fruits of his labour. When the War ended, the government moved to disband the Board and return the marketing of wheat to the Grain Exchange. This prompted such a storm of protest that the Canadian Wheat Board was created to handle the 1919 crop. Then, despite the strongest of Western protests, it was allowed to lapse. Within six months, grain prices fell as much as sixty percent. By 1922, with prices still low, farmers were desperate for action. Some such as E.A. Partridge, grandfather of the Western farm movement and chief founder of the old G.G.G., advocated the reinstatement of the Wheat Board as a prime example of government activity "for securing the greatest good to the greatest number; for using the strength of all of us, to overthrow the undue strength of some of us, that is being used to the injury of most of us."

Other farmers were not convinced they should rely on government for their salvation. They favoured a pooling of grain, a plan which would require farmers to give up individual ownership of grain upon delivery and allow the marketing of it from one large pool, large enough it was hoped to provide some price support. The wild fluctuations of the private market and typical harvest time drop in prices would be overcome by returning to farmers the average price over the entire crop year, as had the Wheat Board. In general, sentiment in Alberta favoured such a pool while Saskatchewan and Manitoba farmers were more insistent on a government wheat board. Prime Minister King, still looking to capture some of the "Liberals in a hurry", as he described the Progressives, finally agreed to re-establish a Wheat Board in cooperation with the provinces. At least two of the three prairie provinces would have to pass concurrent enabling legislation, as well as find the personnel to sit on the Board.

Brownlee, soon to be fully involved with these problems, had his mind elsewhere as he prepared for his annual vacation. Before he left, he sent Greenfield two very firmly worded memoranda. The first dealt with the government's financial situation and the need, as he saw it, to balance the budget. "I feel we are running into a very dangerous and unpleasant position," he wrote, "and that prompt, decisive and drastic action cannot be longer avoided and I wish to put myself on record to this effect." He went on to tell Greenfield that he should order "the most drastic cuts in expenditure." If this were not done, he warned, "I personally would find it very difficult to face another Session on the strength of what we have done so far and attempt to deal with the criticisms and questions which will inevitably be asked." His conclusion pointedly reminded Greenfield of how dependent on Brownlee the U.F.A. group were. It was a strong attempt to spur Greenfield to some action toward balancing the budget by questioning both the future of the Government and Brownlee's part in it.

The second memorandum, on the subject of the province's railways, was in the same vein. The expenditures on railways, almost $5,000,000, accounted for fully thirty-seven percent of the province's budgeted expenditure in 1922.

Alberta's adventure into railways dated back to before the War. The Liberal regime had become fully caught up in the traditional spirit of Canadian railway building, awarding contracts to railway syndicates, floating some bonds and guaranteeing others. After the War, the construction continued apace with even more extravagant assistance. The Alberta and Great Waterways Railway into the province's unsettled north-east, for example, dubbed by some a "rail trap line", was being built at fifty-seven percent over budget and seventy-three percent above construction costs of similar railways in other parts of the country. Despite its generous assistance, the various syndicates collapsed and the province found itself supporting four small railroads; all uncompleted, all losing money at a prodigious rate, and all with a heavy load of bonded debt and associated debt charges.

The largest of the roads, the Edmonton, Dunvegan and British Columbia (E. D. & B.C.) tapped the Peace River country but with the depression, that region was experiencing no growth. The other lines were too small to be viable in themselves but, Brownlee argued, all four had potential and might well be profitable branch lines for one of the two transcontinental systems. His frank memorandum urged Greenfield to begin negotiations immediately with the railway companies in an attempt to sell the lines. The Province had nothing to lose by the attempt, he argued, and much to gain if it could shed their debt burdens and operating deficits.

Having thus unburdened himself, Brownlee left for what he must have felt was a well deserved month's holidays in Victoria with his family. His rising impatience with Greenfield was understandable considering the tremendous responsibilities and workload which had fallen his lot, and the difficulty he was having prompting the Premier to the kind of firm, decisive and pragmatic leadership the situation seemed to demand. Greenfield, still buoyant and charming, enjoyed guiding visitors about the Legislative Building, embroidering his tours with hearty, earthy anecdotes. However, for the practical detail of administration he relied on Brownlee, even to the point of organizing the agenda for Cabinet meetings.

While Brownlee was on holidays, the Assembly met for an unprecedented Special Session. Since its sole purpose was the enabling legislation for the Wheat Board, the passage of which was certain, Brownlee's attendance did not seem necessary. The Assembly met on August 25, discussed the proposed Wheat Board, passed the enabling legislation, and considered, briefly, the problem of natural gas supplies in Medicine Hat and Calgary. By August 31, it was about to adjourn. The last item to consider was the indemnity for the Session. The Government had planned an indemnity of $100 but some Members complained that the trip to and from Edmonton would cost them several days. Greenfield, characteristically eager to please everyone, brought in a bill providing for a payment of $200. At the last moment, Robert Pearson (Independent - Calgary) remarked that Saskatchewan Members had received $250 and Alberta Members were worth as much. This suggestion was carried in Committee without a division, amidst considerable joviality, and the Members set off eagerly for their homes. They were greeted by a storm of outrage.

All across Alberta there were farmers who had less than $250 to show for an entire year of muscle wrenching, heart breaking labour and anxiety and here the M.L.A.'s had voted themselves that amount, derived from those same farmers' tax dollars, for six afternoons of sitting in the comfortable chairs of the Legislative Assembly. All winter long U.F.A. Locals passed resolutions condemning the action. Members were petitioned to give the money back or donate it to relief in the drought area. More than any other single incident, the indemnity controversy ended the identification of the grass-roots U.F.A. supporter with the Government. Instead, the "we versus they" attitude that inevitably arises between the electors and the elected became apparent. U.F.A. M.L.A.'s, thoroughly embarrassed, tried somewhat limply to defend the action. Privately, though, they began to look more critically at their leader. Would they have done something so foolish if practical, foresighted, politically alert John Brownlee had been present?

The situation was not helped any when Greenfield, and his Saskatchewan counterpart, Charles Dunning, were unable to persuade anyone to sit on the proposed Board. Because of this, there was no Wheat Board for the 1922 crop and farmers faced another year of low prices and the speculative vagaries of the Grain Exchange. U.F.A. Locals loosed another volley of resolutions now that it was clear the Special Session had accomplished nothing other than voting each M.L.A. 250 of the taxpayers' dollars.

* * *

Emil Picariello was known to everyone in the Crow's Nest Pass as Pic' and to many, only half jestingly, as Emperor Pic'. Picariello had come to the Pass a poor Italian peddler and junk dealer. He acquired a small confectionery and specialized in the sale of ice cream. He parlayed these two small businesses into the ownership of the Blairmore Hotel, became a town councilor in Blairmore, and was a well-known and popular figure in the Pass. His popularity, however, was largely with the non-English residents of the Pass. Both in Blairmore and nearby Coleman there were sharp ethnic divisions. Most of the merchants and professionals were from English speaking backgrounds, while most of the areas' miners were of southern and eastern European origin. The usual ethnic tensions of such a demography were exacerbated by a sharp difference of attitude over the province's prohibition legislation. The so-called "foreign element" had trouble taking prohibition seriously and it was an open secret that the real key to Picariello's business success was his importation of alcoholic beverages from nearby "wet" British Columbia to a strong local market. The fact that this business was illegal, accomplished by daring night runs in high powered cars along mountain roads, and the fact that Pic' had made several dramatic, not to say flamboyant, escapes from the law, both on the highways and in the courts, had turned him into something of a local hero to many. The so-called "British element" viewed Pic's activities less favourably. While there was division over prohibition itself, they saw the illicit liquor trade as involving a larger issue -- the rule of law. Disrespect for the law was a serious matter and the popular support of this disrespect by the "foreign element" raised the question of which cultural conventions were going to be observed.

The embodiment of Law in the Pass was the Alberta Provincial Police (A.P.P.) detachment at Coleman. Steve Lawson had joined the force there in the spring of 1922 as a regular constable, belying the fact that he had been specially recruited by the new A.P.P. Commissioner, W.C. Bryan. Born in England, Lawson immigrated to southern Alberta early in the century. He served with distinction in W.W.I and subsequently as police Chief in Macleod and Field. He knew the people and the terrain thoroughly and had been assigned specifically to help bring the illicit liquor trade under control.

On September 21, 1922, Picariello and his son, "Young Pic", were discovered in Blairmore unloading a car full of illicit alcohol. Young Pic', fleeing with the car, blasted through nearby Coleman where Lawson joined the chase, firing several shots. One of them connected but "Young Pic" made good his escape to British Columbia. Early that evening, as the sun edged behind the shoulder of the mountain peaks, a sleek car pulled up in front of the A.P.P. barracks where Lawson lived with his wife and five children. Everyone recognized Picariello's high-powered McLaughlin, recognized "Pic" driving and saw beside him a dark young woman wearing a red tam. Lawson, his wife doing dishes and two youngest daughters playing in the back yard, answered a call from the car and, putting one foot on the running board, he leaned into the car and chatted with the occupants briefly. Suddenly, however, he reached across the car and grabbed Pic' by the scruff of the neck. A scuffle ensued and then, shots rang out. Lawson fell back from the car which sped down the street, Pic' leaning out the window yelling at children to get out of the way. Lawson lay crumpled in front of the barracks. His horrified young daughters, who had come round from their play in the back yard to see who had come to talk with their father; saw the neighbours quickly gather, their faces filled with shock and grief, they saw the doctor run from the hospital next door, they heard through muffled sobs that their father was dead -- shot in the back.

Late that night in Edmonton, Brownlee received news of the murder by telephone from Commissioner Bryan. He immediately authorized Bryan to employ special constables, if needed, to apprehend the killers. Lawson was the third officer to be killed that year in a liquor related incident and both men felt it was clearly time to assert the rule of law. For Brownlee this meant strong action by his own Department and strong support of the A.P.P.

Some U.F.A. Locals had criticized the police for a lack of vigour in apprehending bootleggers. Both Brownlee and Bryan believed that the death of three officers in that duty clearly showed that was not the case, and that such critics, by undermining police morale, hindered the prosecution. Brownlee's rebuttal for such critics was to point out that success in enforcing any law depended more on public cooperation than on police activity itself.

To complicate matters, however, the prosecution of liquor cases was also handicapped by the attitude of the courts. It was clear that some justices would not find against offenders because of their personal opinion of prohibition. Picariello himself, had escaped conviction the previous winter when the Supreme Court of Alberta, straining for a gnat, dismissed a Crown appeal. Some argued, with justification, that had the Justices decided that case on the basis of the law rather than on their opinion of Prohibition, Pic' would not have been at large to murder Lawson.

The next afternoon the A.P.P., with assistance from the R.C.M.P., arrested Picariello hiding, ironically enough, in an abandoned brewery in Blairmore. His "female companion" (as the press termed her, although she was actually Picariello's daughter), Florence Lassandra, was arrested a short time later. Feelings ran high in the Pass and an ugly crowd gathered in front of the town hall where they presumed Pic' was being held. He had been, however, spirited away to the Provincial Jail at Lethbridge. The next day Brownlee secured the services of A. A. McGillivray, reputedly the best courtroom lawyer in the province, to act as Crown Prosecutor. There were to be no technical mistakes. Shortly after, surprisingly, Picariello and Lassandra were moved to the maximum security penitentiary at Fort Saskatchewan. There were to be no escapes. When the trial began in early December, Brownlee took the unusual step of appearing at the prosecution bench beside McGillivray. He wished to demonstrate clearly that the Government was going to take a direct and aggressive part in the assertion of the rule of law in Alberta. He was also seated beside McGillivray four days later when the jury returned their verdict of guilty and Mr. Justice Walsh sentenced Picariello and Lassandra to death on the gallows at Fort Saskatchewan on February 21, 1923.

Brownlee was pleased with the outcome. As he remarked to former A.P.P. Commissioner Alfred Cuddy, "while one naturally regrets any decision which means the execution of an individual, I could not help a feeling of relief when the decision of the jury was announced, as undoubtedly the result of this case will mean a great deal to the work of law enforcement in this Province." As it happened, neither Brownlee's involvement in the case nor the controversy about prohibition was over. However, there were still other problems to attempt to solve.

* * *

As early as October 1921, Brownlee had taken up the Natural Resources file. By November 1922, he was attending his second Dominion-Provincial Conference on the topic in Ottawa. The problem revolved around the fact that the three prairie provinces had been, in reality, brought into Confederation as second class provinces. Unlike all the other provinces, the Dominion government retained control of the natural resources of the Prairie Provinces, including all mineral rights, water rights and Crown land. Such colonial status was defended on two grounds: one, that control of Western lands was necessary so that national policies of immigration and settlement might be followed; and second, that administration of the natural resources would be too costly for provinces with relatively small populations. The three provinces did receive subsidies in lieu of control of their natural resources but formal attempts to gain control of them began even before the provinces were created. These attempts were fueled by a belief that the resources were worth more than the subsidy and even more by a desire to be provinces with the same rights and powers as all the other provinces.

In 1920, Prime Minister Meighen committed the Dominion to the principle of turning over control of the resources and from then the discussion involved the terms of such a transfer. As Brownlee explained to the U.F.A., if Alberta was prepared to simply "take over the balance of our resources and give up all our annual subsidies, I do not think we would have much trouble getting a settlement." The problem was to obtain compensation for the resources which had already been alienated by the federal government and for the revenue lost through not having control of the natural resources. Brownlee believed it unfair to consider only the period after Alberta's entry into Confederation in 1905, since in the preceding five years alone, over 10,000,000 acres of Alberta land had been alienated by the Dominion. Of this, 6,400,000 acres of the finest and most fertile land in Alberta had been granted to various Eastern Canadian corporations as subsidies for the construction of railways, not in Alberta, but in British Columbia, Manitoba and Ontario.

This question of compensation for alienated lands was especially important for Alberta. In addition to a total of 10,000,000 acres of land granted to railway companies, another 10,000,000 acres had been granted to homesteaders with no compensation to the province. Other huge tracts had gone for Indian reserves, forest reserves, military reserves, and national parks, which in themselves accounted for tens of thousands of square miles of territory. Alberta had provided fully ninety-five percent of the national park area then existing in Canada. Brownlee was prepared to accept most of these alienations without compensation but argued strongly that there should be compensation for land granted for the construction of railways outside Alberta.

In addition to lands, large tracts of mineral leases, especially for coal and oil, had been awarded by the federal government to various corporations. Such leases contained undertakings which meant that even if the control of the resources was transferred, of the over six million tons of coal being produced annually, for example, over one-half of it would provide no royalties to the province. The absence of control over water rights had already meant that some areas of huge hydroelectric potential had been awarded to private corporations and could not be controlled by Alberta. These points made it obvious that the amount of compensation to be awarded was of vital importance. Since a single cash payment was not realistic, proposals were made that compensation be paid by a continuation of the subsidy payments for a certain number of years, beyond the time the control of the resources was transferred.

At this point the issue was complicated by objections from Atlantic Canada, caught up in the throes of the Maritime Rights Movement (a manifestation of their dissatisfaction with the progress of Confederation). Both in the caucuses of the old line parties, and in the Commons, Maritime representatives refused to accept compensation for the western provinces without comparable increases in the subsidy payments they were receiving. The issue caught on this snag, even though the independent negotiations of each of the three prairie provinces carried on. For Alberta, the chief negotiator on this vital question, indeed almost the exclusive negotiator, was John Brownlee.

Chapter 7: The Alberta Wheat Pool

Winter in Alberta, in the natural order of things, is a time of rest. The fertile farmlands are frozen under restless drifts of snow, streams are bound under thick layers of ice and only tell-tale footprints in the crisp white morning snow reveal that living creatures are about. However, for the organized farmers, winter was not a time of rest. As more than one wit observed. come January, whatever the weather, there was always a bumper crop of resolutions for the U.F.A. Annual Convention. January 1923 was no different; in fact, there was a particularly high yield of resolutions concerning monetary and banking reform.

George Bevington was a leading spokesman and theorist of the economic reform group which challenged the adequacy of the conservative tinkering with existing institutions that Brownlee favoured. They called for much more thorough-going schemes such as an extension of the terms of the Drought Area Relief Act to cover the entire province. This was a clear indication that the real problem was not drought but low farm incomes. There were also demands that the Province charter and operate a bank on a service rather than profit basis and this plan was tied to an elaborate scheme by which the provincial government would completely re-fund the entire farm debt by issuing provincial bonds. These bonds would be secured against notes obtained directly from the Dominion Treasury, thus eliminating the costs "raked off by the middlemen" bankers and dropping the effective interest rate from nine to three percent. In addition to these specific plans, there were calls for more general monetary reform of a stimulative nature The most popular of these theories was the call for "Social Credit" based on the writings of Major C.H. Douglas, the Scottish economic critic whose writings were already so popular that the U.F.A. central office stocked extra copies of his books for distribution to the members.

Some in the U.F.A. attacked "Social Credit" as too inflationary but others found in Douglas' work a solid endorsement of their own ideas about democratizing banking and credit institutions. For Bevington, one of the leading popularizers of Social Credit, such democratization provided the ideological base from which he championed the demand that the Alberta government obtain a federal bank charter and operate a bank to serve the people. Grain companies had been unjust so the farmers had set up their own companies; governments had been unjust so now farmers were busy electing their own governments. Banks were unjust so why not, through their Governments, set up their own banks?

Bevington spoke out strongly in favour of the resolutions embodying these proposals and when he had finished it was obvious that opinion on the noisy, bustling, confused convention floor was strongly in his favour. At this point, Brownlee strode to the platform to fill what he judged to be a desperate need to talk sense to the crowd. Facing him were 600 farmer delegates, all the energy of their pent-up frustration and anxiety coursing toward a solution promising to transform them from victims to masters of the economic system.

"The government fully realizes the serious situation which faces farmers as a result of conditions beyond their control," he began, "but Alberta already has the second highest per capita debt in Canada." Within the next year, he advised, it would be necessary to borrow $13,000,000 to finance the existing debt load, to which a heckler shot back, "Another effort to keep us in perpetual serfdom." If the proposal for refunding all farm debt and amortizing it over twenty-five years were adopted, Brownlee countered, it would "leave every man, woman and child in Alberta paying more to retire debts than in any other province." He appealed to the delegates to have faith in their government to do as much as it could and warned darkly that the financial markets were very sensitive and that the Convention was being watched closely. Loan companies, he cautioned, were preparing to leave Alberta because they expected "certain resolutions to be passed."

His authoritative remarks shifted the momentum of the convention, but not completely. The resolutions calling for an extension of the Drought Area Relief Act and for provincial funding of farm debt were defeated, as he had urged, but not by extreme margins. Passed, though, were resolutions demanding that the federal treasury establish a loan department and that the Alberta Government obtain a federal bank charter and establish a bank in which it had the controlling interest.

The daily press hailed Brownlee's speech as a courageous effort to talk sense to the radical element among his own supporters. By his gritty performance, he had changed the course of the Convention and largely defused the demand that his government take radical action. However, the deeply felt demand for a reform of the monetary, credit and banking systems was only temporarily submerged. When severe hard times returned, it would re-emerge so powerfully that Brownlee's pleas for moderation would then be completely swept aside.

Just as he had cited the attitude of the financial institutions as posing a threat when trying to keep the banking reformers at bay, so he cited the fiercely radical reformers from rural Alberta when asking the bankers for moderation on their part. He investigated complaints about bankers thoroughly. Sometimes he found he had not been given the facts but in other cases he was convinced that a particular branch manager's attitude was entirely unjust. Thus he came to play an intermediary role. One such case, one of several Brownlee appealed over the head of a local official to the senior executive in Eastern Canada, was presented to Sir Frederick Taylor. His letter was written in the firm tone so characteristic of the forthright manner he could adopt when the occasion demanded. It was as no-nonsense as any bank critic might wish..

I note that you approve of the position taken by Mr. Peters [regional superintendent] which, in brief, is as follows: The present indebtedness of this farmer [Mr. McKinney] is $4409. You agree to carry this account for another year providing you obtain security in all as follows: Present security valued at $4000, chattel mortgage covering livestock valued at a minimum of $3000, land mortgage covering 480 acres estimated at a net value of $12,500. In other words, your bank after carrying the account for a number of years, which in May 1921 reached a high point of $6847, and has been reduced since that time by $2438, now takes the position that you must have a total security, at your own valuation, nearly five times the amount of the indebtedness.

You take this position notwithstanding the fact that this man is recognized as a good farmer in one of the best districts of this Province, after he has given ample evidence that he is trying to meet his liabilities and his financial statement shows him to be perfectly solvent. If this is to be considered as an indication of the general banking policy of the present chartered banks, nothing but bitterness can result and it would be useless for anyone to attempt to modify the attitude of the people of Western Canada on the banking question ...

We have arranged a meeting with the Alberta Members of the Dominion House ... to discuss the approaching revision of the Bank Act and I would appreciate a statement from your Bank before that date stating your final position ...

The Bank, faced with the larger implications of its position, reconsidered and allowed the farmer to continue without presenting additional security. To Brownlee this was a vindication of his faith in reasonableness and moderation. He would continue to play the role of intermediary, delicately balancing the arch-conservative bankers on the one hand, and some of the most radical economic reformers in Canadian history on the other; successfully for almost a decade before a complete economic collapse swept reason aside and cast moderation into disrepute.

* * *

When the 1923 session of the Assembly opened in February, Brownlee found himself as Government House leader, replacing a Greenfield troubled with recurrent laryngitis which, some quipped stemmed from chronic procrastination. A chagrined Brownlee, the most persistent voice in Cabinet urging drastic action to balance the Province's financial statement, found himself having to present and defend public accounts showing an operating loss for 1922 of $1,900,000. This meant a total deficit since the U.F.A. had taken office nearly $4,000,000. The time had passed when the continuing deficits could be blamed on previous Liberal extravagances. The Opposition stepped up its attacks and even some U.F.A. backbenchers became restless about excessive expenditures in areas outside their own constituencies. Brownlee, more critical than any of what he regarded as an entirely lax financial management, found himself defending the Government by pointing to sharply increased revenues and such on-going drains as the ill-fated railways with their net operating losses of $1,500,000 per year.

He was much happier tabling the report of the MacGibbon Commission on banking and credit conditions in Alberta. He had been the main advocate in Cabinet of creating the commission and appointing Professor D. A. MacGibbon of the University of Alberta to lead it. The report, recommending strongly against setting up a "provincial bank", had been a major bases of Brownlee's strong attack on that plan at the Convention. In general, MacGibbon's recommendations supported Brownlee's own conclusions. Both saw inefficiencies and inadequacies in the existing banking and credit institutions, and occasional glaring injustices not only to certain individuals but to the West as a region. The report confirmed Brownlee's belief that with more information and moderation, on all sides of the controversy, the existing system could be improved. Such a course would certainly be preferable, he believed, to any wild innovation whose result might be disaster for all.

Brownlee did, however, consider the concept of a provincially operated bank more seriously than some in the U.F.A. suspected. He sought information from New Zealand and New South Wales where such banks had been attempted, and at one point presented a detailed submission on the topic, accompanied by interpretive charts, to the Cabinet. He could see that state sponsored banks had certain merits but he was convinced that the Province had neither the economic nor constitutional base to consider such a scheme. The MacGibbon Report confirmed that judgment and Brownlee was content to rely on an expert opinion rather than feel compelled to act on a resolution which might well have been drawn up extemporaneously one winter's night by a group sitting around someone's kitchen stove.

As the Session ended, Brownlee piloted through the Debt Adjustment Act, a replacement for the Drought Area Relief Act. The name change reflected official recognition that the essence of the problem was economic, not meteorological. Many in the so-called "Drought Area" had objected to the falsity of the term, both from civic pride and out of concern for its impact on land values. The Commissioner under the new Act, still to be E.J. Fream, had slightly stronger powers to protect creditors, both against the debtor and other creditors with inferior claims. The legislation was to be proclaimed in two parts; the first applying only to the previously designated area, and the second extending the services of the Commissioner to any farmer in the province. The lenders raised such a storm of protest, which Brownlee considered entirely unreasonable, about the impact on their business of the second part of the Act that he reluctantly deferred its proclamation indefinitely.

The Session adjourned just as the Picariello case again captured the headlines. The execution of Pic' and Mrs. Lassandra, twice delayed pending various appeals, was finally set for the morning of May 2, 1923. Some of the notables in the Crow's Nest Pass protested to Brownlee about an elaborate public funeral for Picariello which, rumour had it, was being planned by his relatives. Such a "hero's welcome", including an ostentatious procession down the main street of Blairmore, would probably spark more violence in the Crow's Nest and Brownlee set his mind to avoiding such a confrontation. When the King Government announced its decision not to commute either sentence, a group of grief stricken, excitable relatives descended on the Legislative Buildings to demand the release of the bodies to the families for burial. Brownlee, showing courage since his home and family were under police guard, agreed to meet with the families.

Tall, dour John Brownlee, with the detached reserve of the stereotype corporate lawyer, stood calmly confronting wailing women in their black widow's weeds, sobbing behind their veils, while dark suited men alternated between intense demands and violent gesticulations of impatience at Brownlee's firm refusal to release the bodies for burial in the Pass. He did agree, however, to announce his final decision on the disposal of the bodies the next day. After the group left, Brownlee pondered the situation and late that evening met with Roman Catholic Archbishop O'Leary to get his cooperation for a compromise plan. Brownlee was aware that the Criminal Code provided that all condemned prisoners were to be buried within the walls of the prison in which they were executed, unless the provincial Attorney General authorized their removal for burial elsewhere. In practice this had become a mere formality but he sought to use this prerogative, and the Archbishop agreed to support him, and accept the bodies for burial only in cemeteries near Edmonton. The next day, May 1, Brownlee again met the families and informed them of the conditions. Faced with Brownlee's firm position and its support by the Roman Catholic hierarchy, Steven Picariello and Charles Lassandra signed undertakings with regard to the burial of their father and wife respectively. They would be buried by their families, with the blessing of the Church, and controversy in the Crow's Nest would be avoided. Brownlee took pride in achieving the compromise.

Shortly after six the next morning, first the square faced Picariello and then thin, haggard Florence Lassandra were led to the gallows and, after making short statements, were "hanged by the neck until dead". Then the bodies were cut down and the coroner's jury delivered its verdict of "justifiable homicide". Newspapers headlined the executions, with public opinion, following its inevitable course, now showing sympathy for the "Bootleg King" and his "female accomplice". Steve Lawson was remembered, but his murder was now seen as part of a larger tragedy whose final result had been three deaths. The liquor legislation itself, it was argued now, was the root cause of this and other tragedies. More and more public opinion shifted against prohibition legislation. It had not worked, it was claimed. There were too many loopholes, it was a "scientific fact" that the body needed alcohol, alcohol was a medicine, and the use of alcohol was so deeply engrained in the culture that any attempt to outlaw its use was ill advised. Moreover, the attempt to enforce such legislation, it was argued, encouraged criminal activity such as Picariello's. Along with most of the rest of North America, many Albertans began to wonder if government control of liquor sales was not the best solution to the extremes of the uncontrolled barroom on the one hand and total prohibition on the other. Brownlee, personally a prohibitionist, had also come to favour a compromise which would not endanger officers' lives enforcing an unpopular Act. His stance frustrated those who believed strongly that it was the duty of the law to enforce what was "right", not simply what was popular. The pragmatic Brownlee began studying the legislation of jurisdictions which had already opted for government sale.

Disappointed by the lack of effective public support for prohibition on the one hand and irritated by complaints about a lack of its enforcement, he became increasingly impatient with complaints and demands directed to the Government. He believed that the public in general and U.F.A. members in particular were expecting too much and were contenting themselves with demanding government action where individual initiative was more appropriate.

* * *

In June of 1923, Greenfield and Charles Dunning, Premier of Saskatchewan, announced the failure of yet another attempt to persuade any one with the necessary experience, ability and confidence of the public to sit on a proposed Wheat Board. With this setback, and the prospect of yet another year at the mercy of the Grain Exchange, farmers turned more seriously to cooperative marketing or, as it was popularly known, a Wheat Pool. The pooling of wheat, through a cooperative association of producers, democratically choosing the directors of their marketing agency, would be an attempt to reduce the influence of the middleman in the grain trade. It would also be an attempt to overcome the farmer's complete lack of bargaining power in setting the price of his commodities, resulting from his being one of a multitude of sellers delivering a product to a small number of buyers.

The idea of such a Wheat Pool had been endorsed as early as 1920 when the Canadian Council of Agriculture created a Cooperative Wheat Marketing Committee. Rice-Jones made it clear to that committee that the U.G.G. would be more than willing to handle pooled wheat. By the summer of 1923, though, many cooperative marketing proponents were insisting on a new and independent organization to handle all aspects of the Pool. They were encouraged by publicity given to the views of Aaron Sapiro, a flamboyant American lawyer making headlines in connection with cooperative marketing among tobacco growers and fruit producers in the United States. Brownlee had already been introduced to Sapiro's ideas when Snow Sears, a U.G.G. director, had forwarded a copy of the Byngham Cooperative Marketing Act, the enabling legislation Sapiro had drafted for the organization of the Burley Tobacco Growers. Brownlee saw nothing exciting in the legislation and he filed it as simply another piece of the information which

Sears and other Western Canadian proponents of the Pool concept were continually sending him.

Early in July, the U.F.A. Central Board met in Calgary to consider forming a voluntary pool. Brownlee, attending as the Alberta Government's representative, urged that the proposal be studied carefully and the details worked out completely before going ahead with implementation. He disagreed with those who thought there was a possibility of organizing a Pool in time to handle the 1923 crop. Nevertheless, it was decided to go ahead as soon as "practical".

As part of the thorough study of the concept, Brownlee and fellow Cabinet Minister, Richard Reid, were soon off to California where they met with officials of fruit growers' cooperatives and with Sapiro in his San Francisco offices. Superficially, Brownlee and Sapiro had something in common. Both were successful corporate lawyers who, although having no direct farming experience, had become immensely influential in the councils of farmer organizations. However, their personalities and attitudes clashed from the beginning. Brownlee was suspicious of Sapiro's high-energy, fast talking approach. He questioned his methods, motives and, most of all his insistence on haste. Sapiro had already stated that a "Wheat Pool could be organized in a few weeks." Brownlee had advised care and caution, believing that any mistakes could damage Western agriculture and discredit the cooperative marketing concept.

After meeting with Sapiro, the two man committee journeyed to Chicago where the commodity market provided a convenient place to interview those involved in marketing schemes throughout the United States. They returned to Alberta basically unimpressed. There was little new in the American experiments other than the fervour with which they were being advanced as panaceas. Both Brownlee and Reid, a soft-spoken Scot, regarded this enthusiasm as shallow and dangerous if it prompted ill-considered action.

Events in Alberta, though, had not stood still. Sapiro had been invited to address a series of meetings by no less unlikely a source as the Calgary Herald and the Edmonton Journal, the inveterate antagonists of the U.F.A. Brownlee now found Albertans flocking to listen spellbound to Sapiro's dramatic oratory and accepting completely his proposition that where there was a will there was an immediate way. Sapiro's speeches sparked an intense grassroots demand for a Pool and, just as in 1919, U.F.A. leaders found themselves being forced to action by the enthusiasm of their own supporters.

In short order a "Committee of Seventeen" was struck to supervise the formal organization of the Pool. Various sub-committees would look after the details. Brownlee sat on the Elevator sub-committee and chaired the Legal sub-committee. By August 7, it was decided definitely to go ahead with the creation of the Alberta Cooperative Wheat Producers Limited. Despite Sapiro's insistence that the Pool could be organized as an association without capital stock it was finally, on Brownlee's advice, organized with capital stock, priced at a nominal one dollar, to be included within the three dollar initial membership fee. Now, both the instruments for the creation of this novel joint stock company and the form for the contracts which would bind the growers to the Pool organization had to be drawn. Again on Brownlee's advice, the best legal talent was recruited to draft these instruments. A. A. McGillivray drew up the membership contract, with R.B. Bennett, Sapiro, and Brownlee as advisory counsel.

Next, financing had to be secured. Brownlee was quick to assure the Committee that the Alberta government would provide a loan toward organizational expenses. The U.G.G., many of whose shareholders helped to organize the Pool, loaned the Committee a further $10,000. Later, when the banks demanded that the Alberta government guarantee the Pool's fifteen percent operating margin, it was Brownlee who wired his Cabinet colleagues urging them to approve the guarantee. They did, but, in line with Brownlee's previous advice to them, they insisted that the Pool provide some security against the guarantee. Politically cautious Brownlee was protecting both flanks by assisting the Pool and at the same time disarming any criticism that the Government had risked the taxpayers' money on enterprises for farmers.

After financing came the problem of securing handling facilities and the demand, from some, that the Pool create its own network of elevators. Brownlee, for one, viewed such a massive capital expenditure as entirely unnecessary for the implementation of cooperative marketing and as an unwise business risk, particularly in the very early stages of an untried corporate organization. However, J. McFarland, President of the Alberta Pacific Grain Company, made a surprise offer to sell his company's elevators to the embryonic Pool. As a member of the Elevator subcommittee, Brownlee suggested the alternative of Alberta Pacific simply agreeing to handle Pool wheat for a handling charge plus a commission rate to be agreed on. McFarland hesitated to enter such an agreement until it was clear what the attitude of the rest of the grain trade was going to be. Immediately after the meeting, Brownlee alerted his friend, Rice-Jones, to the development and suggested that the U.G.G. be the first to offer to handle Pool wheat, along the lines he had suggested to McFarland. It was clearly better for the U.G.G., or any elevator company, to have the revenue from handling Pool wheat rather than face direct competition from a new, enthusiastically supported elevator company. Brownlee's suggestion was accepted and first the U.G.G. and, within a week, almost all the other companies had agreed to handle Pool wheat. In the longer term though, the strategy was not successful in preventing a separate network of Pool elevators, regardless of how unwise Brownlee thought that to be.

By the end of August, it was obvious that the Saskatchewan and Manitoba Pools and the inter-provincial selling agency which Brownlee believed were crucial to the plan, were not going to be realized in time to handle the current crop. From across Alberta, U.F.A. Locals fired off resolutions calling for a strictly Alberta Pool and urging that Sapiro be recalled to show how it could be done. The Committee of Seventeen decided to try to organize a Pool in time to handle the crop.

The essence of the organization was the grower contracts. It was decided that if contracts representing fifty percent of the total wheat acreage were signed by September 15, 1923, the Pool would handle the crop. Brownlee told the Committee that he doubted it could be done and, as he later maintained, his doubts were well founded. What was being proposed was the creation of a province-wide force of volunteer canvassers to attempt to secure signed contracts from farmers to market their largest cash crop with an untried and literally still unformed organization under legal penalty if they marketed it elsewhere. All this would be done while all farmers, both canvassers and canvassed alike, were in the midst of their crucial harvest operations. The time provided was little more than two weeks. Clearly it was a mammoth challenge and when they succeeded, Alberta farmers had accomplished a feat of grass-roots organization, canvassing and persuasion unequaled in Canadian history.

They had done more than simply sign a petition. More than half of Alberta farmers had formally bound themselves and their livelihood to an untried system. They risked everything. It was a measure of how desperate their situation had become that most believed they had little to lose. If they could escape the exploitive clutches of the private grain traders, it would be worth the gamble. On September 22, 1923, the official announcement was made. The Alberta Wheat Pool would handle the 1923 crop.

Brownlee had been active in every stage of the Pool's formation from the initial study and investigation, the drafting of the incorporation and contract instruments, through the detailed structuring of the operation and finally, the drafting of the contracts under which the other elevator companies agreed to handle the Pool wheat. Often his call for prudence had been overrun by the zeal which spread among the ordinary farmers. His emphasis on caution was interpreted by some as a lack of enthusiasm for the concept but this was only partially true. As future events would show, he was a firm supporter of the Pools as indigenous, broadly based business organizations. His caution was not reserve about cooperative marketing but rather concern that it be established according to solid, traditional business principles. He saw the Alberta Wheat Pool as a new, Western controlled business, not as a revolutionary challenge to traditional business practices. He did not share, or understand the basis of the motivation which propelled most farmers to join and yet he had played a very significant part in the Pool's creation and in giving it its distinctive form and character. His part in that process was not yet over.

All Alberta had been swept by "Pool" enthusiasm but before the harvest was over, the province was embroiled in another controversy -- a referendum on the "liquor question". Despite the U.F.A. dutifully taking the field in defense of prohibition, a large majority opted for government sale of spirits for home consumption and the licensing of premises to sell beer by the glass. The U.F.A.'s only consolation was that the legislation to control this activity, since Brownlee already had it well in hand, would be drafted more carefully and therefore be more successful than it had been in other jurisdictions.

While disappointment among Alberta farmers about the result of the Liquor Referendum was widespread, it was muted both by the enthusiasm surrounding the Wheat Pool and by the general weakening of the vision of building a new and better world. After three or four years of economic adversity and severe assaults upon perfectionist reform movements, many were concentrating on attempting to secure a decent living for themselves and their families rather than on ushering in the Millennium. Farming is at once both a business and a way of life; however, if the business fails the way of life must be abandoned. The enthusiasm of 1921 for spreading the virtues of farm life, and its auxiliary institutions, so as to reform society at large, had withered in the face of severe difficulty in remaining solvent.

What did a typical farm balance sheet look like at this time? One of the few detailed studies of farm production costs in Alberta was done in 1923 by a special committee of the United States Tariff Commission. Based on actual cases in several districts, it determined that the average cost of producing wheat in Alberta, from 1921 to 1923, was 70 cents per bushel. This figure included the cost of land but not of food, clothing, shelters and personal expenses. It also did not include any debt charges.

On the revenue side of the ledger, the average farm gate price for wheat during the same 1921 - 1923 period was 73 cents per bushel. Considering average Alberta farm size of about 350 acres at the time, average yields of 16.6 bushels per acre and typical cropping practices where only one-third of the acreage was in wheat; the net return to the average farmer for his wheat crop during the three year period was about $58 per year. This was neither minimum wages nor a minimum return on capital investment, and certainly not both.

The Wheat Pool was the major attempt to increase the net return to farmers but Brownlee pursued some other avenues as well. He insured that competent legal counsel was retained to represent farmer interests before such federal commissions as the Board of Railway Commissioners. Any increase in freight rates would decrease the net return to farmers. Similarly, he thought it vital that wheat growers be represented before hearings of the Royal Grain inquiry held that summer. He was especially concerned about the operating costs of country elevators. He believed it unfair that the farmer should have to bear the costs of inefficient management either of the company as a whole or any of its branch operations. The Inquiry was, in fact, investigating some other facets of elevator practice such as overages, grade and price spreads; as well as the influence of the Grain Exchange on wheat prices, particularly the influence of short and margin selling and the reasons for futures-cash spreads. Freight rate and grain trade commissions had come and gone before with almost seasonal regularity but it was largely the result of Brownlee's efforts that throughout the decade, Western farmers' interests were represented by some of the best legal talent available.

In addition to a continuing steady stream of routine matters, Brownlee's other major files had also been active. Correspondence on the natural resources control transfer continued intermittently even though Alberta's colonial status meant that it was unable to control policy for the development of key resources. In the Twenties the most prominent of these was hydro-electricity. Here, the Province found itself arrayed against both the federal government and Calgary Power Company, a corporation with head offices on St. James Street in Montreal. Electrification of all towns and many rural municipalities was expanding quickly and Calgary Power, anxious to monopolize this expansion, applied to the Dominion government for water power rights in large tracts of the Upper Bow River watershed, including the immense potential at Spray Lakes. The U.F.A. government did not want to see small town and rural Alberta supplied by a corporation whose main interest was profits for its shareholders, who were largely non-Albertans. Therefore, Brownlee, on behalf of Alberta, made a formal application for a priority permit for the water power rights concerned. Brownlee's old nemesis, Charles Stewart, however, was now the Minister of the Interior and had the responsibility for administering the resources. The Province's application was denied. The water power rights were conferred on Calgary Power Company and hydro-electric development in Alberta remained under the control of private corporations. This was clearly not the wish of either the Government of Alberta or the majority of Albertans.

In addition to the immense number of duties in his office, Brownlee was increasingly called upon by backbenchers to address political meetings in their constituencies. Dissatisfaction with Greenfield was spreading and although he was still a popular figure, he could make an effective speech, it seemed, only by dealing in pleasant generalities. When faced with sharp questioning or when detailed knowledge of legislation or statistics was required, he often appeared at a loss. Some U.F.A. M.L.A.'s, noting a spirit of criticism and unease among their constituents, wanted Brownlee to address their meetings. In the early winter, he accompanied Greenfield on a speaking tour of the central and eastern sections of the province and the combination was effective.

Brownlee was now secure about his leading position and becoming more relaxed in it. He even permitted himself occasional attempts at humour. On one occasion he replied to a request to appoint an issuer of marriage licenses with the note, "This Department deals with every form of crime excepting the issuing of marriage licenses. I have therefore forwarded your letter ... to the Minister of Health."

The year's work load had been incredibly exhausting and perhaps partly because of this, Brownlee was struck down with the first of what would be a series of mid-winter illnesses. He was confined to his house for almost a month with whooping cough. At best this afforded him some time to spend at home with his family. He had purchased earlier a two-story, three bedroom frame home in the Garneau district of Edmonton's south side. The location, 11151 - 88 Avenue, was just one house from the corner which overlooked the spacious grounds of the University to the west. His salary of $6,000 per year as Minister plus a $2,000 sessional indemnity, and a continuing share from his law practice in Calgary, allowed the family to employ a live-in maid and live comfortably but not ostentatiously. Florence's condition had improved but she still required lots of rest and took care to get it and protect herself from infectious diseases.

The boys; Jack, now eight, and Alan, six, were looking forward anxiously to Christmas. Brownlee, recalling his own austere childhood, attempted to make such occasions warm and festive for his own family. Christmas morning found a bounty of colourfully wrapped presents under an elegantly decorated tree in Brownlee's book-lined study-cum-family room. Tracks of coal dust footprints came from the fireplace and crossed the room to the stairs. He solved the mystery for the boys by producing a handwritten note from Santa apologizing for the footprints and explaining that Santa had had to go searching for one of his reindeer and had gone upstairs, only to discover that what he first thought was a reindeer antler was one of Florence's bare feet sticking out from under the covers. Such interludes of relaxation and enjoyment with his family were all too rare for Brownlee who at home displayed a warmer side of his nature than many who encountered him in public would have thought possible.

Chapter 8: Reluctant Leader?

The 1924 U.F.A. Convention jubilantly celebrated the creation of the Alberta Wheat Pool. The party was marred only by the discordant clamour of the "provincial bank" advocates, back riding heir hobby horse. George Bevington was now clearly their leader, after taking his ideas before the House of Commons Select Committee on Banking the previous summer. There, he had attracted attention, colourfully comparing the flow of credit in society to the blood stream in the human body. Wood, Brownlee and others were determined to use the wave of support they enjoyed as a result of the success with the Pool to finally "get rid" of the provincial bank idea. It would be no easy matter.

Political conventions can be easily dominated by small, vocal cliques. They monopolize debates and target key party positions, such as committee chairmanships, where they can be very difficult to dislodge. The "provincial bank" group had controlled the U.F.A. convention the two previous years, aside from the skirmish defeat at the hands of Brownlee. Now, to put an even sharper focus on the struggle, Bevington was challenging Wood for the presidency.

The battleline was a resolution demanding the Government act immediately on the previous year's call for the Province to secure a charter and operate its own bank. Brownlee, drawing on his study of state sponsored banks, moved to undercut this demand. He recommended that the Provincial Treasury expand its public function from merely selling savings certificates to accepting general deposits. The money deposited, he offered, could be loaned to rural credit societies to help alleviate serious deficiencies in long term credit for farmers. These proposals gave more ground than some expected, but he stopped far short of a provincially operated chartered bank. The recent collapse of the Home Bank, and the enforced mergers of others, argued that it wasn't the time to jump into the banking business. The province was in severe financial difficulties. Brownlee stood firm on his belief that even if a Provincial Bank was constitutionally possible (which he denied) it would imperil the entire financial position of the Province.

It was crucial that the resolution be defeated in order to prevent the Government being embarrassed by its own supporters directing it to take an action which it must refuse. Such a refusal would alienate many members at a time when the U.F.A.'s political future was beginning to appear cloudy.

William Irvine, surprisingly recruited to the side of the economic conservatives on this issue, launched an eloquent, ringing attack on the resolution. "If I were Premier of Alberta and I were asked to carry the terms of this resolution into effect, I would not do it," he chided. "I would resign and say 'Go ahead and do it yourselves' and I'm sure that if you attempted it you would come a cropper." Irvine's speech swung the momentum against the resolution and, in the time honoured strategy of conventions, its opponents attempted to have the vote called immediately. Robert Gardiner, chairing the session, and far from a conservative, refused to accept the motion and instead recognized several more speakers. The first of these, Bevington, sensing the momentum turning against him, pleaded with the delegates. "All I want is an endorsement of the principle of using our own credit. I do not say that it is absolutely feasible, but we can make it feasible."

Finally, though, Wood took the platform. Coolly and mercilessly, his gravelly voice rumbled out an indictment which routed his challenger and the "provincial bankers". "The establishment of this bank is not fundamental to the solution of our financial problems," he declared. "The farmers' problem is not that they cannot contract more debts but that they cannot pay their debts because the price they receive for their produce is not sufficient. ... the most important step has been the organization of the Wheat Pool. When the farmer has as much to say about the price of what he sells as others have to say about the price of products the farmer buys, then much will have been accomplished." He concluded fiercely "If you do not understand what you are doing and why you are doing it, don't do it."

Bevington tried a last desperate motion to table the matter for further study but by now the Convention would have none of it. Firmly behind Wood, they overwhelmingly defeated the provincial banking resolutions. The ideas of banking and monetary reform were not, however, swept entirely from the field. Their seeds were scattered widely and awaited only the return of severe economic hardship to reap, in their turn, the victory.

When the Session opened, Brownlee was an even more prominent and crucial part of the Government's forces. When he suffered a relapse and was confined to his house for a week, Boyle telephoned to tell him to rest, that the Liberals would not ask any embarrassing or controversial questions during his absence. They kept their bargain and to Brownlee it was an unexpected bit of chivalry, one barrister to another. However, to the U.F.A. group it was humiliating. Boyle and the Liberals had as much as said that without Brownlee, the U.F.A. were a pitiful lot.

The major feature of the Session was the debate on the Bill which became the Government Liquor Control Act of Alberta. Brownlee, had thoroughly researched and prepared the legislation. He had also secured the services of his former tutor, R.B. Bennett, in drafting the measure. Bennett's fee was $1,000 but Brownlee wanted to be certain he had a "law which can not be set aside on technical grounds." He guided the Bill through a prolonged debate, explaining the various provisions, such as permit costs and licensing regulations. Recognizing that the strong sentiments on the issue cut across party lines, he proposed the unusual course of a free vote and cited several British constitutional authorities to show there was both precedent and ground for having it. In defense of his decision to put the administration of the Act under one man with wide powers, he introduced the Commissioner he had selected, R.J. Dinning, and spoke of his fine reputation. It was typical of Brownlee to prefer placing the responsibility on one man in whom he had confidence, rather than trust in the checks and balances of the three man commission many had suggested. The character of the person holding a position was, for him, more important than the character of the institutional framework.

His care with the legislation did not prevent it from dividing communities all across Alberta. In some cases one faction wanted a licensed premises while another did not and, almost as frequently, two or more groups contested for a license. Brownlee, as in all disagreements, tried to have the parties resolve their differences directly with each other.

Another controversy arose out of the increased attempts to balance the budget. A Mineral Tax Act was passed providing for a nominal tax of three cents per acre on the holders of mineral rights. Immediately, the two largest land owners, the Canadian Pacific Railway Company and the Hudson's Bay Company, which together had been granted mineral rights to over ten million acres in Alberta, protested the tax in Ottawa. The Dominion Government quickly disallowed the provincial statute, amazing a wide segment of Alberta's population, outside the U.F.A. as well as in. Brownlee, who argued the Alberta case, attacked Ottawa's action on three grounds. First, it had become constitutional practice for the federal government to use its power of disallowance sparingly and only when a province enacted legislation clearly outside its jurisdiction as defined by Section 92 of the British North America Act. Brownlee contended that the Mineral Tax was a direct tax, on property within the province, and as such clearly within its competence. To disallow such an Act was a blatant infringement of provincial sovereignty. The second objection was that the disallowance arbitrarily denied the Province a basic right, access to the courts, to have the constitutionality of the Act determined. The third ground of attack was on the reasons for the disallowance which, after some delay, the Minister of Justice, Ernest Lapointe, released. Brownlee rejected them out of hand, calling them erroneous and claiming Lapointe must be "unfamiliar" with the land-holding system outside Quebec. The protest was futile. The disallowance remained and whether the reasons for it were erroneous or not, Lapointe was not about to supply any others.

The summer of 1924 saw renewed activity in cooperative marketing. Within Alberta, a livestock pool and three major dairy pools were organized. Brownlee was an active consultant to all of these, drawing up their instruments of incorporation and the various contracts. He was especially involved with the livestock pool since it planned to take over the U.G.G.'s own livestock business in the province. He was still the U.G.G.'s chief counsel and during the difficult negotiations creating the livestock pool his cool presence as an intermediary became crucial in order to avoid squabbles. He was in a very delicate position. First, he did not believe there was enough business in Alberta to warrant two farmer owned livestock concerns but he saw there was no hope of resisting the enthusiasm for a "pool". As he confided to Crerar, "I am a little bit afraid the pool movement has become more or less of a fever in this Province and will not be brought to a sane basis until some commodity has been organized with disastrous results."

Second, there was a true dilemma to which he applied his typical approach of weighing the alternatives and foreseeing the possible consequences of each decision, just as the good chess player visualizes the consecutive positions of both the white and black pieces. "If I give assistance to the Committee in organizing the Provincial Pool it may prove a failure in a short time and, of course, there would be some reaction both against myself personally and against the Government," he reasoned. On the other hand, if he refused to help, the livestock pool would be organized anyway and harm the U.G.G. business. Therefore, it would be better to keep involved since, "I might be of some assistance in bringing the two organizations together."

Thus he intellectualized his way through problems but, did he apply the same approach to his career and his personal life? Did he project consecutive consequences of situations so skillfully that he could often "happen" to be in the right place at the right time. Was this what his college friends meant by the comment that "there was always something indirect about Brownlee"? Did this explain his accumulation of college offices, or even his heir apparent role in the U.F.A. Government? Was he really a master at manipulating people and events while not seeming to do so? There would be many steps in his career which would raise these questions and another one was about to unfold.

Wheat Pools were now formed in Saskatchewan and Manitoba and a Central Selling Agency was being formed to market the wheat of all three Pools, either to millers or for export. Each provincial Pool appointed directors to a Board to control the Central Selling Agency and Brownlee worked closely with this group, both in designing the original framework of its organization and advising on policy matters. In the process he formed a close relationship with A.J. McPhail, who became President of the Agency and almost changed the course of Brownlee's life.

It had been Brownlee and Wood who, one evening over supper, persuaded McPhail to accept the presidency. Brownlee also urged him to hire a top flight manager for the Central Selling Agency. McPhail approached a number of prominent men in the grain trade but, being frugal, he balked at the high salaries they demanded. He considered $5,000 a suitable salary but Brownlee convinced him that one could not economize if one wanted a top-rated professional. For $5,000, he argued, one got a $5,000 manager but if the best candidate demanded $10,000 it was well worth paying that.

By late August all the contracts were signed, arrangements with the banks completed, seats on the Grain Exchange and Lake Shippers' Clearance Association purchased and, in fact, everything was ready for the operation of the three Wheat Pools and the Central Selling Agency except that a general manager had not yet been hired. Now McPhail turned the tables on Brownlee and offered him the position at a salary of $20,000 per year. Could Brownlee have been surprised by the offer or its attractive terms? He talked to McPhail, and others, frequently about his desire to leave government and return to law or business management. He had influenced the selection of several of the Agency's Board members, including McPhail's choice as president. He had convinced McPhail that a general manager was vital and that the salary should be generous. All the while, by his assistance and advice he had been demonstrating that he was as qualified as anyone for the job. It was one of Brownlee's more obvious maneuvers but, was it really so obvious? Was the general managership his true objective?

He was forced to decline the position by the strenuous objections of the leaders of the Alberta Pool and the U.F.A., especially Wood. They knew that the Alberta Government needed Brownlee and several of them were coming to suspect that without him, the U.F.A. might not retain its hold on the Legislature. Both positions were important but it would be easier to find another general manager than to replace Brownlee in Edmonton. Clearly, retaining the Government of Alberta was vital, as the assistance to the organization of the Pool had shown, and it was there he appeared indispensable. Had this been his true objective, to underscore his indispensability by raising the spectre of his possible departure? Was he driving home his importance to the U.F.A. so that when thoughts turned to the question of Government leadership his claim would already have been staked?

U.F.A. Members were already closely reviewing their situation and a group came to feel that for the sake of their movement's future, Greenfield would have to be replaced. George Johnston, George McLoughlin, William Shields, Donald Cameron and A. B. Claypool were among those who feared that unless they changed leaders they would lose the next election. It was obvious that Greenfield had little interest in the detail of his position and, in short, was not doing his homework. Almost as disturbing, he no longer counted his closest friends among the U.F.A. group. Rather, he was spending more and more time with a crowd of cronies who headquartered at the Corona Hotel. As soon as Brownlee learned there were plans afoot to remove Greenfield, he contacted the Speaker, 0. L. McPherson, a leader of the dissatisfied Members, and told him that if they asked for Greenfield's resignation they would receive his own along with it. This threat threw a wrench into the plans. The group had simply assumed that Brownlee was the best choice to succeed Greenfield. Grudgingly the plans to replace Greenfield were set aside. Brownlee had put aside the crown for the first time.

It was not long until Brownlee was again demonstrating the value of his work on behalf of Western agriculture. Appeals were necessary to try and prevent the complete abrogation of the Crow's Nest Pass freight rates, one of the few benefits Western farmers had received from national transportation policies. Trough timely action by U.F.A. M.P.'s and vigorous governmental and legal support from Edmonton, the Board of Railway Commissioners' decision to abrogate the rates was eventually overturned, although only in part.

Brownlee also turned, with renewed determination, to the problem of balancing the budget. He decided to use his own Department as an example of the rigorous economies that were needed throughout the government service. He cut staff and ordered his officials to explain every instance in which costs had exceeded budgeted estimates. He finally got some support for his efforts when Richard Reid, who replaced Greenfield as Provincial Treasurer, presented a detailed brief to Cabinet recommending thorough cost control by all Ministers and the creation of a Purchasing Department to co-ordinate spending on supplies. Brownlee advised Reid to "insist that this be brought back before Cabinet at an early date."

Meanwhile, there was the continuing stream of routine matters which always required attention. Not least of these were the frequent requests that he use his position to benefit certain individuals either by securing them jobs or intervening for them before the courts. With only very rare exceptions he refused such requests and insisted that the formal channels be strictly followed. One example of this was his handling of a request from Howard Ferguson, Premier of Ontario, asking Brownlee to intervene on behalf of a relative of a former M.P.P. from Wentworth being charged in Edmonton. Ferguson cited the man's fine family background and suggested, indirectly, that Brownlee should get him off the charge and send him home to his family in Hamilton. Brownlee firmly declined such intervention and the accused was sentenced to twenty-three months at hard labour on a charge of gross indecency.

The final two months of 1924 were ones of almost continual travel for Brownlee and on one trip he took his boys to visit their grandparents in Brigden, while he attended yet another round conferences in Ottawa. They had an enjoyable time with the elder Brownlees. Christina had a collection of red plush furniture which, to the young boys, looked remarkably like the seats in the train. They took delight in arranging it in rows and playing the roles of passenger and conductor. Other boyish exuberances were less charming. On one occasion, the door to the cellar was left open and Christina, crossing her familiar kitchen the dark, fell in, breaking her arm. Perhaps the grandparents had mixed feelings about seeing the children off for home.

For their part, the boys were almost distraught that they would have to leave behind the household cat. They pleaded with their father to be allowed to take it with them and only desisted when he told them there would be an even better surprise waiting for them at home. Sure enough, when they arrived they were bowled over by a young bloodhound that Brownlee had acquired as surplus from the A.P.P. canine corps. It was the first of a series of large dogs which the family owned and which Brownlee enjoyed. It was a favourite pet until it developed the habit of chasing children on bicycles and, once it perfected the art of catching them, it was replaced.

* * *

As Brownlee looked ahead to 1925, the prospect was a daunting one. The central problem was the province's poor economic condition and central to that was the continuing plight of its farmers. The year was to see some recovery in wheat prices but that was quickly absorbed by the debt obligations of the previous years. As Brownlee had feared, the slight sign of returning prosperity launched zealous collection activity from some creditors. Most noticeable of these was Associated Mortgage Investors of New York which invested its clients' money in Western farm mortgages. After a period of being cooperative, it suddenly became one of the most aggressive collectors in the province. Both Brownlee and Fream intervened directly with the owners to attempt to achieve a more reasonable attitude and ameliorate the bitterness that such relentless hounding of debtors generated against all lenders. Even some municipalities became aggressive collectors of tax arrears. Fream found himself overwhelmed with cases but the Debt Adjustment Act helped control creditor rapacity and allowed a more balanced alleviation of financial obligations.

But that was a mere palliative. Attempts to improve the farmers' financial position significantly had had little success. The Wheat Pool was a magnificent organizational achievement but the gains it meant in improved handling charges were marginal. The top flight legal advisors Brownlee had secured to represent farmer interests were hard pressed to win even a draw against the intransigence of private corporations and the federal government. An irrigation scheme to alleviate drought problems in small areas of the south promised no immediate relief. In fact, calls for assistance to such projects as the Lethbridge Northern Irrigation District seemed to promise that, in the short term at least, irrigation might well be just another large financial "drain". There was the additional frustration that irrigation would improve substantially the market value of land owned by the C.P.R., which was so efficient at avoiding taxation by the province. Brownlee, for one, was not anxious to invest large sums in a scheme which would benefit a company which was not willing to bear some of the costs.

The agricultural sector was not the only one facing problems. In the coal mining areas, a continuing slack market meant no prospect of relief for the hard hit miners. They protested short shifts and frequent lay-offs by staging a prolonged strike. The attendant unrest and violence was a cause of concern, especially for Brownlee who was more sensitive than his colleagues about potential criticism of the Government on the issue.

Greenfield had promoted the export of coal to Ontario by special unit trains during the off-season of grain movement. In order to compete on the Ontario market, Alberta coal needed one of two things; either a subsidized freight rate of about $3 per ton or a tariff against American coal of an equal amount. The federal government was reluctant to subsidize freight rates and rejected out of hand the notion of a tariff, even though tariffs had proven so advantageous to Eastern manufacturers. The attempt to diversify the province's economy had come to nothing. In any event, neither coal, nor oil, nor natural gas, the latter two being produced in the Turner Valley and near Medicine Hat, could contribute substantially to the provincial economy until the ownership and control of the natural resources was transferred to the Province.

While the main advantages of the transfer of the natural resources would be the long term economic ones, there would also be short term political ones. J.R. Boyle, just prior to handing over his Liberal leadership to C. Mitchell and escaping to the bench, advised Prime Minister King that "it is generally conceded here that the Greenfield government is doomed in the next general election unless something extraordinary happens. That extraordinary thing which Greenfield wants to happen now is obtaining from you the natural resources at once."

Certainly the U.F.A. needed a breakthrough on at least one major issue on which to campaign. The transfer of control of the natural resources, the most symbolic of the issues, would have provided an ideal achievement to offset the lack of progress in balancing the budget or restoring agricultural prosperity. Whether King delayed acting for such political reasons or not, the federal government was exasperatingly slow.

At a conference in January of 1925, Alberta accepted the federal offer of a transfer of control plus a continuation of the subsidy for three years. O.M. Biggar was appointed by the federal government to draft an agreement and he and Brownlee had several sessions painstakingly framing all the clauses. Greenfield, naively, began to portray his anxiousness to have the agreement announced.

In late January he wired King to ask when Biggar's report would be ready. In March another wire asked when it would be considered. King advised that there would be no time to study the matter until after the House prorogued. In May, a special Ministerial committee met to discuss the draft agreement, clause by clause. On the Dominion side were King, Motherwell, Lapointe and Charles Stewart, with Biggar as counsel. Alberta was represented by Greenfield and Brownlee.

The first meeting was on May 19 and subsequent ones were held at leisurely intervals into June. On June 7, Brownlee left for Edmonton, all the clauses having been re-drafted and discussed. Greenfield telephoned King to say rather forlornly, that since the matter was so important he was prepared to stay in Ottawa "a day or two longer" in hope that an agreement could be concluded. Four days later King informed him that the federal Cabinet had decided it would like to have the summer "to study the agreement and all its implications." Greenfield returned to Edmonton empty handed. Normally, there would have been a summer election but with nothing to announce the prudent thing to do was wait.

The federal government was apparently stalling on the natural resources control transfer, but there was one other major issue -- provincial railways. As Brownlee had advised, if the burdensome lines could be sold, the U.F.A. could announce the solution of the railway question and campaign on the promise of balancing the budget now that an annual expense of $1,500,000 had been removed. However, neither transcontinental system was interested. Finally, though, as the existing lease on the E.D. & B.C. neared expiry at the end of July, both systems made offers to lease the line. At this point the Royal Bank, the major mortgage holder of the line, announced that it would not agree to any further lease unless the Alberta government redeemed the stock it held as security for its mortgage. The amount demanded was $2,000,000, an amount beyond the province's resources.

With the breakdown of the railway negotiations another split in the U.F.A. emerged. Vernor Smith, the Minister of Railways, came out strongly in the Members' meeting in favour of the government discharging the mortgage held by the Bank and becoming the owners and even the operators of the railway. Brownlee leaned toward this approach but took care not to become embroiled in the controversy. Greenfield opposed the government's assuming ownership and this stand made him unpopular with his supporters, many of whom were already questioning his leadership. Finally the group which had planned to ask for his resignation the previous year reassembled and George Johnston and O.L. McPherson agreed to bell the cat and ask Greenfield to resign. Not entirely surprised, he agreed but the next day, acting apparently on advice from his cronies, he reversed his position. By this time, Brownlee was aware of developments and again threatened to resign along with Greenfield. He had put aside the crown a second time.

In theory, Brownlee had other political options. There had been rumours that summer of his being invited to enter the Dominion Cabinet. Now, with the federal election over and King heading a minority government, a tentative offer of a portfolio was relayed via Crerar. King was toying with the idea of getting "rid of both Motherwell and Stewart and [having] their places taken by men who have the confidence of the Progressives -- possibly Brownlee in Alberta and Bracken in Manitoba." Brownlee had a lively interest in the national political scene but the situation in Alberta was still such that it could only be an academic interest.

Finally, those trying to oust Greenfield enlisted H.W. Wood and confronted Brownlee at home. "If I had the ability, I'd damned sure take it," Wood urged, "but it's you, John, who has the ability." Brownlee relented, providing he received a personal assurance that Greenfield did not doubt his loyalty. Someone left immediately and soon returned with the Premier, almost his old hearty self, in tow. There was no possible grudge, he boomed, he hadn't wanted the job in the first place and if Brownlee would take over, he would give him every assistance he could. With this agreement, on November 23, 1925, following Greenfield's formal resignation at Government House, John Brownlee agreed to form a Ministry.

Figure 4

John Edward Brownlee
Premier of Alberta
November 23, 1925 - July 10, 1934

(Photo courtesy of Glenbow Archives - NA-1451-11)

Chapter 9: Premier of Alberta

The major issues which confronted Brownlee as Premier were four: balance the budget, dispose of the provincial railways as a financial burden, secure control of the natural resources, and win the next election. All were interrelated and progress on the first three appeared essential to the latter. He immediately set about implementing his business-like approach to these issues.

First, he called a meeting with several of the U.F.A. M.P.'s to co-ordinate efforts to obtain the control of the natural resources, protect freight rate agreements, devise a system of rural credits and otherwise assist the Province in obtaining its objectives. The M.P.'s were in a unique position to help since the King Government's hold on office was so precarious that a withdrawal of U.F.A. support would mean its immediate defeat.

Having secured the cooperation of this important bloc, he next sent off a series of telegrams to Prime Minister King urging immediate action on special freight rates for Alberta coal, the rationalization of the Province's railways and, of course, the transfer of the control of the resources. "There appears to be no reason why it should not be possible to have the agreement as concluded placed before Parliament at the opening of its next session," he blithely informed King. "May we be assured that this question will be included in the Speech from the Throne?"

Before he could follow up on these initiatives, he was struck down with "congestion of the lungs." Even more serious, Florence contracted the illness and, given her previous condition, her life was thought to be in danger. The news reached the Prime Minister who "was shocked to hear that Brownlee's wife is dying of tuberculosis and that he has an affected lung and has to go South." For two full weeks, he was confined to his home under a doctor's care. By Christmas he and Florence had recovered sufficiently to travel to Victoria for a week of rest before he returned to his duties. His wife stayed behind hoping the change in climate would help.

Brownlee was in Edmonton barely long enough to re-pack before leaving for Ottawa where he had dinner with King and discussed the country's political situation during a pleasant fireside chat in Laurier House. He reassured King that the Progressives

119

would support the shaky Liberal Government, especially once the Speech from the Throne (with its announcement of the natural resources control agreement) was made public.

He was accompanied on this trip to the East by Vernor Smith, provincial Minister of Railways, and together they saw Charles Dunning, recently become federal Minister of Railways. They tried to persuade Dunning that the Dominion should take over the Province's railways. Next, they went to Montreal where they met with the head officers of the Royal Bank. Although the Bank had originally valued its E.D. & B.C. shares at $2,000,000, Brownlee was able to conclude an agreement for their purchase for $1,300,000. This move gave the Alberta Government much more latitude. It could now sell, lease, or even operate the railroads and act in negotiations as a principal rather than as a highly interested third party. Brownlee and Smith took immediate steps in this direction and, while still in Montreal, made direct offers for the sale of the railways to Sir Henry Thornton, President of the C.N.R. and E.W. Beatty, President of the C.P.R.

Back in Ottawa on January 9, 1926, there was one more important piece of business to attend to at the Prime Minister's office. As King described it, "at noon Brownlee of Alberta and Smith, a member of his Government -- a Conservative -- came in with Lapointe and Mr. Stewart and signed the agreements for the transfer of the Natural Resources to Alberta. "

Thus, in little more than a month after assuming the Premiership, Brownlee had made significant progress on all the important issues facing his Government. Part of the reason for this was the fact that whether he was dealing with bank or railway presidents, federal Ministers, or even the Prime Minister himself, he was accepted as one among equals. Unlike a Greenfield or a Wood, he did not lack a formal education or have to rely on advisors to explain the intricacies of financial or legislative detail. He projected an air of competence and confidence so that he was able to deal with issues more authoritatively than any other Albertan of the day. King referred to him as "Brownlee of Alberta" and that term, for the next decade, would sum up his place in Canadian affairs.

Before leaving Ottawa, he had another private chat with King. The October federal election had left the Liberals with fewer seats than the Conservatives but, since the latter were short of a majority, King proposed continuing in office. He had, himself, been defeated in North York and sought Brownlee's opinion about the chances of succeeding in a by-election in any of the four Alberta seats won by Liberals. Brownlee replied very frankly in a handwritten, confidential letter giving King an astute assessment of his chances in each riding. "There will also be the advantage of a winter election which may keep the farm vote from being recorded," he advised and concluded, "Regret I cannot assist you more."

Many of Brownlee's U.F.A. supporters would have been shocked to learn that he had given as much assistance to King as he had. The reality was, though, that less than a third of Albertans had supported U.F.A. federal candidates while almost sixty percent had voted for the Liberals or Conservatives. The truth was that when it came to federal politics, many in the U.F.A., leaders included, had preferences as between the Liberals and Conservatives. Brownlee, to a degree which reassured his father, preferred King and the Liberals. Others, among them U.F.A. M.P.' s W. T. Lucas (Camrose) and A.M. Boutillier (Vegreville), favoured the Conservatives under Meighen. Given the tense Parliamentary situation these preferences became crucial for on January 15, Lucas and Boutillier supported a Meighen amendment and brought the Liberals within three votes of defeat.

Why had they supported the Conservatives? Crerar was one insider who speculated that, "the Conservatives held out promises, I think to both Lucas and Boutellier [sic], that if they got into office they would be looked after and Alberta would be relieved of its liabilities under the northern railways ... I do not wish you for a moment to get any impression that Brownlee was a party to anything of this kind, for I am sure he was not," Crerar went on, in a confidential letter to Robert Forke, nominal leader of the Progressive group, "but I think also you should know that his Minister of Railways ... was using his influence, especially with Lucas and Boutellier, to get them to support Meighen, and I am sure that this deal in railroads was one of the considerations held out to them."

Had Smith been intriguing with his old friends behind his Premier's back, or was Crerar underestimating Brownlee's capacity for indirection? Brownlee must have left Ottawa with the sense of having wrought a major coup. No matter which party came to the top in the volatile cauldron of Ottawa politics, Alberta stood to receive a major gain: either the control of the natural resources from the Liberals, the disposal of the railways with help from the Conservatives, or even both. Not incidentally, such a major gain for Alberta would also be a significant boost to the Brownlee Government's chances for re-election.

* * *

Once Brownlee was back in Edmonton, there were such details to attend to as a request from the new Poultry Pool for his photograph to put on their office mantelpiece. He had given copious assistance to this virtually all female organization, formed under the chairmanship of Mrs. R.B. Gunn, one of the leaders in the U.F.W.A. Also, the Livestock Pool needed some more assistance and its chairman assured Brownlee that, "you are the only man whom we can get to represent us, who has the confidence of all parties." It was evident that with his new duties as Premier, even the work-devouring Brownlee would not have the time to look after the growing legal needs of the Pools. He soon added a well regarded young lawyer, M. M. Porter, to his private practice in Calgary, mainly to handle the Pool files. Porter was to serve as counsel for the Alberta Wheat Pool for almost thirty years.

Now, the George P. Smith case captured the headlines. The preliminary investigations of Harry Brace, a former Pinkerton detective Brownlee had assigned to the case, had been thorough and revealing. A further judicial inquiry resulted in warrants being issued for the arrest of Matthew Esdale, a printer, J. W. Jeffrey, former King's Printer, and Smith, former Liberal Minister of Education. Smith declined to return from his new home in Hamilton but the case went to court nonetheless. Brownlee, still Attorney General, sought the best possible barrister to prosecute what promised to be an important action. A. A. McGillivray, who had handled the Picariello case, was now provincial Conservative leader so Brownlee turned to A. L. Smith, a Calgary lawyer with a fast growing reputation as a skilled cross examiner.

The evidence revealed that while George Smith was Minister, over $18,000 worth of printing contracts had gone to Camrose Job Press. At the time, Smith claimed to have sold his interest in that company but Brace had uncovered an agreement by which Smith had continued to receive a share of the profits. He had also directed large contracts to Esdale Press of Edmonton, owned by Matthew Esdale, a staunch Liberal supporter. The highlight of the trial, however, was the bizarre history of a cheque for $5,820.

The prosecution strategy, apparently devised by Brownlee and A. L. Smith, was to drop the charges against Esdale and Jeffrey in return for their appearing as witnesses against George Smith. Jeffrey testified that on the day after the Liberal loss in 1921, Smith called him into his office and directed him to authorize a large printing of extra copies of the Education Act, to be done by Esdale Press. Jeffrey authorized payment even though there was no evidence the printing was ever done. Esdale Press did not enter the payment in its regular books. It was alleged that Esdale had opened a special bank account for the deposit of that cheque and had immediately re-issued the amount ($5,820) in the form of a cheque payable to George P. Smith. R. D. Purdy, manager of the Alberta Wheat Pool, had been, in 1921, the assistant manager of the bank where Smith cashed the cheque. Brownlee, a friend of Purdy, had discussed the case with him at least as early as November, 1925.

Despite what appeared to be conclusive evidence, the Crown failed to win a conviction. The strategy of dropping the charges against Esdale and Jeffrey backfired. First, it enabled the defense lawyer, McKinley Cameron, to argue that the Crown's case rested on the testimony of two who were admittedly dishonest. Second, the prosecution of George Smith alone enabled the Liberal Edmonton Bulletin to claim that the charges were politically motivated. This argument had more impact than Brownlee expected because the majority of Albertans saw the matter as one of simple justice. If three men had conspired to defraud the public purse, all should have been prosecuted. Numerous resolutions from U.F.A. Locals questioned the morality of dropping some of the charges. Another prosecution error was to change the charge from "conspiracy to defraud" to "theft". The latter charge put a larger burden of proof on the Crown to show that George Smith had ended up in possession of stolen funds. The jury decided the evidence was not conclusive and brought in a verdict of not guilty. Mr. Justice Ives, the trial judge, dismissed the case without comment. U.F.A. Locals, however, were not as reticent and Brownlee finally had to take the unusual step of publishing a letter from A. L. Smith, accepting full responsibility for the way the prosecution had been conducted. But, had Brownlee been a little too clever, trying to out maneuver the defendants instead of relying on the moral strength of his case? More than he realized, the conduct and outcome of the case were a blow to his prestige. Brownlee had intended to remind the U.F.A. of "villainous conduct of the Liberals", but the conduct of their own champion had fallen short of the purity of principle which would have won their enthusiastic support.

* * *

On February 11, the first session of the Legislative Assembly with Brownlee as Premier began. Perhaps the biggest surprise came a week later when Brownlee, amid cheers from his supporters, announced that the public accounts for 1925 showed a surplus of $188,019 instead of the expected deficit. The U.F.A. had finally achieved a balanced budget. With the transfer of the control of the natural resources thought to be imminent and the disposal of the burdensome provincial railways nearer than it had ever been, the Government, for the first time since assuming office, could look ahead with some optimism. Total provincial revenues were under $12,000,000 but with good management and normal growth the province had a right to expect that the worst conditions were over. That the picture had changed so markedly in the three months since Brownlee had assumed the Premiership augured well for his own future as well.

There were, however, to be some complications. On February 24, O.M. Biggar arrived to discuss a number of minor differences between the natural resources agreement as signed and the Bill that King proposed introducing in the Commons. One of the changes involved attaching a rider which required the Province to administer the remaining school lands and the school lands fund "for the support of schools organized and carried on therein, in accordance with the provisions of Section 17 of the Alberta Act."

Brownlee approved the change on the understanding that it merely tied the use of the school lands fund to school purposes.

No one in Alberta took any further notice of the change until almost the end of the Session when the Orange Sentinel of Toronto raised an alarm about Alberta being forced to use some of its school lands fund to support separate schools. Brownlee immediately telegrammed King to say that it had been brought to his attention that the change he had agreed to could provide an "opening for raising the whole question of provincial rights in relation to education. It was never suggested to me, by or on behalf of your government that this was necessary or intended and was never contemplated by me." He suggested three possible amendments: one dropping the reference to Section 17, a second substituting "in accordance with the laws of the Province", and a third retaining the reference but adding a clause to the effect that nothing in the agreement to transfer control of the natural resources should limit the jurisdiction already accorded, the Province. Mackenzie King replied that "to change it now would raise the very question it is desirable to avoid raising."

The federal Cabinet, having gained the change which Ernest Lapointe wanted in order to disarm potential objections from French-Canadian Nationalist leader, Henri Bourassa, refused to allow the Alberta Government to retract that change. The political reality was that the majority of King's seats were in Quebec. The inclusion of the reference to Section 17 was thought necessary to reassure French-Canada that, in transferring the control of the natural resources, the rights of the Catholic minority to separate schools had been protected. From this point of view, any further change would be likely to initiate yet another squabble between Quebec and Ontario over the character of the institutions under which Westerners would live.

Brownlee, too, was anxious to avoid any religious-ethnic controversies but it soon became apparent that the matter which most alarmed Albertans was not the school question but the intrusion of the federal government into an area of exclusive provincial jurisdiction. King chose to interpret the Alberta position as defending the validity of the Alberta Act and offered to submit the matter to the Supreme Court. Brownlee firmly challenged this construction and protested, "We see no necessity for initiating proceedings to test the [Alberta] Act," but King proceeded on his determined course.

With seemingly nothing to be gained by further exchanges with Ottawa, Brownlee referred the question to the Assembly which ratified the natural resources agreement and amended the contentious clause to state simply that the school lands fund would be used to support schools "organized in accordance with the laws of the Province." Almost immediately afterward, Brownlee called a general election for June 28, 1926.

* * *

Brownlee stood firmly on the Government's record, calling it "Five Years of Progress". In speeches throughout the province he challenged electors to review that record, asking themselves two questions: first, had the Government shown itself to be honest, conscientious and sincere, and second, how had it conducted the ordinary, everyday matters of business. What his audiences saw on the platform was an extraordinarily tall man, well over two hundred pounds now, fixing them with a rivet-like gaze from behind the strong lenses of his circular wire framed glasses. Almost forty-three, he had a commanding presence but it was neither attractive nor engaging. He spoke for the most part as though exercising a routine duty, showing only hints that he could be a more effective and forceful speaker. His tone and manner reinforced his conception of government as "essentially the administration of business."

In his campaign speeches he touched on all the issues and reviewed the accomplishments. Of the struggle to overcome financial adversity, he said proudly, "We end our five-year period with the problem of finance practically solved." Of his contribution to the formation of the Wheat Pool, he remarked nonchalantly, "I am satisfied that the farmers of this Province know how the Wheat Pool was formed." In concluding his various addresses, he returned to the sentiments the U.F.A. had expressed in 1921. "The present election of 1926 is going to answer one great question," he proclaimed, aligning himself squarely with the expected rhetoric about the "evils of partyism". "Are we going to return in this

Province to Government based on the two-party system, or are we going to continue to work for a better [way]?"

The future of the Natural Resources Bill remained a concern but he came to recognize that "the question is not now [a] serious issue in [the] campaign." Having secured the public announcement of the transfer of control in the Throne Speech, and having signed a formal agreement, he had shifted the onus for action to the federal Government. Even King admitted to himself that "Brownlee has the best of the position thus far ... The whole trouble is due to Lapointe's fears of Bourassa, and allowing an unnecessary section to be added to the bill."

As Brownlee came to recognize the strength of his position, he became less insistent on an immediate transfer and began to see other items, such as the proposed boundaries of the National Parks, which might benefit from closer study. He continued to object strongly to King derailing the matter by a referral to the courts, but he tried to soften criticism of the delay by U.F.A. M.P.'s. He had some success in restraining those such as H. E. Spencer, with whom he had a close relationship, but others, notably Lucas and Boutillier, continued to pursue their own objectives and vote against the King administration. The failure of the federal government to live up to its promise to transfer the control of the resources was clearly one factor in the wavering support of many "Progressives" which was soon to lead to the tumultuous dissolution of Parliament and another federal election. Just on the eve of that happening, Brownlee and the provincial U.F.A. won their election.

It was the first time that a Farmers' government had won re-election. Even more impressive, it had done so with a larger majority than after the initial victory. The final results which, thanks to the U.F.A.'s introduction of the preferential ballot and to the number of recounts, took almost one month to determine, were: U.F.A., 43; Liberal, 7; Labour, 5; Conservative, 4; and Independent Labour, 1. The U.F.A. had held forty seats at dissolution. One of their gains was in Edmonton where J. F. Lymburn, a lawyer with non-partisan credentials whom Brownlee had named Attorney General about a month before the election, headed the poll. Lymburn, a forty-six year old native of Scotland, had lived in Edmonton for twenty-five years. His lack of political affiliation recommended him well to the U.F.A. and his continuing reputation for integrity and competence made his appointment a material strengthening of the Cabinet. As well, in naming a new Attorney General, Brownlee was freed from considerable responsibility.

The election results disconcerted the provincial Liberals. Their hopes of regaining power, optimistically predicted by the Edmonton Bulletin, had been dashed. Their new leader, J. T. Shaw, the former U.F.A. endorsed Member of Parliament, had been handicapped throughout the campaign by the ready fund of quotations from his previous affiliation, with which the U.F.A. were able to attack the credibility of his new position. Likewise, the Conservatives under A. A. McGillivray fared poorly. Although Brownlee admired him highly as a barrister and friend, he believed that McGillivray made a tactical error by revealing his entire programme just after being named leader so that by election time he had "nothing new to say." Brownlee also thought that, like Meighen, McGillivray had a "first class intellect but was out of touch with the feeling of the people."

Despite the election win, all was not well within the U.F.A. Some Locals had become moribund and there was difficulty, Brownlee observed, "in two or three constituencies in even getting a nomination meeting together because the Locals had pretty much passed out of existence." In part, this decline resulted from the absorption of the natural local leaders into one or other of federal politics, provincial politics, farmer owned companies, cooperatives or Pools. Another reason was simply waning enthusiasm. For a group which prided itself in grass-roots-only fund raising and organization, such a deterioration in involvement and local leadership did not auger well for the future. Brownlee recognized this danger but his warnings went unheeded. In those constituencies where enthusiasm had failed, his corporate organizational approach was necessary to fill the void. Such direction from the centre was antithetical to U.F.A. principles but the members refused to address themselves to the long range, larger implications of the necessity for Brownlee's action.

As soon as the campaign was over, he took his family for a holiday in the East. The presence of the Premier of Alberta in Brigden, Ontario attracted notice, with requests for interviews from local reporters and discreet invitations to address various clubs. In the main, though the usual seclusion in which the Brownlees lived was respected. William was intensely proud of his son's success and fascinated by the political world in which he now traveled. Christina, while regretting such developments as the end of prohibition, also basked in the accomplishments and rectitude of her son. On the return journey, Brownlee took his sons to the Mayo Clinic for further check-ups and treatment by reputedly some of the best doctors in North America. While there, he insisted that Florence, too, have a thorough examination. She, but not Brownlee, was surprised that she received a completely clean bill of health and the advice to resume a more active life.

However, politics could not be escaped for long. Brownlee did not want the issue of the contentious school clause in the resources agreement to be played up in the election rhetoric of the federal campaign. "We are living in peace here and wish to continue to live at peace," he commented and made it clear to the Liberals, through Crerar, that if they raised the issue he would be forced to go out and defend his position. It was an effective threat since any slim hope the Liberals had for election wins in Alberta depended upon support from those who had just voted for provincial U.F.A. candidates.

Mackenzie King's hope of absorbing "Progressives" through gradual "fusion" with Liberals had been disappointed in Alberta. Charles Stewart, fighting hard to retain his influence, remained adamantly opposed to cooperation with what he and die-hard provincial Liberals were now beginning to term "the Brownleeites". Brownlee's strong showing in the election made it completely unnecessary for him to solicit Liberal cooperation, unlike the situation in Saskatchewan and Manitoba where political fortunes drove Liberals and Farmer groups together. Brownlee had the strongest mandate of any Western Premier but, ironically, this strength would isolate him and, in the long run, make him more vulnerable.

However, for the time being his position appeared unassailable even though he continued to keep alive rumours that he might leave politics behind, telling A .J. McPhail for example, that he was "still ready to come to the Pool." Keeping other options open eased the pressures on him and, more importantly, strengthened his position with his caucus and his Cabinet. By demonstrating on the one hand his indispensability, and on the other keeping alive his potential exit, he created a situation in which he had considerable power to pursue his own objectives.

Chapter 10: International Wheat Marketing

From his position of power, and having nipped any potential Liberal criticism in the bud, Brownlee was able to look rather philosophically at the 1926 federal election campaign unfolding. "It may be that the people of Canada are exercised over the constitutional question," he reflected, "but I am personally rather inclined to doubt it." Once again, he under-estimated the role of the emotional in politics, for Mackenzie King rode the "constitutional question" that he had manufactured, to a comfortable majority.

Meanwhile, Brownlee's routine work continued, sometimes giving rise to unpleasant incidents. On one occasion, A. M. Matheson, (U.F.A. - Vegreville), frustrated by Brownlee's procrastination at providing an additional police station for his constituency, warned, "I will be sorry if it becomes necessary for me to take this matter on the floor of the House." Brownlee replied calmly, "I personally would not wish you to feel any hesitation in raising this question on the floor of the House." Faced with this challenge, Matheson backed down, admitting he felt "duly and properly squashed." It was obviously counter-productive for a backbencher to alienate himself from Brownlee and futile to attempt to appeal over the Premier's head to the public on such a small matter. Ironically, it came to be true that Brownlee was less sensitive to the concerns of his supporters than to those of his opponents or the press.

Such sensitivity may have been part of the reason why, in the fall of 1926, Brownlee accepted the resignation of E. J. Fream as Commissioner of the Debt Adjustment Bureau. Fream had helped literally thousands of farmers to deal with their indebtedness. His competent handling of mammoth responsibilities had, no doubt, relieved the Government of much pressure to initiate more radical measures to assist debt ridden farmers. However, in 1926, rumours surfaced that he was exceeding his authority and disbursing funds to his staff in an irregular manner. Brownlee ordered an investigation which revealed that Fream had authorized some salary advances and bonuses without observing the usual rules of civil service financial accountability. As soon as these were questioned, Fream, himself extremely sensitive to criticism, resigned. It was a sad conclusion to a friendship.

Fortunately, there were happier times. In November, the U.F.A. held a gala banquet in the ornate main ballroom of the Palliser Hotel in Calgary. They were honouring H. W. Wood, and welcoming him home from a three month cruise to Asia and Australia. Brownlee proposed the Toast to the Guest. It was one of the warmest addresses of his life. He began on a note of gentle, good humour, describing his friendship with Wood over the years. "I have had the pleasure of playing rummy with him ... He loses many a nickel in the course of an evening. Once in a while he wins a nickel, and if you could see the smile of satisfaction that comes to his face when he wins a nickel, you would see our President in one of his lighter moods," he declared to generous laughter.

He went on to describe the great gains which democracy had made, both around the world and in Alberta, and the great contribution that Wood had made in the latter sphere. He was fulsome in his tributes, describing Wood as "working and struggling in honesty and sincerity and devotedly to further the interests of the people, ... his own personal interests ... relegated to the background." It was a moving tribute and showed clearly Brownlee's capacity to master the occasion. Wood, in thanking the 350 people assembled in his honour, paid special thanks to his "old friend and disciple." The occasion was undoubtedly one of the high points in the history of the U.F.A.. As well, it underlined the fact that Wood was passing into the role of "the grand old man", and as he did, Brownlee's ascendancy became even more pronounced.

As 1927 began, Alex Ross, a casualty in the general election, resigned from the Cabinet. Brownlee defended the lateness of the move as necessary to allow Ross to complete the season's work. "I thought this to be only following good business principles," he commented. He replaced Ross as Minister of Public Works and Labour with O. L. McPherson, one of those most insistent on the U.F.A. taking political action in 1919. He had a reputation for bold (some said head-strong) action, as his leading role in the removal of Greenfield had shown. The Speaker in the previous Assembly, he had also been a Director of both the Alberta Wheat Pool and the Central Selling Agency. In adding McPherson, Brownlee strengthened the farmer element of his Government.

Although he claimed the Labour Members were still his "second favourite group", his decision not to replace Ross with another labour Member set him clearly apart from such federal U.F.A. Members as William Irvine, who was beginning to work toward closer cooperation with Labour.

Another of Brownlee's appointments caused even more controversy. Naming Herbert Greenfield as the Alberta representative in Britain, seemed an obvious sinecure for the former Premier. Some backbenchers were embarrassed about defending the decision. Brownlee urged them to defend it strictly on merit, pointing out Greenfield's unique qualifications for the position of representative of the Province and how he could benefit Alberta in establishing business contacts and intelligently recruiting and advising immigrants. Greenfield did perform well in his London office with his engaging personality and familiarity with Alberta. He kept up a steady stream of correspondence with Brownlee and acted as a resident guide for Albertans visiting Britain.

In January, Brownlee was in Ottawa to help argue the case for the exemption of the Pools from income tax. They had been exempt but as they expanded their elevator network and began paying patronage dividends, the private grain corporations pleaded unfair competition. The federal government responded with plans to impose income taxes on the Pools' elevator systems. Brownlee and McPhail argued "that the Elevator Company is a subsidiary of the Pool and if the Pool is exempt, the Elevator Company should be ... Any surplus we have at the end of the year is simply an excess charge, and belongs to the farmers." Partly because of this intervention, but probably more because the tax promised to damage future Liberal election chances in the West, the plans for an income tax on Pool elevators were shelved.

Brownlee was the key-note speaker at the 1927 U.F.A. Annual Convention. He was becoming a master at such formal addresses. His style, formal and dignified, suited a "Premier's Address", but he had developed lately a greater capacity for the human touch and the humourous. His literary quotations and allusions seemed more natural and less obligatory. In fact, his penchant for poetic quotations became so pronounced that some political opponents used them to caricature him. When he spoke to the U.F.A. now, he was not as before simply an expert appendage to the organization. In a subtle yet very real way, he had become the centre. It was he now, rather than Wood, who personified their power. When he spoke of them "fostering an active, aggressive public opinion" and making a great "contribution to the welfare of Alberta," he was interpreting for them their place in reality. As Wood had done, he gave them an understandable description of the events in which they were involved and made them feel proud by explaining the significance of their role in the world. In this way he moved beyond being a mere source of information and became a source of inspiration. In short, many were beginning to have faith in John Brownlee. He had assumed the mantle of leadership and, far from that mantle having the usual formalizing and distancing effect, it seemed to make him more understandable, more human, and thus more attractive.

In the Legislative Assembly, when the Session began, he was relaxed in his dominant role, moving easily from the dignified personage of Premier to champion of his group and terror of the Opposition. Better prepared, more expert, and with more information at his ready recall than anyone in the House, he was able to toy with his opponents, colourfully describing their ineptitude and impotence in the last election, to the hearty laughter of his backbenchers. "Then finally along came June, 1926, and the old dilapidated wreck, with the windshield broken and four flat tires -- I hope you do not think I am alluding to the four Conservative Members -- its engine knocking and its gas tank leaking, limped into the garage from its great adventure."

His mantle of leadership was nowhere more evident than in the Assembly. Interestingly, he now abandoned the former practice of occupying the seat at the end of the front row to the immediate right of the Speaker, and began the custom of the Premier's desk occupying the centre of the front row. This central position in the chamber and his towering height, both subtly reinforced his dominance.

The major subject before the Assembly was the handling of the railway question. After acquiring control of the E.D. & B.C. and the Central Canada Railway by purchasing the common stock from the Royal Bank, the Government faced the question of whether to sell, lease, or operate the lines as a public utility. To sell, Brownlee pointed out to the Opposition, required a buyer, and neither the C.N.R. nor C.P.R. was interested. This was understandable in view of the enormous debt load of the lines and their annual operating losses. As for leasing, the C.P.R. allowed its five year lease to lapse before proposing to renew it at terms less advantageous to the Province. Vernor Smith argued that the Government should forget the leasing of the lines and operate them directly. Brownlee was less doctrinaire in his support of public ownership. He insisted that the leasing option be kept open for a time in case a proposal was received which would result in a greater reduction of the liabilities than would operating the lines. His principal concern was the balance sheet.

The eventual decision to operate the lines was eased by the fact that Smith was a business acquaintance of John Callaghan, one of the few successful railroad contractors in Alberta. He was financially well-to-do but he agreed to abandon his semi-retirement for one reason -- he loved the Peace River country. Soon after the decision, he was appointed Superintendent of Railways and set off, with Brownlee and Smith, on a first hand inspection of the acquisition. Brownlee enjoyed the trip immensely. In a Packard touring car, specially fitted to travel on railway tracks, they had an unrivaled view of the line and surrounding countryside. From time to time they stopped and Callaghan showed where maintenance had been inadequate or improvements needed to be made. Callaghan was known almost as well for his laconic speech as for his railroading knowledge and Brownlee was still inept at small talk but he returned with a much fuller understanding of the state of the Province's railways and a stronger conviction that his Government had made the right decision. He was also convinced that with sound management, the E.D. & B.C. could be turned from a financial burden into a paying proposition, and thus a salable item.

Strangely, the achievement of this was aided greatly by one of the most unlikely heroes of the Peace River country – Herman Trelle. Trelle's ideas about how grain should be grown had so infuriated his father that he had thrown Herman off the family farm. Nevertheless, in the fall of 1926, he won first prize for samples of wheat and oats at the Chicago Exhibition. The Americans, as is their wont, called this a World Championship and Trelle won instant notoriety as the World Champion Wheat Grower. The fact that he had grown his grain 600 miles north of the United States, in the northernmost grain growing area in the world, added a colourful dimension to the glowing press accounts. To Trelle, his celebrity status was no more than he deserved, but a wider result was that Alberta, and the Peace River country in particular, received an enormous amount of publicity which renewed interest in the area and sparked the beginning of a period of growth and prosperity. With increased traffic into the north and renewed optimism, the Government's decision to operate the railway, and its timing, looked like strokes of genius.

What Brownlee had to defend in the 1927 Session were the traffic agreements reached with the C.N.R. The E.D. & B.C. was, after all, only a branch line, and the C.N.R. had contracted to ship the line's freight over its transcontinental system. Awarding this contract to the C.N.R. was an astute move in which Brownlee took some pride. As the traffic on the line increased and a more optimistic tone swept the Canadian economy, the C.P.R., having leased the line for several years, would know exactly what it was losing. On the other hand, the C.N.R., now handling traffic coming off the line, would know exactly what it stood to gain by adding the line to its system. The stage had been set for the resolution of Alberta's railway question in a way that not even the wildest optimist of 1926 could have predicted.

Also during the Session, Brownlee announced a second successive small surplus in the public accounts. Increased spending on provincial highways was forecast and approval was given to pave two test sections of the Calgary to Edmonton highway and the driveways of the Legislative Grounds with a tar saturated sand found in large quantities near Fort McMurray. There was talk of extending the Alberta and Great Waterways Railway to tap this resource but in view of the costs involved the consensus was to delay. At the end of the Session, Brownlee made his first radio broadcast, one of a series on the Alberta Wheat Pool. He pointed out to his listeners that no less than thirty-two of the U.F.A. M.L.A.'s were members of the Pool. Radio was still in its infancy but already exploding in popularity, especially among rural Albertans. Unknown to Brownlee, the "Back to the Bible" broadcasts of Calgary high school principal William Aberhart were already popular in many rural homes.

Brownlee was still maintaining his contacts with Pool executives and was included in the twenty-two man Canadian delegation to the Second International Cooperative Wheat Pool Conference in Kansas City in early May. He was one of five speakers to the evening banquet on the first day of the Conference, his address following that of the United States' Secretary of Agriculture. Brownlee could not forbear mentioning that he represented the province in which the championship wheat and oats had been grown, before stating that the major problem before the delegates was how the farmer could be assured "of receiving not occasionally, but with reasonable regularity, the cost of production plus an adequate and substantial return for his labor and investment." He admitted that technological advances were making life on the farm "more pleasant" but the fundamental problem of making farming "a profitable industry" remained. The Canadian Pools had made a contribution in this direction, he declared, pointing to the price increases since their formation. Admittedly other factors had had an influence but a comparison of the Winnipeg and Chicago markets, he thought, supported his contention that the Pools were "a very substantial factor" in the upward price trend.

In concluding, he touched on the international factors bearing on wheat marketing. His remarks reflected a growing realization that the world had a large surplus wheat producing capacity. This explained the pronounced instability in world wheat prices and their downward shift when the crop of any major producer came on the market. Such a decline could quickly wipe out the profit margin of wheat farmers in several exporting countries. Brownlee suggested that major producing countries would have to limit their exports in order to insure price stability for all. This, he declared, was "the international aspect of the problem which cooperative marketing agencies have to solve." He could hardly have imagined that thirty years later he would still be attending international conferences attempting to work out such a cooperative solution.

Upon his return from Kansas City, he was one of the "prominent personages" present at a giant rally to kick-off the sign-up campaign for a second series of Alberta Wheat Pool contracts. The array of governmental, business and farm leaders present underscored Brownlee's belief that overwhelming support from all segments of society was the main reason for the unparalleled success of the Pool. His own example was an important factor in prompting that support. Even more exciting, during the summer the manager of the Prince of Wales' ranch signed a contract. The Royal Family supported the Alberta Wheat Pool.

* * *

By late June, John and Florence Brownlee and their traveling companions, the newlywed McPhails, were enjoying the "wonderful scenery down the St. Lawrence, dinner at the Captain's table, and the sight-seeing in and around Quebec City." The next day, as the ship poked its way toward Europe through fog and drizzle, the fog horn blasting every minute, McPhail, something of an exercise nut, insisted that Brownlee join him for a walk about the deck and some exercise in the gymnasium. On the following day, McPhail recorded proudly in his diary that the two walked nearly three miles on deck. Thereafter, he exercised alone. For Brownlee, much of the pleasure of travel was the opportunity to relax.

They arrived in Liverpool on July 4, 1927, and were met by the London agent of the Central Selling Agency (now more popularly known as the Canadian Wheat Pool), M. McIntyre, and immediately began touring grain exchanges, elevators, and talking with British "grain men". By July 7, they were welcomed in London by a thrilled and genial Herbert Greenfield. McPhail headquartered at the London office of the Canadian Pool, where McIntyre acted as the chief of the Pool's several overseas agencies. These offices arranged sales and funneled market information back to Canada for co-ordination and decision by the Central Board.

Brownlee, accompanied by Greenfield, met with financial and immigration officials. He wanted prospective immigrants routed through Greenfield so they could be screened more effectively and be better informed about Alberta conditions. He also wanted to meet personally with financial figures to make himself and his "firm" better known to potential investors. By impressing these people that a solid business manager was in charge of a Province with considerable potential, financing might well be more readily available and at lower rates.

The main purpose of the trip, however, was to investigate first hand the overseas grain trade and to explore the possibility of dealing directly with British and European customers, at one time considered a utopian idea. Traditionally, the ownership of a quantity of wheat changed hands many times from farmer to grain buyer to exporter to shipper to importer to miller and finally to the customer. Many farmers believed the Winnipeg and Liverpool grain exchanges multiplied the number of these ownership changes, which, in view of the world wheat surplus, decreased the farmer's share of the price. In short, the size of the pie was limited so the more people who had their fingers in it, the less there was for the farmer. As well, many farmers believed, grain exchanges encouraged speculative trading which distorted the natural law of supply and demand. Removing people from the trading of grain whose only motive was to make a profit for themselves was another long held utopian dream of the Western farmer.

Brownlee was far from an utopian but he was a firm believer in business efficiency. He was always collecting information about alternative business methods. He had long been convinced there were advantages to cooperatives, as long as they were run along solid business lines. Thus, he wanted to look closely at the possibility of the Canadian Pool dealing directly with British millers or, preferably, British cooperative associations. A producers' cooperative dealing directly with a consumers' cooperative seemed a very progressive step indeed.

The trip was not all business though. In the evenings they often went out as a foursome, one night to the Winter Garden Theatre to see a performance of <u>The Vagabond King</u> and on another night to the motion picture, <u>Ben Hur</u>, which McPhail, a motion picture fanatic, declared was "as good as any sermon." One highlight was an invitation to dinner at the Parliament Buildings followed by seats in the distinguished visitor's gallery from where they heard a speech by Winston Churchill. For Brownlee that really underlined the contrast between the England he saw now and that he had seen as a college freshman twenty-two years before.

Brownlee and McPhail were next off to the Continent where they toured the Pool agencies and met in rapid succession with "grain men" in Paris, Brussels, Antwerp, Rotterdam and Hamburg. Two men who represented over half the wheat growers of Western

Canada and more than 200,000,000 bushels of high grade milling wheat created comment among the grain traders and politicians of Europe.

The next week the foursome went to Scotland for meetings with the United Cooperative Bakers' Association, one of the oldest British cooperatives and a prime prospect for direct sales from the Canadian Wheat Pool. The meetings were punctuated with bus tours of the loch country, visits to castles and abbeys, and shopping for new wardrobes to take home. They even saw the brown lees of the highlands which, centuries before, served as the origin of Brownlee's family name.

Brownlee and McPhail ended their tour with a much fuller knowledge of the facilities, personnel, and methods of the European grain trade but they had little to show in the way of firm contracts to buy Western Canadian wheat. While the product was excellent and the "salesmen" sincere, the Europeans were concerned about after sales service and, even more important, about the local and regional repercussions of dealing directly with Canadians. A miller, for example, who took that step might find himself ostracized by British grain traders and thus totally dependent on a source of supply many thousands of miles away. Beyond this, no European miller used Canadian wheat exclusively. The practice was to blend in Canadian wheat to improve the milling characteristics of domestic wheat. Millers would be dependent on European grain traders to supply their domestic requirements and this made it unwise to alienate the local network of contacts. All of these factors were even more pronounced on the Continent where a spirit of jealous nationalism was growing. France and Germany, both experiencing severe financial difficulties, were moving toward increased self-sufficiency, especially in foodstuffs such as wheat. The attempt to break into this market in the spirit of international co-operativism was, to say the least, naive. It may even have contributed, as some would later charge, to an acceleration of protectionist tendencies by raising the prospect of large volumes of Canadian wheat coming on the market. Nevertheless, McPhail was convinced the network of overseas agencies should be expanded and Brownlee returned singularly well qualified to assume the general managership of the Canadian Pool. They were all back in Montreal by the end of August.

In November, Prime Minister King chaired the much heralded Dominion-Provincial Conference of first ministers. It had been called originally to discuss Senate and constitutional reform but, like so many such conferences in the years ahead, by the time the Premiers gathered around the table, economic matters seemed much more pressing. There was surprising progress on the natural resources question, with all agreeing to the suggestion by Saskatchewan's James Gardiner that the unalienated lands should be turned over and the subsidy continued in perpetuity.

The problem of most concern to Brownlee was the increasing difficulty in balancing provincial budgets. While there were sharply increasing public demands for education, health and welfare services, all provincial responsibilities; provincial revenues remained relatively fixed. As long as a modicum of prosperity prevailed, the situation was only a growing irritant but what would happen if there was a serious decline in revenues as a result of economic adversity? According to the Eastern press, prosperity was rampant and the future rosy. To Brownlee and other Westerners this was not apparent. Grain prices were down from their 1926 high and while the decline had been offset by higher yields, given the world wheat surplus, basing Western prosperity on high yields was not a comforting position. Urban unemployment was another symptom of economic sluggishness. Every Western city faced a year-round demand for unemployment relief, rising in winter to serious proportions. Brownlee focused more on the cause of this situation than on the additional funds that would be needed to meet the expenses. He blamed it squarely on federal immigration policies. The federal government had accepted the argument of the Railways and other large corporations that more people meant economic growth, lower per capita costs and ultimately more prosperity, and so federal policy had been to vigorously recruit immigrants.

Brownlee argued that immigration should be curtailed to allow for the economic consolidation of those already present. There was no need for, or wisdom in, artificially induced immigration, he believed. If Western farmers and Western governments were allowed to consolidate their economic situation and if federal policies were aimed at assisting in this direction, a degree of prosperity would arise which would attract immigrants without any sales campaigns. Brownlee's analysis had no impact on federal immigration policies .

The Dominion-Provincial Conference over, he accepted two speaking engagements in southern Ontario. The first of these, at Simcoe, allowed him to visit his childhood haunts at nearby Port Ryerse. After his evening speech to the Norfolk Canadian Club, many came forward to share remembrances of his childhood or of his parents and grandparents. His three aunts still lived in the area and Simcoe considered him, proudly, as a native son. Both in Simcoe and, the next night, in Brantford, he spoke encouragingly about the recent Conference, asserting that "East and West are closer together than they have ever been."

Chapter 11: Railways Sold

For over half a century, railways dominated the Canadian experience. The major political issues and enormous economic ventures of the great transcontinental systems had their microcosmic duplicates in communities across the land. Yet for most Canadians it was not the economics or politics of railways that excited their imagination but the haunting whistle of the steam locomotive echoing through the chill of a winter's darkness or the platform rumbling beneath their feet as, with bell tolling, steam hissing and the screech of steel on steel, a freight swept into the station. Even more romantic were the great passenger trains, winding their way from sea to sea. Was there a prairie boy in the back pasture, fetching home the cows, or a miner's wife in a shack between the rock ridges of northern Ontario, whose thoughts, upon seeing the "transcontinental" pass, did not drift to wondering who was on board and where they were going?

In the first week of 1928, John Brownlee was, again, one of those aboard the "magic carpet made of steel". Always with a full briefcase, the clickety-clack of the wheels served him as background noise for writing letters or reading reports. The white linens and silver service in the dining car passed unnoticed if there was a political or business figure with whom to have a serious talk about current events. The endless ribbon of trees, rock and water hurtling by the windows were ignored to continue a discussion in the lounge car where Brownlee, who now smoked discreetly after dinner, might take a rare bit of relaxation. For him, the trip was routine. He was going to have yet another talk with King about natural resources and provincial railways.

The natural resources question was now stalled before the Judicial Committee of the Privy Council which, finding itself faced with the puzzle of a referral by the Dominion of a Supreme Court ruling in its favour, waited for other submissions. Alberta, in order to underscore its objection to the referral process, declined to appear. There the situation remained as the months passed.

As for railway matters, the previous November, Brownlee had suggested to Dunning a "joint conference with your self and heads of C.N. and C.P.R. to consider joint acquisition of the lines."

No conference had been called so Brownlee now arranged his own individual meetings. He found Sir Henry Thornton, of the C.N.R., now much more receptive. Thornton had visited the Peace River area the previous summer and had become a convert to the boosterism with which the area was promoted in prosperous times. As well, the notion of joint acquisition of railway lines, once dubiously regarded, was now finding favour as fierce competition between the two transcontinental systems was leading to obvious duplication. Brownlee left for home with the understanding that a joint offer to purchase at least the E.D. & B.C. would soon be forthcoming from the Railways.

Another factor in the changed attitude toward the provincial railways was that they were at last making money. John Callaghan, now Deputy Minister of Railways, provided competent management, while large crops, a small influx of settlers and a general note of prosperity combined to increase traffic steeply. Since freight volumes are the major factor in railway revenues, the expansion, particularly of the Peace River district, promised even higher revenues in the future. As it was, the Province's four lines had an operating surplus in 1927 of $476,000 despite large capital expenditures to upgrade roadbeds. Of course, the massive debt charges meant that they still were a net drain on the treasury. However, they had quickly become much attractive, as was underlined by the sale of the Lacombe and North Western to the C.P.R. The total remuneration, including assumption of bonded indebtedness, amounted to $1,500,000 but the point Brownlee stressed was that the Province would be relieved of annual debt charges in excess of $150,000.

Once the Session began, the sale was quickly ratified. There was even more excitement when a joint offer to purchase the E.D.&.B.C. was announced. To the surprise of both sides of the House, Brownlee recommended against accepting the offer. The total remuneration proposed was $15,000,000, well under the value of the line, but even more unsatisfactory, he argued, were the terms of payment. No payment would be made until mid-1930, leaving the Province completely responsible for the large debt charges for over two more years. Also, of the $8,000,000 cash, one million would be paid annually and the four percent interest would apply only to the annual installment. This meant an effective interest rate of one-half of one percent. Brownlee argued that more might be derived from operating surpluses if the line were retained.

Another disadvantage was that the offer did not include the Alberta and Great Waterways. It would be inefficient to maintain the Department of Railways to operate only one line. Future offers, Brownlee informed the House, would be expected to be significantly higher and include all three remaining lines. He appeared confident such offers would be forthcoming.

Despite the obvious progress on the railway question, the Session was long and controversial. Among the standard issues was the struggle to balance the budget. Despite rigorous control of expenditures, and increased revenues such as the $2,500,000 profit on liquor sales and almost $3,000,000 from the increase in gasoline tax from three to five cents per gallon; the rising demand for government spending in health, education, welfare, and highways more than offset any gains. As Brownlee had pointed out at the Dominion-Provincial Conference, the ratio of public service costs borne by the federal government was declining, enabling it to enjoy large surpluses, reduce taxation and lower the national debt.

A new burden for the Province, its share of the new Federal Old Age Pension, promised to equal fully one-third of the existing federal subsidy. Brownlee recommended that Alberta not enter the scheme until the federal government agreed to assume a larger share of the costs. They had already, he declared, pared many necessary expenditures from the estimates. He knew that many were "impatient at still being told the Province is not able to bear further financial burdens" but, he warned, it was as necessary to be frugal as it had been in 1921. With the capital debt continuing to increase, the "time is not yet ripe to assume further heavy burdens." The Assembly agreed to a one year delay while further attempts were made to have Ottawa pay a larger share. However, by the time the year passed, it was obvious from the letters and resolutions to the Ministers that the sentimental momentum to have the twenty dollar per month pension for every needy citizen over seventy years of age could no longer be resisted.

Another perennial problem was the financial situation of the farmers. With high yields and "dollar wheat" common, many were at last making progress in liquidating their debts. Some were even adding the newly popular gasoline and Diesel tractors. Brownlee noted wryly that the banks and mortgage companies were all actively lending again despite continuing criticism of so-called restrictive legislation.

With the need for special measures in the south-east no longer apparent, he introduced amendments to change the Debt Adjustment Bureau from an agency to meet special and temporary situations, to an ongoing one to which any farmer in the Province might voluntarily submit the administration of his financial affairs in order to satisfy creditors. The intent was to create a province-wide financial or credit counseling service. The introduction of the amendments prompted an immediate stream of well orchestrated telegrams expressing the outrage of the lending institutions and containing the standard threat to withdraw from the Province.

Brownlee regarded the contention that the proposed amendments represented a virtual debt moratorium as ludicrous. He believed the proposed changes were not understood but in a series hastily called conferences with the money lenders, it became obvious that it was futile to argue the reasonableness of the amendments. Reluctantly, he withdrew the measure. He was disillusioned by the episode. In the future he would be more suspicious about the real attitudes and motives behind the money lenders' complaints. Conversely, he became more aware of the plight of farmers dealing with these same lenders. As he remarked to one banker, "for years in this Province legislation having much the same effect existed under our Assignments Act for the benefit merchants and traders, but apparently the protection given to merchants and traders cannot be applied to farmers."

He began to be convinced that the large institutional lenders were, as a group, attempting to convince the borrowing public that the provincial Government was responsible, through its debtor protective legislation, for forcing lenders to adopt such iniquitous policies as higher interest rates for Western Canada and issuing credit instruments patently unsuitable for agriculture. Thus the struggle between debtor and creditor interests began to intensify with both groups attempting to pressure the government away from the role of neutral umpire which, to Brownlee, was the ideal. Given that 1928 was an expansionist period of relative prosperity, Western debtors lacked sufficient motivation to supply the counter-vailing force which would have allowed Brownlee to resist the creditor objections. When economic adversity struck, debtors would promptly demand much more active government intervention on their behalf than could be provided simply by an umpire.

Meanwhile, the federal Government finally agreed to subsidize freight costs so that Alberta coal could be shipped to Ontario at a rate of $6.75 per ton. An Alberta Coal Standards Board was set up to advise on production and marketing. The production of hydroelectricity, however, was still in limbo, at least to the extent to which its development would be by public enterprise. A new source of enormous potential, the Ghost Falls on the Bow River, was now the object of conflicting applications for development from the Province and Calgary Power Company. Charles Stewart proclaimed that, "So long as these resources are under Federal control, the responsibility for administration must rest with the Federal Government." Then, despite the fact that Manitoba had been given priority rights on a similar project in anticipation of the transfer of control over its natural resources, he again foiled Alberta's opportunity for public power by leasing the Ghost Falls rights to Calgary Power. Stewart's long standing bitterness toward Brownlee was now heartily reciprocated.

Stewart was one of the few federal Liberals whose attitude corresponded with that of certain provincial Liberals who, frustrated by what was to them their inexplicable failure to regain power, attacked Brownlee more and more directly. They chided the U.F.A. Members with being unable to think for themselves and being totally dominated by Brownlee. The Liberal Edmonton Bulletin now referred to Government supporters almost exclusively as "Brownleeites". Eager to come up with embarrassing issues, it charged that the Hudson's Bay Company was profiting more from Greenfield's London office, than Alberta. Brownlee admitted that the office was leased from the Company but denied that settlers recruited by Greenfield were being directed to Hudson's Bay land. Later, Brownlee's appointment of Alex Ross as Chairman of the Workmen's Compensation Board was criticized as politically inspired. The Liberals were obviously envious.

The most controversial measure of the Session was the Sexual Sterilization Bill. This was a response to pressure from the U.F.W.A. and a segment of the medical profession, which in turn was in line with an international reformist thrust which argued that many forms of mental incompetence were genetically transmitted. Experts of high repute, both in North America and Europe, declared that if a concentrated programme of negative eugenics was applied, most forms of mental disability could be eliminated within three generations. Feminist leaders in Alberta had argued for some time that sterilizing the severely retarded would assist in their treatment. Nellie McClung, the heroine of the political enfranchisement of women, now popularized the case of a pregnant, simple-minded girl and made an impassioned appeal for sterilization to save such girls, and their children, from horrendous consequences. There were many inmates of asylums, it was contended, who might be safely discharged if their reproductive capacity were removed. The main argument, though, was that sterilization would prevent the mentally defective from reproducing themselves and thus reduce the incidence of mental disease.

Critics of the proposal objected to the assault on human dignity, the invasion of privacy, and awarding to the state or medical profession such far reaching and easily abused powers. Cases were cited of individuals improperly admitted to mental hospitals due to improper diagnosis or even conspiracy by relatives. The prospect of being sexually sterilized during such an admission was a frightening one. Brownlee, however, maintained, "there is no need to fear that because a person is unfortunate enough to become temporarily an inmate of a mental hospital that that fact will put that unfortunate one within the provisions of the Bill." Despite this assurance, there was no safeguard in the Bill itself which stated simply:

(4)   When it is proposed to discharge any inmate of a mental hospital, the Medical Superintendent ... may cause such inmate to be examined ....

(5)   If upon such examination, the Board is unanimously of opinion that the patient might be safely discharged if the danger of procreation with its attendant risk of multiplication of the evil by transmission of the disability to progeny were eliminated, the Board may direct in writing such surgical operation for sexual sterilization of the inmate as may be specified in the written direction and shall appoint some competent surgeon to perform the operation.

It was required that the inmate give permission for the operation but, if the Board considered the inmate incompetent, the nearest relative or guardian could grant permission.

After midnight, following one last stormy all day "squabble", the Bill was passed. The issue divided the U.F.A. Members. Thirteen were absent from the vote, including A.M. Matheson who, earlier, had tried to have the debate adjourned. M. J. Connor (U.F.A. - Warner) abstained. The rest, including the entire Cabinet, supported the measure. The Labour Members were also divided, three voting in favour while the other two voted with the Liberals and Conservatives against the Bill. The final count was: Ayes, 31; Noes, 11. The next day, posters calling for the sterilization of George Hoadley, the Minister of Health, appeared along Jasper Avenue.

Why had Brownlee proceeded with the Bill? Over the years he showed himself to be generally sympathetic to reforms advocated by the U.F.W.A., albeit somewhat patronizing as to their practicability. Probably more important in this case was that the measure also had the support of the medical establishment. He was a great respecter of professionals and experts. This deference was built into the Act by, first, requiring that the operation be recommended by the institution's Medical Superintendent and, second, by providing that the Board of Examination would be nominated jointly by the Senate of the University and the Council of the College of Physicians. Neither body objected to nominating candidates, as the Council had done earlier regarding a proposed board to regulate Chiropractors. That a sterilization could only take place with the unanimous approval of such an array of professionals seemed to Brownlee complete assurance that no unreasonable action or medical abuse would take place. As well, given his sensitivity to political criticism, if there had been a significant opposition, he would have been much less likely to disregard the covert resistance of some of his own supporters. He apparently concluded that the Sexual Sterilization Bill had the majority approval of a broad cross-section of society.

Finally, the Session was over. It had considered over eighty pieces of legislation. Each year the work load grew larger, not simply because the population was growing but more because citizens were demanding more government services. The delivery of those services required more and more complex policy decisions and administrative capacities. The increasing demands on the governmental system fell most heavily on Brownlee, in part because he had more ability than any of his colleagues. Some backbenchers freely admitted that they did not prepare themselves on issues, knowing "Brownlee will handle it." At the same time, he did not delegate decision making. His Ministers were expected to administer the routine of their departments but on larger policy questions he took it as his responsibility to present the issue for discussion, first by the Cabinet and later by the U.F.A. Members. His main instrument in these meetings was logical analysis, since his approach, which required him to plumb a matter exhaustively, was to review the background of the issue thoroughly, summarize the question in problem form, list the possible solutions and the pros and cons of each, and describe the criticisms which might be made of each decision and how they might be countered. By the time he had completed his presentation, there was usually little left to decide. His colleagues were asked to supply any information he had missed and present viewpoints or arguments he had not considered. Given Brownlee's thoroughness and expertise, there was usually little to say on either count. As well, the listing of potential solutions together with their advantages and disadvantages, usually made the best solution obvious. Thus, Cabinet meetings were not so much decision making sessions as opportunities to discuss decisions at which Brownlee had already arrived.

* * *

The summer of 1928 was to be a summer of cooperative conferences. In June, Brownlee attended the Third International Wheat Pool Congress, held in Regina. The Congress, attended by representatives of some of the largest British cooperative societies, as well as by representatives of wheat pools throughout the English speaking world, rejected Aaron Sapiro's notion of a World Wheat Pool. The very concept of such a Pool confirmed for Brownlee his suspicion that Sapiro's aim was more personal aggrandizement than fostering co-operativism. Later in June, the Canadian Cooperative Congress, held in Lloydminster, decided that a consumers' cooperative association should be formed in every province. Early in July, the Alberta government helped play host to a Cooperative Institute held at the University of Alberta and featuring addresses by prominent international authorities on co-operativism. Later in the month, Brownlee traveled to San Francisco where he spoke to the American Institute of Cooperation.

Brownlee was a sincere supporter of co-operativism. Through helping to organize the Wheat Pools, the other pools, and now the increasing number of consumer cooperatives, he played a major part in the evolution of legislation to provide for the special type of joint stock company which he regarded cooperatives as being. He thought cooperatives encouraged the broadly based, democratic, citizenry involvement in important institutions; and the familiarity with sound business principles which were both essential to real social progress. These two elements: good citizenship and good management, were basic to Brownlee's creed.

In between conferences of co-operators, a new President for the University of Alberta had to be selected. Dr. H. M. Tory was resigning, after twenty years at the helm, in order to accept the Chairmanship of the National Research Council in Ottawa. A number of candidates applied or were suggested but the short list came down to two; Dr. R.C. Wallace, Professor of Geology at the University of Manitoba, and John Bracken, Premier of Manitoba. Brownlee wrote confidentially to T. A. Crerar, asking him for his own opinion and those of his close friends A. B. Hudson and J. W. Dafoe, on the relative merits of Wallace and Bracken for the post. Crerar replied that all favoured Bracken on the ground that he had greater administrative experience although lesser scholarship. Despite this advice, Wallace was chosen, partly to avoid the criticism of having made a "political" appointment and partly because of concern for Bracken's health. Also, Brownlee was anxious to make some changes in the University's operation. Within two weeks of the new President assuming his duties, he was called before a Cabinet committee in Brownlee's office to discuss additions to the University Board of Governors, changes in the relationship between the University and the University Hospital, the creation of a town planning division, and the enlargement of the Department of Extension's services to rural areas.

The summer of 1928 was one of ideal growing conditions, both for field crops and the grass on the golf courses. Brownlee was on the links as often as possible that summer before leaving in mid-August with his family for holidays in Victoria. In this era, before super-highways and high-speed automobiles detached the traveler from the environment, the trip by car was an adventure. Clattering down narrow, dusty gravel roads chiseled into the side of canyon walls, chugging around hairpin switchbacks, and rumbling over hollow sounding wooden bridges crossing dashing mountain streams, the Brownlee family crossed the great mountain ranges of British Columbia. Young Jack, twelve, and Alan, ten, were at an age to enter fully into the adventure and the journey was without mishap until the final leg. Nearing Banff on the homeward trip, the family car was making good speed down a long incline when Brownlee pointed out the unusual occurrence of being passed by a single wheel. Seconds later it became obvious that the wheel was from their own car and they jolted to a stop, laughingly watching the wheel far down the road bounding high into the evergreens.

* * *

Shortly after returning to Edmonton, Brownlee announced the sale of the Province's railways. Both the total price of $25,000,000 and the terms of payment were far superior to the earlier rejected offer. The new offer came from the C.P.R. with an option, subsequently taken up, for the C.N.R. to acquire fifty percent ownership. The payment was to consist of the assumption of almost $9,500,000 in bonded indebtedness, and installments of $5,000,000 paid in 1929 and 1933, with the balance including interest at four percent payable in 1939. The disposal of the lines lifted a burden of over one million dollars a year in interest charges.

The total price meant recovery of most of the capital worth of the lines but the more than $15,000,000 paid over the years in debt charges was written off as the "contribution to the opening and development of the north country." Brownlee concluded his announcement by commenting simply that he believed the Province had gone "about as far as it could go" in terms of the price, and that it was "well out of the railway business."

What accounted for the sale of the railways at a price which, even six months previously, was almost unimaginable? In part it was due to the rising current of optimism generated by returning prosperity. Even more responsible was the enormous crop of 1928, a total wheat production not surpassed for the next twenty-four years. On the basis of these huge volumes, the lines showed a surplus for the year of over $810,000. Another important factor, many concluded, was John E. Brownlee. His ability to meet heads of government and business as an equal, his skill as a negotiator and his keen business sense all seemed confirmed by the deal. It was an enormous boost to his prestige.

The Province's success with railways led directly to demands Alberta set up a hydroelectric utility. It was argued that the Department of Railways had shown that "given good management, utilities can be carried on as efficiently under public as under private ownership." Brownlee had promised for some time that as soon as the financial condition of the telephone and railway systems improved, power development would be seriously considered. With reductions of over $1,000,000 in annual expenditures and of more than $9,000,000 in capital debt as a result of the railway deal, the time seemed opportune.

Two developments marred the otherwise buoyant atmosphere of the autumn of 1928. The first was widespread early frost which lowered the grade of the large crop and overnight reduced farm incomes by ten to twenty-five percent. The second was that Brownlee, who had contracted a severe cold while at the Coast, reached a point of nearly total exhaustion and was ordered by his doctors to take a complete rest for two or three months.

Thus, he was given an opportunity to delegate responsibility. He established Cabinet committees, each assigned to cover certain topics, and prepare for the debates that might be expected in the 1929 Session. However, his memoranda to these committees were so frequent and so thorough that it was obvious he did not find the situation restful. He reminded his Ministers to hold meetings, what to put on their agendas, what arguments to consider, and in general continued to act as a forceful chairman, albeit by way of memoranda. John Brownlee was thorough indeed and his thoroughness negated the prescribed rest.

Figure 5

The principal U.F.A. Cabinet Ministers.
Left to right (top): Perren Baker, George Hoadley,
John Lymburn, O. L. McPherson, Irene Parlby,
Richard Reid, and Vernor Smith

(Photo courtesy of Glenbow Archives - NA-1074-3)

Chapter 12: Control of the Natural Resources Gained

The U.F.A. Convention of 1929 dealt with the usual vast array of resolutions. The major ones passed included: unanimous support for the creation of a public power utility, strong endorsement of the proposed new School Act, a call for the creation of a government controlled central bank for Canada, a plea for immediate adoption of the Old Age Pension, and approval of a study of a scheme for state medicine. There was sharp criticism of the Government's withdrawal of its Bill to extend the provisions of the Debt Adjustment Act. The Stettler Provincial Constituency Association charged that it had been withdrawn "through the influence of the financial and perhaps legal interests," and protested that "the Members of the Provincial Legislature [should] give more consideration to our needs and pass the Act as amended."

For his part, Brownlee considered Convention resolutions a very poor basis for Government policy. Some within the U.F.A. believed that the Cabinet should be bound by the will of the Convention but he rejected this emphatically, both on the principles of ministerial responsibility and responsible government, and because of his deep commitment to reason. Only the most naive observer of a Convention in action could fail to notice that a loud voice often overwhelmed logic and that the herd mentality was more in evidence than rational analysis and intellectual consistency. Brownlee was prepared to consider Convention resolutions but only calmly in the quiet deliberations of the Cabinet room, adding the advice and information of experts where necessary and weighing the impact, political and otherwise, on all groups in society. "We must reach our conclusions not from the consideration of how our decision may affect an individual organization," he said frequently, "but rather from the standpoint of the general good of the Province."

Such an approach led to caution. The Convention was unanimous in its call for a public power utility but Brownlee did not find it that simple. "I am not ready to say that adequate capital can be provided without hampering and handicapping other vital Provincial needs." He explained, "So far we have not been given control of our power resources by the Dominion Government and

157

even when this takes place we will have to face the problem of acquiring plant, equipment and, possibly, goodwill by process of arbitration, with all the danger of a prohibitive price being fixed." Another issue on which his caution proved the guiding force was the proposed new School Act. Two years earlier, Perren Baker, the Minister of Education, had declared that, "educational progress must proceed along two general lines: 1) providing for full time operation of sufficient schools, both primary and secondary, and 2) improving the quality of teaching." His two broad objectives won ready acceptance. Five times more students now wished to go on to high school than twenty years earlier. A generation which had glorified the value of farm life now measured its success in terms of the number of its children pursuing other careers. Opportunity must be delivered to all, including rural, students.

The educational reformers contended that the small local school boards would have to be scrapped. As long as the thousands of small school districts, each with its own board policies, tax rate, budgeting strategy, salary provisions, and employment terms continued to exist, they argued, it would be impossible to standardize and improve the quality of instruction. Baker's new School Act proposed massive consolidation and centralization. The School Division, roughly the geographic size of the municipality, and containing dozens of school districts within it, would become the new administrative unit. With an eye toward the expected resistance to the loss of local control, the proposal provided that each school district elect a trustee to sit on the division board.

All matters relating to teachers, including salaries, pensions, and basic employment conditions, would become Provincial responsibilities. Only in this way, it was thought, could serious progress be made toward improving the quality of teaching. As well, it would help eliminate the numerous complaints about poor salaries and working conditions in some rural districts. The standardized salaries, it was hoped, would help overcome the tendency of better teachers to gravitate to urban schools where, because of the larger tax base, higher salaries could be paid, while their less able and less experienced colleagues ended up in rural schools. The standardized staffing expenses were to be provided for by standardized mill rates.

The U.F.A. Convention heartily endorsed the proposed changes but it soon became clear that a large majority of rural people, though usually a less articulate element, opposed the new scheme. The split revealed the disturbing fact that, as participation rates declined, the U.F.A. was becoming less and less representative of the general attitudes of rural communities. As with any narrowly based group, it was being increasingly dominated by the vocal and fanatic proponents of pet schemes. This left the majority without an organization to articulate their concern over the loss of local autonomy and, even more significant, their fears about the impact of the school reforms on the family and the community. Would not older students have to live away from home to attend the regional high schools? Would not centralization mean the closing of many rural schools? Would it be safe for small children to travel long distances to school over uncertain roads during winter blizzards? In most rural districts the school was the focal point of the community. It was there that the important seasonal social events were held, that meetings took place, in short, where those of all ages developed their sense of community. What would happen to their cooperative community spirit once the local schools were closed?

Brownlee became aware of these feelings and how deeply and widely they were held. "The Government is not seeking to ride roughshod over the views of the people of this Province," he assured, withdrawing the Bill before it came to a vote in the Assembly. Personally he strongly favoured the reforms, both because they promised a more efficient school system and because "all leaders of educational thought, either in Canada or elsewhere have condemned the present system of the local school board and have advocated a broader basis." He told those urging the change to work during the ensuing year to educate public opinion so that if the Bill were passed, there would be wide enough acceptance of it to insure it could successfully be implemented.

Brownlee's caution and his recognition that public opinion sometimes differed from the thrust of U.F.A. resolutions were also evident in his handling of the continuing demand that the Debt Adjustment Act be extended to apply to the entire province. The demand was suddenly blown into the forefront of U.F.A. concern by what came to be known as the "Barritt Case". In 1918, R.W.

Barritt was a well-established farmer in the Mirror area, owning 480 acres and over 100 cattle, free of liabilities. Following the disastrous drop in cattle and grain prices in 1919 and 1920, he was left heavily indebted to the local bank. To clear this debt, he took a mortgage in 1922 from Canada Permanent Mortgage Corporation of Toronto for $6,000. By 1928, despite what everyone agreed were determined efforts to pay the interest and principal, the arrears stood at over $9,200. By then there had been considerable involvement in the case by the Debt Adjustment Bureau, various M.L.A.'s and Ministers, including Brownlee, and the executive and Convention of the U.F.A. The Barritts were active U.F.A. members and Mrs. Barritt, especially, had put their situation forcefully before the Convention on several occasions, making it a *cause celebre*.

For its part, Canada Permanent made it a point of honour not to yield in the face of what it regarded as U.F.A. "political pressure". Despite the contest of wills, the interventions resulted in two extensions and an offer to compromise for $7,000. Throughout the summer of 1928 the crop promised to provide the final solution to the Barritt debts but first hail and then the early frost turned $7,000 of hope into $560 of harsh reality. Canada Permanent foreclosed and the Barritts lost their farm, their home, and by the winter of 1928 were dependent on the charity of their neighbours.

The Barritt case was not unique but thanks to the focus the U.F.A. had given it, it became symbolic. Barritt and his wife had done their best, deprived themselves and their family to make payments on the mortgage and had, in fact, paid a considerable amount in interest; yet they had lost everything. Every farmer could feel Barritt's profound sense of injustice, not simply about the nine percent interest charged when the legal maximum specified by the Bank Act was seven, or that uncontrollable economic reversals had meant the loss of everything, but rather that the entire burden of economic misfortune seemed to rest on the debtor. The whole thrust of the law protected the creditor from any loss of principal or interest while attempts to protect the debtor were, in the final analysis, ineffective. Thus the calls for an extension of the provisions of the Debt Adjustment Act marked the beginning of a resurgence of the demand for governmental initiative and intervention on behalf of debtors. "The money [the citizen] has invested in his equity in the property ... is lost to him and his money is as sacred as any money the Company has loaned on the property involved," one complainant protested. "To so pursue the honest citizen to pay up for financial losses incurred through temporary shrinkage of value ... of the land in question, is absolute slavery and unworthy of any civilized government today."

Brownlee was not touched by any such deep sense of injustice. On the Barritt case, as in any other, he would go as far as to suggest a compromise but he would never question the traditional assumptions and practices of business. This led him to a middle ground which irked those with deep feelings on the subject who regarded his comment that, "it is true the mortgage bears interest at the rate of 9%, it would still be considerably in arrears if the rate had been 7%," as a heartless quibble. "The whole success of the efforts of ... the Debt Adjustment Bureau," he went on, "depends upon maintaining an attitude of reasonable fairness in dealing with claims. Unless we are to say that individuals or companies who lend money in this Province in good faith must wait indefinitely for repayment, whatever may be the contract or agreement at the time, there comes a limit to the extent to which the Government is justified in interfering in any one case."

Thus, what to Brownlee was "reasonable fairness" was to Barritt criminal injustice. To people who wanted vigorous government action to make their homes and farms as inviolable as the laws of contract, Brownlee argued for the status quo in which a Minister might put in a good word with the president of the mortgage company for an extension (during which interest would continue to be charged). That failing, the machinery of eviction, backed by the laws and courts, would begin its inexorable push to clear the farmer from his land. Given the variance in the two attitudes, there was the potential for considerable tension. Yet all of this was happening at a time which would come to be known as a peak of prosperity. Who would listen to Brownlee's arguments for "reasonable fairness" if ever there was a serious economic downturn and every district in Alberta had its Barritt case?

Throughout all of 1929, Brownlee held back the rising tide of demands and expectations being placed on the provincial government. He argued for financial caution and stressed the need to avoid any new, large capital commitments until the provincial debt was substantially reduced. His position became even more difficult to maintain when a surplus in the public accounts of $1,578,823 was announced. It was Alberta's largest surplus yet and the second largest for the year among Canadian provinces. It drew attention to Brownlee as the main factor in the continuing budgetary restraint and fiscal caution. For Brownlee, already typed as cold, reserved and aloof, a Scrooge-like reputation did nothing to enhance his image. One of his constituents informed him bluntly that his

> "attitude towards strangers is most unfortunately remote and unfriendly. Your manner neither invites confidence or goodwill... a little ordinary civility and candour such as one meets with in ordinary life, would have put matters right and would have been more worthy of one in your position."

Despite such criticism, he remained convinced that he was right and that his correctness was ultimately in everyone's interest regardless of what they might think of him for the time being. As he told one of those who protested his lack of action in the Barritt case, "I cannot see this case in the same way you do, and yet I feel that I am not shutting my eyes to the needs of the farmers of this Province, either collectively or individually."

The final important matter dealt with during the Session was Alberta's position on the natural resources question. King and Brownlee had finally come to a tentative agreement on a new wording of the contentious school lands clause. The Natural Resources agreement would now state that schools in Alberta would continue to operate "in accordance with the laws of the Province, but in keeping with the letter and the spirit of the constitution." This wording, sufficiently nebulous that it could be argued that it supported either separate schools or provincial jurisdiction over education, appealed to both King and Brownlee.

Brownlee thought that the proposal to base the continuing subsidy on the present population, under which Alberta would receive $526,000 annually compared to Saskatchewan's $750,000, was unfair since Alberta had larger mineral resources and had had more resources alienated. As well, he was confident, Alberta's population, and production, would soon equal and perhaps even exceed that of Saskatchewan. He proposed negotiating a sliding scale which would see the subsidy increase as the population grew.

The Assembly unanimously approved giving him the freedom to negotiate a more favourable settlement than those previously suggested. His position throughout the remainder of the negotiations was that Alberta was entitled to terms at least as favourable as those granted the other two prairie provinces.

Not all the problems to be dealt with concerned large issues or influential people. There was still a mass of routine duties and a large volume of correspondence from people who turned to the Premier as the final hope for a solution to their problems, regardless of how strictly personal they might be. One clear example of this was a letter to Brownlee which began starkly,

Dear Sir,

My husband has been going out with another woman since December 1927 and sometimes stays with her two or three days ...

The obviously distraught woman went on to argue that her husband was well intentioned but could not overcome temptation on his own. As a result, children and other innocent parties suffered. She went on to argue,

There is so much good in all of us, if there is only something to turn us the right way in moments of weakness and surely that is one reason for our laws ... there should be a law against adultery ... if you find some such law could be helpful, I hope we shall very soon have it.

Unlike a later age when such a letter would not have passed the initial screening secretary, Brownlee replied personally to this pathetic plea but his totally typical response offered little encouragement.

Whatever may be the merits of your suggestion, under the British North America Act jurisdiction with respect to criminal law has been placed entirely in the hands of the Federal Government so that the problem you mention can only be dealt with by that Government.

At times, however, he did become involved in purely personal matters and no better illustration of this exists than the case of Herman Trelle. Trelle was still winning numerous prizes and awards for his wheat and other crops, including the so-called World Championship of Wheat, which he was to capture no less than five times. Other than win championships, he could do little right. His finances were a disaster, partly, as he pointed out to Brownlee, because the prizes usually had only nominal cash values. Trelle argued, with justification, that he should be more generously rewarded in view of the benefits Alberta and the Peace River district had gained from his grain growing success. Brownlee agreed and a number of grants were made, averaging about $500 per year. The provincial Department of Agriculture also advertised and distributed the seed Trelle sold. Through this assistance he was able to escape from the irony, which struck him more than anyone, of living in near abject poverty in a made-over grain bin while letters and telegrams of congratulations poured in from the world's notables. By 1929, Brownlee had become a confidant for Trelle and frequently assisted him more directly. For example, when Trelle's health failed requiring him to spend six months in a Winnipeg sanitarium, Brownlee had all the travel arrangements made, including a nurse to accompany Trelle on the train. He also directed officials of the Department of Agriculture to supervise the harvesting and marketing of Trelle's crop. Both Trelle and his wife looked on Brownlee as a mentor and a reliable friend.

By mid-July, Brownlee was eagerly preparing for what would become known as his "northern trip". Accompanied by Commissioner Bryan and other officers of the A.P.P., he went by train to Peace River, then down the Peace in an Alberta designed river cruiser. He enjoyed the trip greatly, away from the routine of the office, often out of touch with any signs of human habitation. The party camped along the way, Bryan snapping some candid photographs of the Premier shaving before a mirror hung precariously on a tent pole, and hanging his laundry to dry after washing it in the cool river water. Brownlee, himself, was developing an interest in photography and took many pictures along the way. From Lake Athabasca, they continued down the Mackenzie River to Fort Smith. Thus, Brownlee became the first Premier of Alberta to cross the Province's northern boundary. The homeward journey was up the Athabasca River to Fort McMurray and then by rail back to Edmonton. The trip had taken the entire month of August but it left him with many fond memories of the scenic northern wilderness, the great rivers and the ice cold lakes, the Indians and the trappers and the isolated outposts of traders and police. Upon his return he announced that the government would establish numerous parks and campsites so citizens could enjoy the natural beauty of Alberta. With August now over, he only had time to take his family for the typical Alberta holiday of a week in the mountains, before returning to the rigours of office.

Essentially, it was a very comfortable time for Brownlee and his Government, with no foreseeable reason to anticipate any change, or a challenge from political opponents. Prime Minister King, when he visited Edmonton in November, could see for himself that "Brownlee's administration of the Province stands very high." Only some sort of bold stroke would begin to restore either federal or provincial Liberal fortunes in Alberta. King was seriously considering such a stroke -- inviting Brownlee into his Cabinet. During his visit he raised the prospect with him personally observing that Brownlee was "a dour sort of person wrapped in mystery, not too frank." However, despite his caution and indirection he certainly did not discourage the offer and King was not one to allow personalities to interfere with political objectives. King was still pursuing his goal of absorbing the "Progressives" and if he were "to take Brownlee into the Federal field" it might go a long way to "reconcile Liberals and Progressives" and immediately establish a large base from which to rebuild Liberal strength in Alberta. King was even more pleased to find in Calgary, on the return leg of his tour, that the provincial Liberals were most agreeable to Brownlee being removed from the provincial scene.

Doubtless, these provincial Liberals were thinking more of their own future than that of either Brownlee or King. If Brownlee left the Premiership, it would create an entirely new and, from the Liberal point of view, promising political situation. However, in the interval between King's Edmonton and Calgary visits, his Minister of Finance, J. A. Robb, died. The vacancy meant new opportunities for Cabinet reorganization. Charles Dunning was promoted to Robb's portfolio and T. A. Crerar entered the Cabinet as Minister of Railways. Thus it was Crerar and not Brownlee who was to be the new Western figure in King's Cabinet and provide at least a degree of fusion with one-time "Progressives".

Brownlee and King were soon meeting again, this time in Ottawa, to discuss once more the natural resources question. There appeared to be good promise of agreement at last. The contentious school lands clause had been defused by the artfully nebulous phrases, the Dominion had agreed that the subsidies would be continued in perpetuity, and later that they would increase along with the population. On Wednesday morning, December 11, 1929, Brownlee, accompanied by Hoadley and Lymburn, met King, Stewart and Dunning in the Prime Minister's office. Brownlee insisted that first the unemployment relief situation should be discussed. He asked if the federal Government would help the provinces and municipalities meet the situation as it was likely to be "a hard winter" in view of "the stock [market] failures, crop failures, etc.". King smugly replied "that on the same grounds we might ask them for help." He would "give no undertaking for the future, beyond trying to get public works, etc. carried on as largely as possible." It would be some time before King would realize that unemployment was a serious national problem and not just a suddenly popular complaint by the provinces, bent on raiding the federal treasury.

As for the question of the transfer of control over the natural resources, Brownlee, with some trepidation, announced that Alberta was no longer willing to accept the terms to which it had previously agreed. The Turgeon Commission had recently recommended that in addition to the perpetual subsidy, Manitoba should receive a once only cash settlement of something over four million dollars. Brownlee, committed to the position that Alberta's terms should be at least as favourable, now asked for a similar cash payment. King protested that the payment "was to put Manitoba on a par with Alberta and Saskatchewan ... there had been a period in which Manitoba had received no subsidies." Brownlee countered that "since Confederation much more of Alberta's lands had been alienated than Manitoba's for Federal uses, 13,000,000 [acres] for railways as versus 4,000,000 in Manitoba and each got the same stretch of railway in their province."

By this time, Brownlee had noticed that "Mr. King was rather sadly disappointed." King suddenly stood up from the table and, as he himself admitted, "I got a little hot and told Brownlee to put his proposition into writing & we would give an answer after

Christmas. He was anxious for a further interview today. I told him we would not give it." With this, King left abruptly by a side door. Brownlee, not to be outdone, departed abruptly by another door, leaving a frantic Charles Dunning to try and cool the tempers and effect a reconciliation. By mid-afternoon he had both leaders convinced that the other wished to resume the discussion. This led to a short afternoon meeting at which both were apologetic, but Brownlee subtly warned King of the position the Leader of the Opposition, R.B. Bennett, was taking, that "Alberta should get something more than Manitoba for alienations."

King presented Brownlee's terms to his Cabinet and argued in favour of settling with Alberta. Charles Stewart strenuously opposed agreeing to Brownlee's demands but by now King was determined to pursue a strategy of settling with Manitoba and Alberta in order to undercut Saskatchewan Premier Anderson's attempt to secure even better terms. All three Prairie Premiers were in Ottawa that week. Bracken was ready to sign an agreement but Anderson, at least according to King, merely wanted a controversy and had been suitably obnoxious. If an agreement were signed with Bracken and Brownlee, it would leave Anderson odd man out and make it obvious that he, rather than King, was to blame for an agreement not being signed with Saskatchewan.

Armed with Cabinet support, King invited Brownlee and Dunning for dinner at Laurier House and after the meal, in King's memorabilia filled library, the three discussed frankly the past negotiations and the current situation. They soon settled that the agreement transferring control of the province's natural resources to the Alberta government should be signed within the week. The matter of whether an additional cash payment should be made would be left over, to be studied by a commission. Brownlee also had reservations about the federal plans for developing resources within the National Parks, urging "against their being used for revenue purposes to any extent." Stewart strongly favoured large scale private development within the Parks but King again brought his weight to bear on the side of the Province. He was becoming more impressed with Brownlee, commenting, "Brownlee strikes me as knowing his subject and his province, and as such being superior to Mr. Stewart, who is handicapped in his dislike of B.[rownlee]."

The agreements with Manitoba and Alberta were ready for signing on Friday but Bracken made a suggestion, with which King quickly agreed, that in view of Friday being the thirteenth day of the month the signing be postponed to Saturday. Consequently, at 3:30 on the afternoon of December 14, 1929, amidst the glare of photographers' flood lamps, the historic documents were signed. King supervised the ceremony but Ernest Lapointe (at the time in Europe) and Charles Stewart were to be the signatories for Canada, while John Brownlee and George Hoadley affixed their signatures for Alberta. The document contained a clause, upon which Brownlee had insisted, to the effect that if Saskatchewan should eventually be awarded better terms, the agreement with Alberta would be amended so that Alberta would "enjoy rights equal to those which may be conferred upon or reserved to the Province of Saskatchewan."

The main purpose of the natural resources agreement was to place Alberta "in the same position as the original Provinces of Confederation are in virtue of section 109 of the British North America Act." That section provided, as follows:

... the interest of the Crown in all Crown lands, mines, minerals (precious and base) and royalties derived therefrom within the Province, and all sums due and payable for such lands, mines, minerals or royalties, shall, from and after the coming into force of this agreement and subject as therein otherwise provided, belong to the Province, subject to any trusts existing in respect thereof, and to any interest other than that of the Crown in the same, and the said lands, mines, minerals and royalties shall-be administered by the Province for the purposes thereof ...

The agreement reiterated that Alberta would be bound by all previous agreements made with respect to lands and resources and mentioned specifically the rights granted to railway companies and the Hudson's Bay Company. The financial terms called for an annual payment to Alberta of $562,000 until the population reached 800,000. The payment would then become $750,000 and, after the population exceeded 1,200,000, it would be $1,125,000.

These terms were immensely more favourable to Alberta than those abandoned in 1926. The Dominion, having virtually fulfilled its Western lands policy objectives, and finding administration costs more than any foreseeable future revenues, was amenable to a generous settlement. Also, bringing the Western provinces to a position of equality with the others was an obvious and important step in completing the Confederation. In one bold stroke it would erase a political liability for the Liberals in the West and substitute a boost in prestige for the Government across Canada. As King mused two days later on the eve of his fifty-fifth birthday, the settlement was a "great triumph".

It was an even greater triumph for Brownlee. The inferior constitutional status of their provinces had irked Westerners for a quarter century. It had been an important factor in a continuing feeling of alienation from the effective decision making processes of Canada, and thus had become a perennial political issue. Every Alberta administration had addressed itself to the problem of having control of the natural resources transferred to the Province. Brownlee himself had grappled with the question for almost a decade but now, at last, he had succeeded both in obtaining control and in securing additional benefits of such value that everyone in Alberta hailed the agreement. The psychological effect of finally being recognized as an equal and coming into possession of an immense inheritance produced spontaneous demonstrations of celebration and a spurt of optimistic editorials about the future. Albertans knew the resources were immense: over 89,000,000 acres of land, the world's largest coal deposits, enormous hydroelectric potential, forests, a wide range of precious metals and, still not completely realized, one third of the world's supply of oil and natural gas. There was cause for celebration.

And celebration there was. A crowd of more than 3,000 gathered in below zero temperatures and a biting north wind to welcome Brownlee at the C.P.R. station. As he alighted, the Edmonton Newsboys' Band struck up a rousing arrangement of "Hail, Hail, The Gang's All Here". A large bonfire was touched off and fireworks exploded in the cold darkness. Striding to the top of a makeshift platform, Brownlee accepted the welcomes of the Mayor and the President of the Chamber of Commerce. When he stepped forward to speak, a voice in the crowd yelled, "Three cheers and a Tiger for the Premier." It was indeed a "warm, wholehearted and spontaneous welcome, testifying to the regard the Premier is held in by all." He spoke briefly, telling them that a new era was opening for Alberta, the prosperity of which would depend on the inspiration they could obtain from the possession of such untold resources.

"The transfer means more to Alberta than to other provinces," he assured the crowd, "for the reason that our resources have not been located to the extent that the other province's resources have. It also means a lot to Alberta to have control of her oil resources at their present stage of development," he concluded, to another spontaneous burst of cheers. Then, he was escorted through the biting frost to his car which squealed away over the frozen snow toward his home on the South Side. It was the most enthusiastic reception ever for Brownlee -- a fitting recognition of his greatest achievement. John Edward Brownlee was at the peak of his political career.

Figure 6

Brownlee's greatest triumph, the signing of the agreements which
finally gave Alberta control over its lands and natural resources.
Prime Minister W.L. Mackenzie King is seated in the ornate chair in
the centre; Brownlee to his left. On Brownlee's left is George
Hoadley and on King's right Charles Stewart, having difficulty
swallowing Brownlee's ultimate victory. As the calendars on the
wall attest, the date is Saturday, December 14, 1929. The rare
Saturday meeting was in deference to King's suspicion that signing
the agreements the day before, Friday the 13th, would not have been
auspicious. The transfer laid the basis for the prosperity of every
Albertan alive today.

(Photo courtesy of the Provincial Archives of Alberta
A10924)

Chapter 13: Prices Fall

The signing of the natural resources agreement entrenched Brownlee's political supremacy so firmly that his opponents only fulmination was against his "one man government". Alberta's prospects seemed even rosier than Brownlee's. The record 1929 surplus of over $1,800,000 showed that the Province was on a firm financial footing. Adding the almost limitless opportunities for expansion through the control of the natural resources prompted even Brownlee, to whom the balance sheet was the ultimate test of reality, to comment sanguinely, "Capital debts alone are totally different than capital debts plus resources."   However, despite the optimistic predictions, the next decade would see Brownlee's political career completely destroyed, the U.F.A. totally routed from the political scene, and Alberta forced to become the first Canadian province ever to default on a debt payment.

The signs of what would become the world's worst depression were beginning to be noticed when Brownlee addressed the U.F.A. Convention in January, 1930. The stock market crash of the previous autumn, to which future commentators would attach such significance, had attracted little attention. Even Brownlee, who subscribed to the Toronto and New York financial papers, did not attach overriding importance to it.   Nevertheless, with unemployment in Alberta necessitating relief payments of $3,000 a day, grain prices unexpectedly soft and falling, and the banks nervous and sharply more restrictive, there was a mood of concern and uneasiness at the Convention. Brownlee, in common with political leaders across North America, cautioned against "any feeling of pessimism". To the U.F.A. delegates, so steeped in the rhetoric of progress and advancement, he suggested remembering, "we are traveling a road that has its winding curves, and we go through the valleys and up over the hills. We take strength because of what has been accomplished in the past, and we look to the future with courage and with hope just in proportion as we have the spirit to travel that road."

By the time the Legislative Session was under way, there were even more clouds on the economic horizon. The world wheat surplus finally resulted in a steady down turn in prices when sharply reduced European demand, partly the result of the ending of American loans to

Europe, was combined with large scale dumping by the Soviet Union and the Argentine. By the first week in February, the price of Number 1 Northern in store at Fort William had fallen from a high the previous summer of $1.78 per bushel to below $1.20, dangerously impairing the Pool margin of fifteen percent above the initial payment to farmers of $1.00 per bushel.

The banks demanded the Central Selling Agency prepare to liquidate stocks of wheat to cover any impairment of the margin. The Pools held large carry-overs from both the 1929 and 1928 crops and the prospect of large volume forced selling on an already soft and declining market caused further tremors in the price structure. Also, the nervousness of the banks soon led the Pools to a day by day and then an hour by hour uncertainty about their credit position. Faced with the very real possibility of destruction, the Pools turned to their most reliable source of support, the governments of their respective provinces. Brownlee, Bracken and Anderson met with pool officials in Regina and later with bank representative in Winnipeg. The result was that each government guaranteed the banks against losses on loans to the respective provincial Pools.

Brownlee assured the Assembly that there was little chance of actually having to assume any loss since a large volume had already been sold at prices well above the margin and thus, "wheat would have to sink to a level never reached on Canadian markets before the Provincial Governments would suffer any loss." However. politically cautious Brownlee sought and received an additional security, which Bracken and Anderson did not, that should any advances be made under the guarantee they would be regarded as loans against the assets of the Alberta Wheat Pool.

The guarantees had come none too soon. During February the price for Number 1 fell to a low of $1.07 per bushel and in March to about $1.00, a figure which translated into an Alberta farm gate price of roughly 70 cents or the approximate cost of production. By this time, Brownlee was aware, perhaps to an extent greater than any other political leader in Canada, of the seriousness of the situation. In one of his most impassioned Legislative speeches, he pleaded for a concerted effort by all levels of government and business to meet "a situation which may spell disaster to every farmer or business man in the West, a concatenation of world conditions which may eventually drive Canadian producers and exporters alike from certain world markets."

He went on to advocate that the federal Government guarantee a minimum price to farmers of 70 cents per bushel, enough to possibly sustain them in operation and prevent them becoming any further charge on the Provincial government.

There were more than economic or even political considerations at stake in the support of the Alberta Wheat Pool. The pool was the proudest achievement of the organized farmers; regarded by them as their special contribution to social progress. In a Confederation in which it seemed to Westerners that the most important decisions were made by those distant, uninformed and uncaring; the pools had been a successful indigenous institution which promised Westerners a new control over their own circumstances. Thus their collapse would mean frustration and embittered alienation at again being manipulated by external forces, and a desperate search for some new means of bringing those forces under their control. No prairie government could afford not to come to the aid of the pools, yet there was no feeling that any of the administrations were acting merely because it was the political thing to do. Brownlee, for one, was a sincere supporter of the pools, both as businesses beneficial to Western agriculture and as vehicles for democratic citizenship.

* * *

Throughout the Session, Brownlee hinted and political pundits predicted that a provincial general election was imminent. It was obvious after his triumphal homecoming that he and the U.F.A. administration were at a crest of popularity. In one of his major political disappointments, he was unable to convince a majority of either Ministers or backbenchers that an early election should be called. The resistance stemmed from the sense of fair play which so deeply imbued the U.F.A. view. The criticism of the Liberals' snap election in 1921 had not been idle chatter. There was a deeply held belief that such maneuvering was a type of trickery symptomatic of the corrupt practices condemned by the derisive term "partyism". Thus an early election, motivated only by its obvious political advantage, was distasteful to the majority. Some argued the vote should not be held until at least the fourth anniversary of the last election in June, while others even suggested a delay until 1931. Finally, a compromise was reached and, in keeping with another U.F.A. belief that long campaigns were more democratic, on April 24 writs were issued for an election on June 19, 1930.

Brownlee dominated the campaign. Critics and supporters alike referred throughout to the "Brownlee Government" rather than to the U.F.A. or Farmers' government as they had in 1926. Even Brownlee himself concluded many speeches with the hope that "the people of this constituency will not fail me." He spoke at meetings across the Province, often at three or four scattered points in one day. The major thrust of his appeal was for a mandate to administer the natural resources. The choice, he claimed, lay between the experienced incumbents and the inexperienced Liberals and Conservatives who had nothing to offer but promises. He stressed that there was little real criticism of his Government and, unlike the case in 1926, "you hear from one end of the Province to the other the opinion that the Government will be returned and the peculiar argument is advanced that this Province needs a strong Opposition." He offered an analysis which would become typical of the entire political history of Alberta.

"An Opposition is a thing that is no more needed in the public business of this Province ... than in the management of the affairs of any of our large corporations. The C.P.R. or the Bank of Montreal handling assets nearly as large as the assets of the Province and dealing in sums of money much greater, do not believe that their Board of Directors should be divided into Government and Opposition. The Directors sit around a Council Chamber without any division and face the problems of their great corporation in the interest of the corporation itself. After all, Governments today are nothing but big businesses ... but there is a difference: big business deals in dollars and cents and physical properties, the Government also deals with these and with the welfare of the people of the Province."

In each of his sixty-seven speeches in thirty-eight constituencies and in his two major radio addresses during the campaign, his message was the same: a calm, analytical review of the record, a detailed rebuttal of the opposition points, and a summation which left his fate clearly, but confidently, before the rational review of the electors. From town halls to country school houses he went, speaking on behalf of both U.F.A. and Labour candidates. In Edson, for example, he spoke at an evening dinner in support of Christopher Pattinson, the

Labour Member and a steady backer of the Government. Typical of Brownlee's schedule, he spoke that afternoon at a picnic for farmers about twenty miles from Edson. The picnic, and his speech, were halted by rain which made the road almost impassable. The group including Brownlee was late for the evening dinner but the return was only made possible because the Premier himself stepped into the mud to put his shoulder to the car to free it from several mud-holes. The car belonged to the mayor of Edson, A. D. MacMillan, and on the outward journey Brownlee, now somewhat less inept at small talk with strangers, chatted idly to the MacMillans and their teenage daughter, Vivian, about the girl's future after her imminent high school graduation. This idle chat with an unknown girl in an obscure corner of the Province was ultimately to be regarded as one of the most significant conversations of his life.

* * *

The election results were as expected. The U.F.A. won forty seats, down three from their strength at dissolution. Brownlee and three others were acclaimed. The other party totals were: Liberals - 9, Conservatives - 6, Labour - 4, and Independents - 4. Disturbing for the U.F.A. was the sharp reduction of their previous large majorities. Irene Parlby, for example, won by less than ninety votes. As well, the loss of three rural seats to Independents and one, Pincher Creek, to a Liberal indicated a disturbed and volatile electorate not apparent in the overall seat totals. Brownlee mentioned the reversals in his post-election address but made no changes in his Cabinet. He did, however, remind his supporters that he had advised an earlier election and assured them privately that if they had waited another six months they would have been beaten. However, they had won and it was clear to everyone that Brownlee's leadership and hard work had been the major reason for that victory.

There was little respite following the election. In June, wheat resumed its downward slide moving below the $1.00 mark for Number 1 in store. All summer the price declined and the numbers of unemployed in the cities grew. Brownlee hit out hard at the professional organizers and agitators who began working among the unemployed, ordering Lymburn to prepare a list of known Communist leaders so that he could "get the necessary machinery started without delay for the deportation of all of these persons. The sooner this procedure is started the quicker the influence of this action will be circulated among these people so as to have some beneficial effect in subsequent events this year." Brownlee was to maintain this completely uncompromising attitude toward Communist organizers and Communist infiltrated groups such as the Farmers' Unity League and the Ukrainian Labor-Temple Association.

On the grain front, the nervousness of the banks grew until suddenly the head offices overruled previous agreements and refused to advance the Pools any more money "except on security of warehouse receipts ... and then only up to the actual market value of the grain." With the price of Number 1 now well under $1.00, but the Pools still committed to an initial payment to farmers on the basis of $1.00 per bushel for Number 1, the banks were forcing the Pools into buying and selling at an increasing loss. As chance would have it, Brownlee arrived in Winnipeg on the day the banks withdrew from their previous credit agreements, on his way East with his family for their annual August holiday. He was immediately drawn into the crisis negotiations and by that afternoon had arranged by long distance telephone for the banks to advance the Pools two million dollars in interim financing to cover them while a full discussion of the situation was held. The three prairie Premiers guaranteed the banks against any losses on that amount. Then, in Brownlee's own words, "Bracken put on his best bib and tucker along with myself and we went down together and for a solid month, instead of having a holiday, I was back and forth between Toronto and Montreal working out the problem of the pool indebtedness."

On Tuesday, August 5, Brownlee and Bracken, assorted Pool officials, and the general managers and various legal advisors of the seven major banks met in Toronto. McPhail, still president of the Central Selling Agency, was not impressed by the so-called captains of finance, concluding sadly, "Most of the General Managers showed a surprising amount of ignorance of the matters under discussion and a great deal of stupidity in their ability to understand explanations. ... God help the country if these are the kind of men who carry such large responsibilities."

The banks eventually agreed to continue supplying credit to allow the Pools to continue handling the 1929 crop but only after securing another letter from the three Premiers guaranteeing to stand good for any loss. The next week the discussions moved to Ottawa where the three Premiers confronted the new Prime Minister, R.B. Bennett. The financial guarantees on the 1929 crop were now in the millions of dollars and rapidly moving beyond the capability of the Provinces. Even more perplexing was the problem of the coming 1930 crop. With provincial resources already overstrained and the price continuing to fall, only the federal treasury could offset any further Pool losses. Brownlee, Bracken and Anderson had again rescued them from financial collapse but, of necessity, for the last time. From now on the Pools would have to depend for their survival on the uncertain likelihood of assistance from the federal Government. They cautiously set an initial payment for the 1930 crop of sixty cents per bushel, basis Number 1 in store, thirty cents below the prevailing price.

On October 1, 1930, control of her natural resources was finally officially transferred to Alberta. However, there could be little celebration about future development when the present basic industry was experiencing its most severe reverses ever. Within two weeks, Brownlee was in Regina at a conference of pool officials wrestling with the final liability for over-payment on the 1929 crop -- over $25,000,000. He suggested that final payment reserves for the 1928 crop not be paid out but instead be applied to the 1929 overpayment. This and others of his suggestions such as debiting the pool reserves of those who had received over-payments, were criticized as an unfair transference of the Pools' financial plight to the hard pressed individual producer. Brownlee's concern was to try anything which would get the Pool back on a solid financial footing and protect against political criticism; "If it were brought up in the Legislatures that the Pools had paid out money while heavily involved financially."

Serious as was the situation with the old crop, even more serious problems now loomed ahead for the new crop. The price again began moving downward, reflecting massive world over-production in the face of constricting European markets now aggravated by Russian dumping. In early November the price broke sharply through the margin and Brownlee immediately wired Bennett:

> ... Decline to present levels causing utmost discouragement of agriculture throughout the West. Stabilization at some reasonable price absolutely essential to revival of confidence necessary agriculture and fundamental to return better conditions throughout Dominion. Respectfully urge that

Dominion place credit Canada behind this industry. ... Cannot too strongly urge some action necessary prevent great revulsion public opinion ...

Bennett replied that the existing wheat prices were the inevitable consequence of a world-wide over supply of 400,000,000 bushels. Westerners of all walks of life, and especially farmers, regarded as fundamentally unjust this complete exposure to the rigours of the world market by a Prime Minister who was such an enthusiastic supporter of the tariff as an instrument to protect manufacturers from international competition.

Against this background, wheat prices reeled downward, finally collapsing through the sixty cent initial payment and again forcing the Pools into a loss position on every bushel handled. There was an almost exact replay of the events of July. The Pools were within hours of total financial collapse. The three Prairie Premiers met far into the night in Bracken's office with Pool and bank officials. The banks finally agreed to keep long positions margined on the strength of yet another document signed by the Premiers guaranteeing them against loss. McPhail was also forced to sign an agreement "to appoint a General Manager [for the Central Selling Agency] suitable to the banks." He suspected the banks were preparing to;

"close out the pool and take over the wheat, ... all the banks have grain men on their boards. . . . a number of grain firms already offering their services to sell the pool wheat. The vultures are gathering. I told them there was no mysterious manner by which the wheat could be sold. "

The next day, the banks' head officers in Toronto and Montreal reneged on the financial agreements and once more Brownlee, Bracken and McPhail were on their way to Toronto for a conference with the general managers. With the total resources of the Pools already pledged and the prairie provinces in a position where they neither could nor should commit themselves to any further guarantees, only the federal Government could salvage the Pools.

At a conference in Ottawa with Sir George Perley, Acting Prime Minister in Bennett's absence, the Western suggestions for federal assistance, drafted by Brownlee in his characteristic "if-not-this-then-this" style, were ignored, despite wheat prices continuing to plunge to record lows. When Bennett himself was contacted, in

London at an Imperial Conference, he cabled only the foolish proposal that the federal government might lend the provinces money to protect the banks against loss. In the absence of any federal assistance, the banks returned to their demand to appoint a general manager. After considering several names, McPail advanced two to Jackson Dodds, the General Manager of the Bank of Montreal and spokesman for the bankers. The two were Brownlee and John McFarland, one time president and general manager of the Alberta Pacific Grain Company. Dodds immediately selected McFarland because he was both a "grain man" and probably Bennett's closest friend; thus, "if he can be got into the pool it will probably do more than anything else to get the Dominion Government to do something."

McFarland returned from England, where he had accompanied Bennett to accept the post. His first move was to close the Pools' overseas offices, thus ending their brief experience as a fully integrated wheat marketing entity. For a time there was the charade that McFarland was an officer of the Canadian Wheat Pool Board but it was soon apparent that he was to operate as a power unto himself, answerable only to the Prime Minister and the syndicate of bankers who had engineered his appointment. McPhail concluded that, "McFarland has no understanding of the farmers' viewpoint whatever, or any idea other than to perpetuate old methods of doing business. It will be a relief indeed, when, if ever, we are in a position to let him go."

Such a day was not to come. McPhail and the rest of the Board would soon disappear from the grain marketing scene, leaving McFarland to operate as a virtual one man precursor of the reestablished Canadian Wheat Board as the sole exporter of wheat. The dream of a farmer owned and controlled international sales mechanism had died. What H.W. Wood had told the U.F.A. was the ultimate achievement of the organized farmers had been almost completely destroyed within a year.

Also symbolic of the ending of an era was the fact that 1930 was to be the last year of Wood's Presidency of the U.F.A. Determinedly resisting pleas that he slay on, he refused nomination at the 1931 Convention. His exit meant the end of the religious zeal which had once characterized the U.F.A. It was to be the end of an era for Brownlee as well, for as Wood's biographer has commented,

As long as Wood was the head of the provincial association, there was little or no danger that a radical policy would be adopted by the farmers which, in turn, might force the Government to break with its parent body or to follow a course which might alienate its non-U.F.A. supporters.

With the ascension of Robert Gardiner to the presidency and, perhaps more important, of Norman Priestley to the position of Secretary, the U.F.A. leadership lurched sharply to the left. In so doing, the new leaders alienated themselves both from the Legislative group and from the vast majority of the rural electorate. Farmers soon found the U.F.A. aiming squarely at what was basically a foreign intrusion of socialism thinly disguised behind familiar rhetoric. At the same time, the policies of the Provincial Government were frustratingly cautious and obviously ineffective. Rural voters very quickly found themselves without a legitimate leadership accurately articulating and responding to their concerns, at a time when they were faced with the most drastic commodity price collapse ever experienced by Canadians.

This was the essence of the great depression for Western Canadians. The "currency" of farmers was falling precipitously in purchasing power. It was like run-away double-digit inflation but an inflation that hit only selected parts of society, especially farmers, while leaving others untouched. As an illustration, the U.F.A. prepared a graphic brief translating the cash price of various farm implements into bushels of Number 1 wheat at the net price to Calgary shippers on October 21 of selected years. For example, an eight-foot binder had sold in 1906 for 319 bushels. In 1926, the same binder sold for only 231 bushels. In 1930, the price was already 552 bushels, in 1931, 987 bushels, and by 1932 the binder cost 1,715 bushels of Number 1 wheat. In other words, the farmers' 1926 currency was, six years later, worth less than thirty cents on the dollar.

The collapse was not confined to wheat. The prices of other grains dropped to even lower levels and, discrediting the much offered advice to diversify. The prices of cattle, poultry and eggs tumbled as well. Hogs and cream resisted the steep declines but only briefly. Especially in the case of cream, when large numbers of farm families began selling the cream from their milk in a desperate bid to earn some cash to meet expenses, the price fell. Thus, there was soon no agricultural commodity in Alberta whose price equaled the cost of production.

Chapter 14: The Collapse of the Pools

The severe financial hardship was not confined to farmers. During the winter of 1930 - 1931 unemployment levels in Edmonton and Calgary reached record proportions. In part this was the result of the severe drop in the purchasing power of farmers. Employers caught with slumping sales and large inventories cut costs by laying off staff, while farmers' sons and daughters flocked into the cities, hoping to escape the grinding poverty of the farm by finding wage employment. Later, conditions became even more severe, and another wave arrived even more desperate because they had left the farm because the farm could not afford to feed them. A generation was coming of age whose search was not for some the ideal opportunity, but rather, a desperate, scrabble for a means of survival.

Brownlee grappled with the unemployment problem by assisting existing municipal or other channels to relieve cases of destitution. Provincial resources were clearly finite and already strained beyond their ability to cope, he thought, and thus he continued to press strongly for Dominion financial assistance. He could not forbear reminding federal authorities that he had long argued for a more controlled immigration policy to protect against such an over supply of labour. Also, the impact of the agricultural depression on business, he asserted, clearly vindicated his proposal of a guaranteed floor price for wheat, an alternative whose "cost would not have been greater than what some of the schemes will cost."

The severe economic depression meant both a sharp decline in government revenues and a steep increase in expenditures to cope with the various relief programmes. This combination made balancing the provincial budget impossible. Most citizens were financially hard pressed so there was little scope for increasing taxation. Thus the emphasis had to be on cutting expenditures. Brownlee took an early, vigorous and continuing part in this effort. He pursued possible spending cuts to the smallest detail, refusing to accept collect telegrams, personally supervising and ruthlessly cutting government advertising and even forgoing such luxuries as an electric lift for the Legislative Buildings until "it is absolutely necessary."

However, all was not yet retrenchment and economic woe in Alberta. The U.F.A. tradition of progress and cooperative spirit could not be killed overnight. The Alberta Cooperative Oil Pool, the newest consumers' cooperative, was formed at this time to purchase farm fuels and lubricants at bulk prices and pass the savings along to farmer members. Because of the depression the Oil Pool was able persuade previously haughty Imperial Oil to supply it. Faced with sagging sales as many returned to horses to cut costs, Imperial Oil could not ignore the large volume which a contract with the Oil Pool represented. Brownlee assisted in organizing the Pool by supplying legal advice and drafting the long term contract between the two companies. He showed his characteristic foresight by including a clause giving the cooperative the continuing option to renew. This little known contribution proved to be one of his most important and longest lasting achievements on behalf of the organized farmers of Alberta. For decades, the U.F.A. Cooperative, the successor of the Oil Pool, was able to receive its bulk fuel and lubricants on an assured contract delivery basis, and pass significant savings along to generations of farmers.

But, despite the creation of another Pool, it was the collapse of the agricultural economy that was on everyone's mind. The 1930 crop was above average in yield, one-third larger than that of 1929, but, even so, the drop in the average farm price for wheat from $1.02 to 45 cents per bushel meant that farm income was down more than fifty percent. The Dominion Government still had not responded with any support or relief. After the forced appointment of McFarland as *de facto* manager of the Central Selling Agency, the federal government gradually assumed, in an unplanned way, the guaranteeing of the banks' risk for money to handle pool wheat. Even the provincial premiers were not told the size of these guarantees.

Western farmers had, from the beginning, severely criticized the Winnipeg Grain Exchange and bitterly denounced futures trading as an entirely negative force in the market. Much of the energy behind the demand for a Canadian Wheat Board after 1919 came from the antipathy toward the so-called open market and its speculative practices. The Wheat Pools attractiveness was partly because they promised an alternative to the speculatively manipulated Grain Exchange. Now the Pools were collapsing following the forced closure of their overseas operations, together with the disastrously low prices. Thus came a ringing renewed demand for regulation of the grain trade through a national wheat marketing board, a demand which was not to be met until the summer of 1935.

In the meantime, Bennett named Sir Josiah Stamp, an Englishman, to head a Royal Commission "to determine whether or not the sale of grain futures is injurious." Brownlee attended the elaborate luncheon of Eastern bankers and politicians who welcomed Stamp to Canada. There was doubt across the West that the Commission would seriously consider recommending against trading futures contracts. There was also suspicion, justified as it happened, that the appointment of a commission was motivated more by the desire to examine the operations of the Pools themselves and "come up with revelations which will discredit the Pools ... thus enabling the Government to resist any demand for a financial guarantee on the new crop." The Stamp Commission held a series of hearings across the West, paused briefly in Chicago and New York, but added little to previous studies. Its conclusion, that "futures trading, even with its disadvantages ... is of distinct benefit to the producer in the price which he receives," was believed by very few farmers.

While Stamp was ambling about, concern among farmers over financing the seeding of the new crop was growing. Despite being urged to save seed, many had either been forced to sell all their crop to attempt to feed and clothe their families or chose to follow the common practice of buying seed grain as part of the operating expenses of the spring season. In both cases, the severe shortage of cash due to the low prices and the extremely restrictive credit policies of the banks meant that many farmers feared that they would not be able to plant a crop. This led to pressure on the prairie governments, and numerous requests to Members of Parliament, for assistance to insure that all farmers were able to seed a crop.

Brownlee was anxious for the federal Government to give an early commitment that it would help bear the costs of such assistance but he would make no direct promises of help himself. He was convinced that such assurances would encourage banks, municipalities and individual farmers to avoid their responsibilities and try to shift them to the imagined infinite resources of the Province. He was prepared to assist in those cases where there was no other alternative but only quietly, so as not to encourage everyone turning to government. He believed, "People will demand, as a matter of right, work or relief measures of any kind if made applicable to the whole of the Province, even if they could get along without same if not offered as a general policy." This view was confirmed by abuses of relief programmes which soured the attitude of many, including Brownlee, toward those demanding assistance. The tragedy of this was that the privation of many who honestly deserved help was intensified by the caution and, ultimately, the cynicism which many officials developed. Brownlee exemplified the tone in a letter to H. E. Spencer.

> In one camp [for the unemployed], within a few days of enlistment the men raised money among themselves for a boxing bout and every evening engaged in gambling, apparently having the funds for such things, while in another camp the men were called on strike by one of the leaders within a few days because we would not supply him with a horse to go a short distance for water. Men who are hungry do not act in this way.

The tendency to regard government as a panacea was anathema to Brownlee. He was fundamentally committed to balancing revenues and expenditures and maintaining the solvency of the Province. His approach led to criticism that he was callous to individual human suffering. His counter argument was that the Province was a bastion against economic adversity. If the Province were to fail financially, as Brownlee could see was a very real possibility, there would be much greater human suffering.

This sort of stand caused a widening gap between him and the U.F.A. M.P.'s. The federal group painted Alberta conditions in the somberest tones, trying to move the Bennett administration to more energetic and responsive programmes of relief and reform. Brownlee, on the other hand, wishing to maintain as strong a Provincial credit-worthiness as possible and protect the record of his Government, tried to be optimistic and discounted the more horrendous rumours being circulated. He maintained that while there were difficulties, "the people", faced them with courage and determination. He was convinced that, particularly in the urban centres, most complaints came from professional agitators and organizers who were interested, for their own purposes, in creating unrest, bitterness, and demand for change. He ignored this calculated rhetoric but he did respond generously to cases where ordinary individuals displayed "a good spirit." One farmer, for example, who applied for relief work as a teamster, admitted that he had made mistakes which were magnified by the depression. His crop had been seized twice by the Rumely Machine Company but, he observed, "you cannot blame people as they need the money. I do not want to be kept by the municipality... if I could get teaming for my three boys and myself then we could pull through the winter." Brownlee ordered immediate action, telling O. L. McPherson, "I rather like the tone of this man's letter and would like to assist him in any way that we can."

Not all letters were as easy to respond to positively. Another farmer, after pouring out his anger and humiliation at being denied credit by the local banker despite offering his land, stock and machinery as collateral, compared Canada unfavourably with Russia. "The Alberta Government and the Federal Government are supposed to have at the head two of the smartest men in Canada," he went on, "but unless they take some of the special privileges away from the banks we are doomed."

Brownlee had urged the bankers not to withhold credit where reasonable security was offered. He received agreement in principle on this and further agreement that the banks' head officers would review any cases he brought to their attention. He found himself in virtually the same position he had been in a decade earlier, attempting to act as an intermediary, or in some cases as a referee, between debtors with radical ideas for reform and ultra-conservative bankers. He counseled reasonableness to both parties, citing possible repercussions from unreasonable attitudes. However, his advice was now less heeded. Farmers were no longer as significant a political force and agriculture was not as dominant a sector of the economy. Both factors meant that bankers had less motivation to adopt so-called reasonable attitudes when the severity of the depression in agriculture counseled ruthless restraint on the part of money lenders in order to protect their investments. On the other hand, many Western debtors soon concluded they had little to lose and were, therefore, much more anxious to explore so-called radical alternatives, from creation of a government controlled central bank, through sweeping credit and monetary reforms. to a complete restructuring of economic and political institutions.

The political impotence of these alternatives at the federal level was readily apparent. Thus Alberta debtors very naturally turned to the level of government where they could more realistically expect to be heard -- the Province. Brownlee often replied to requests for Provincial action on behalf of debtors with considerable patience, explaining, "There is, however, a very distinct limit to what we can do. We have no control over currency, banking or interest rates. These questions are all left by the B.N.A. Act to the Dominion." To the suggestion that the Province should take over all farm mortgages and lower their interest rate, he pointed out, "We would have to pay cash to mortgage to the mortgage company, which means that we would have to raise the money somewhere to pay off these mortgages which total many millions of dollars. ... The Government hasn't the money and can only obtain the money by borrowing and paying the rate of interest which is required by the financial market. ... in the meantime, we still require roads, schools, public health and so on and to give these services, the Government must keep itself in a solid condition."

Despite such patient explanations, Brownlee was discouraged. David Duggan, the new Alberta Conservative leader chatted with him one evening and found him "very weary of public life. The present Session has been a real strain on his physical resources. He has intimated to me that he possesses the natural ambition of his profession, which is to go to the 'Bench'." As Duggan coyly put it, in his letter to Bennett, "I refrained from any discussion with respect to the effect his resignation would have on the political welfare of his or any other party."

It was still obvious that if Brownlee were to leave the premiership, it would create almost a complete political vacuum in Alberta. Bennett and Duggan were naturally (as Brownlee must have expected) very interested in this possibility and its impact on their own political futures. By suggesting the possibility, Brownlee had done much to make Conservative leaders attentive to his position and had subtly encouraged them to be more cooperative in case they wished to 'use' him for their own ends at some future time. There was yet another angle to the maneuver which illustrated Brownlee's political astuteness. During the Liberal regime in Ottawa, he had been careful to cultivate both direct and indirect channels to the Prime Minister. Now, through his personal friendship with Bennett and the relationships he was actively fostering with Duggan, and with Ray Milner, the most influential Conservative in Alberta, he was assuring himself of similar access to the Conservative administration.

Conditions continued to deteriorate during 1931 necessitating greater relief expenditures at the same time as Provincial revenues were being reduced. As part of the effort to cut expenses, all but two agricultural colleges were closed. Their enrollments had slumped because farmers were unable to finance such relative luxuries for their children. The colleges, the pride of their communities, had promised to help stem the drift of young people away from the farms; therefore, their closure was another stark symbol of the poverty and lost hope which afflicted the West.

The situation of the Pools also continued to deteriorate. McFarland found the sale of wheat difficult. Pool Directors were not informed of his activities and had to content themselves with rumours that Bennett had authorized him not to let the price of Number 1 fall below 50 cents. Farmer organization leaders went to Ottawa in late June hoping to secure some type of federal assistance for Western agriculture. Following the decision of the Saskatchewan Court of Appeal against the notion of a compulsory pool, sentiment had shifted strongly in favour of the re-establishment of a national wheat marketing board. Brownlee was the principal speaker for the combined delegation which presented the case for a Wheat Board to Bennett. The Prime Minister appeared sympathetic, mentioning that the constitutional difficulties of creating a national marketing board could be overcome with Provincial cooperation.

Following the presentation, the farmer leaders seriously discussed trying to continue some sort "of an inter-provincial set-up with Brownlee in as general manager or general counsel." Again, it was H.W. Wood who scuttled such plans. He was no longer president of the U.F.A. but he was still chairman of the Alberta Wheat Pool and his influence was still great enough that he was able to convince Brownlee, yet again, that he was of more value to the farmers as the Premier than as general manager of a rather uncertain inter-provincial organization. This was to be the last major intervention Wood would have in Brownlee's life.

Soon Brownlee had adopted a position which accelerated the move toward each Pool elevator company buying, handling, and selling wheat entirely on its own. He told the Alberta Pool executive that "the Pool would be expected to pay interest on its debentures in the current year and both interest and principal installments in the following year." He also demanded that the Alberta Government have: "1) the right of consultation re: Pool management, and, 2) the right to veto any capital expenditures and declarations of dividends and to place two observers at Pool Directors meetings." There was even more. He insisted the Pool apply the interest it was paying on members' reserves to retiring the debt and that it raise its sales commission charge from 3/4 of a cent per bushel to the going rate of one cent. To the strong objection that "the Alberta Pool was built on a service basis instead of for big profits" he replied that it was absolutely vital that the Pool arrive at some means of retiring the massive debt it faced. If his advice were followed, the Pool should "be profitable enough to retire the total indebtedness over a period of twenty years without any trouble."

Wood declared that if Brownlee believed such terms were necessary to save the Alberta Pool, he would support them. R. D. Purdy, Pool Elevators general manager, and McPhail were less acquiescent. Although both were long time friends of Brownlee, they did not hesitate to say that they thought his terms unduly harsh and likely to influence the federal government to be less accommodating.

By mid-August it was clear that Bennett was not going to establish a Wheat Board to handle the 1931 crop and that there might be no financial support for the Pools in the coming year. Again Brownlee was off to Ottawa as part of a delegation to meet the Prime Minister and bank officials to negotiate a line of credit for the provincial Pools. Perhaps because they were now operating in almost exactly the same manner as privately owned grain companies, thanks in part to Brownlee's insistence, the banks promised ample credit would be available to finance the elevator operations. An initial payment for the year's wheat of only 35 cents per bushel was agreed upon and Bennett announced that a bonus of 5 cents per bushel would be paid to all producers.

The idea of Brownlee continuing as an official spokesman for the Pools was dropped quietly when Bennett made it plain to Pool leaders that, "He did not want to back the pools with Brownlee in the picture." McPhail speculated that Bennett was afraid that Brownlee's involvement might lead to "a great farmers' organization [being] built up which might be used for political reasons." However, the days when the Western farmer would be the basis of a strong political movement were over, as was foreshadowed the very next day when Bennett discussed the final arrangements with the Pools with McFarland, while pool officials were left to cool their heels in an outer office. McPhail, who would die suddenly less than a month later at the age of forty-seven, was convinced that, "Farmers are the only men who will remedy farm conditions." Whether he realized it or not, though, farmers were never again a major force on the national scene.

In a way too, Brownlee's forcible restructuring of the Alberta Pool's financial operation onto a more traditional basis was the final act of a drama. For three decades, the desire for democratic direction had wrestled with the need for practical business administration within all farmers' companies. Brownlee had always believed the practical considerations of the business must take precedence over the policy desires of the members. The newly truncated Pools and the other farmers' companies, such as the U.G.G., which were to survive and eventually flourish in the future would keep this principle firmly in mind. In 1931, however, Brownlee's insistence on strictly orthodox business management was regarded as contrary to the basic spirit of the pools. Many farmers believed that the real, service oriented pools died during this time, replaced by organizations still called pools and cooperatives but which were, in fact, little different from the privately owned corporations with which they competed.

Whatever the merits of this belief, Brownlee immediately set about to restore confidence in the Pool, not as a commercial expression of the farmers' spirit and way of life, but as a competent and reliable firm which would safely handle the farmers' grain. Since there had been considerable criticism of the proceeds of one crop being used to retire debts associated with another, all Pool members were released from their delivery contracts and Brownlee announced that there would be "a complete cut-off from previous years' operations" and no farmer would be "liable for any debts or obligations of past years." He undoubtedly regretted the collapse and break-up of the Wheat Pools. He regarded them as a great achievement and had, of course, been an important factor in their creation. However, he had also played an important role in re-organizing them to face realities. He firmly believed that no institution, Pool or Province, could survive without a "sane and practical financial footing." Solid financial operation was also a strong defense against political criticism.

* * *

Somehow during the summer, Brownlee found the time to take his family for a holiday on the Earl Cook ranch near Pincher Creek. Cook, an M.L.A. since 1921, had been one of the U.F.A. casualties in the 1930 election. The Brownlee family (Jack and Alan now in their early teens) enjoyed the foothills ranch life as well as the side trips to the new Waterton Lakes Park. Florence, more active than she had been since the early days of her marriage, joined in the hikes and even the trail rides. Also accompanying the family was Florence's niece from Ontario. The Brownlee "family" now generally included such extras. Cecil Rice-Jones, retired from the U.G.G. and a Winnipeg alderman, sent his daughter to stay with the Brownlees for a period while she studied nursing at the University of Alberta. Florence often assisted the Dean of Women with teas for groups of co-eds and Vivian MacMillan, the daughter of Edson's former mayor was a frequent visitor in the home. The Brownlee boys were healthier and more active than they once had been, sometimes being required to accompany their father to the office on a Saturday to do their homework under supervision. In general, the Brownlee household was more active, yet more relaxed than ever before.

There was no such relaxation on the farms. The Hanna region, especially, experienced drought and, although the area affected was a small proportion of the total agricultural land, it had both an economic and a psychological effect. Banks became even more restrictive and soon a new crisis resulted from their refusal to advance farmers the necessary funds to buy binder twine. After all the adversity of low prices, the perils of nature, and severe privation had been overcome, and with an average crop ready for harvesting; the threat of the banks to withhold the means of harvesting that crop raised a storm of outrage.

Brownlee, in Ottawa at a conference with the Prime Minister and the bankers when the first reports of such refusals came in, quickly realized the banks were attempting to force the Provincial Governments to guarantee them against losses on binder twine loans. He regarded this as unreasonable and an irresponsible avoidance of legitimate risks. However, the other two prairie Governments were not as shrewd and were quick to promise such guarantees. The best Brownlee could do was agree to a programme of guarantees but insist that it be kept secret so there would be no unnecessary requests for such credit. Farmers were informed that if they had been refused binder twine loans they should reapply. What was not publicized was that the banks circularized their branches to approve all such loans, on the strength of Provincial guarantees.

The banks' action was, to Brownlee, additional evidence that banking and credit institutions needed some reform. He pointed out the unfairness of blanket higher interest rates for Western Canada regardless of the merits of the individual loan, especially when the rates charged went well above the maximum rate of seven percent specified in the Bank Act. The banks argued that both the risks and costs of operating in the West were higher. Brownlee asked what it would cost them to reduce the interest rate to the legal seven percent. The Bank of Montreal estimated it would cost them about $125,000 and lead to the closing of branches and a consequent loss of services to farmers. In view of the many small prairie villages with two or more bank branches, Brownlee was not impressed by this argument.

Another serious financing problem involved the schools. Bennett wanted to announce that the Dominion would stand a percentage of the loss involved in Provincial guarantees to banks of loans to school boards, proclaiming that no child in Canada should be denied an education because of schools being forced to close. Brownlee "objected to any [public] announcement and requested we be allowed to quietly meet the situation as it developed [since] any general statement would mean the municipalities would throw up their hands and the banks would insist on Government guarantees." Brownlee believed his approach was vindicated by the fact that; "Manitoba has given guarantees to forty-four municipalities totaling several $100,000 ... while in this Province, by having competent officials arrange conferences between banks and municipalities, we have so far kept all schools operating with practically no provincial guarantees."

By fall, however, the situation was more serious. Continuing record low prices for farm produce, combined now with crop failures in some areas, meant that a growing number of both rural and urban residents could not pay their taxes. As a result, school districts found themselves without funds. Several means of coping were attempted. Two of the more popular were reducing teachers' salaries and shortening the school year. In a society so deeply committed to education as a means to social progress, there was widespread resentment and frustration at the enforced curtailment of educational opportunities. These feelings led to demands on the Province to keep the schools open and again Brownlee played "Scrooge" in order to enforce the maximum amount of local belt tightening and thus minimize the demands on the Provincial treasury.

He regarded as completely unreasonable the demand for undiminished services by the same people who were insisting on a reduction in taxation or even a moratorium on the payment of debts and taxes. However, as Albertans prepared for a third year of severe financial privation, the view that the situation was a "temporary recession" was discredited and replaced by a consensus that there was a fundamental economic breakdown. In consequence there was growing impatience with the conservative and orthodox solutions insisted upon by Brownlee.

He ordered staff cuts. At the beginning of 1930 there had been 2,566 permanent civil servants. By the end of 1931, there were only 1,600. However, 40,000 Albertans were now on direct governmental relief. In preparation for a long, cold winter, he initiated a survey of coal supplies and appointed former U.F.A.

Secretary H.E.G.H. Scholefield to co-ordinate the now massive relief network and investigate any complaints of shortages or abuses.

Even more serious, from his point of view, the now precarious financial position of the Province worsened quickly as the international monetary system began to collapse. Soon the many issues of bonds payable in United States currency carried sizable foreign exchange premiums to be paid as well. A series of frantic telegrams to Bennett was necessary to obtain interim credit from the Dominion treasury so that Alberta would not be forced to default on a bond interest payment in New York on October 1, 1931. All Western provinces were forced to turn to the Dominion for emergency financial support. As a condition of such support, Bennett insisted on more stringent provincial budget cuts and moved quickly toward forced consultation on provincial spending. Of course, Brownlee could not inform the public of these conditions without worsening an already difficult predicament. Unfortunately for John Brownlee and the rest of the people of Alberta, conditions in 1932 were to be much worse.

Chapter 15: Poverty in the Midst of Plenty

In January, 1932, the Province of Alberta was within hours of defaulting on a $3,000,000 bond maturity. The traditional New York market was no longer absorbing Canadian securities. Brownlee's urgent telegrams finally moved Bennett to action and the maturity was refunded by a loan from the Dominion while other liabilities were covered by floating a new Sinking Fund Debenture series for $15,000,000. The new series, paying a record six percent interest and discounted on placement to 95.25, was the most costly financing Alberta had yet been forced to acquire. Brownlee, putting the best face on it, announced the issue had all being taken up and that that testified to the Province's continuing good credit rating. However, much of the subscription was by the Imperial Bank of Canada which had only moved on the strength of guarantees secured by stocks of gold transferred from the federal treasury to the Bank. For all practical considerations, the federal treasury had become the bank of last resort for Alberta.

To Brownlee, of course, the necessity of rapidly increasing the public debt in order to finance even the drastically curtailed expenditures was a horrendous situation. He continually pressed the federal government to assume a larger direct share of relief programme costs and slowly Bennett moved in that direction. For example, the Dominion finally began paying a larger share of the old age pension. Brownlee did not miss the opportunity to remind people that he had counseled caution with respect to such schemes.In fact, he came to regard the depression as an object lesson to citizens on the importance of sound financial foundations and as a vindication of his previous fiscal conservatism.

The new U.F.A. president, Robert Gardiner, although not mentioning Brownlee by name, bitterly denounced his policy, declaring, "the only remedy [offered] for the present evil of under-consumption by those who control the system, is to curtail consumption still further by what is erroneously described as economy." The U.F.A. Convention was now firmly controlled by the most radical element and passed resolutions urging: nationalization of the monetary system; public ownership of land, radio broadcasting and hydroelectric power; a drastic horizontal reduction of debts; and the cancellation of all interest payments until the price of farm commodities equaled the cost of production. Brownlee regarded some of these schemes as insane but his policy was to ignore such proposals and their supporters whenever possible, rather than precipitate an inflamed controversy "at a time when it is difficult to get a fair expression of opinion on any question."

The situation he faced when the Session began in February was even more daunting. The previous year's deficit of $2,500,000 had been the first of his premiership but the current public accounts showed a deficit well over $4,000,000, despite the economies. Brownlee's response was to order more drastic cuts, while Richard Reid made a number of minor tax revisions in a budget designed to exhaust every possibility of raising more revenue. Corporation taxes were revised upward with Brownlee taking special note of the fact that Calgary Power Company, with a net revenue of $451,452, had paid provincial taxes of only $1,000.

The most promising source of new revenue appeared to be a provincial income tax, a major piece of legislation during the Session. It provided basic exemptions of $750 for single persons and $1,500 for the married, and was graduated from one percent of taxable income, upwards. It was hoped the new tax would generate about $1,300,000. As an indication of the severity of the agricultural depression, fewer than 100 Alberta farmers had incomes sufficient to be taxed under the programme.

Another major item dealt with during the Session was the continuing waste in the Turner Valley natural gas field. The problem was a long standing one since even before World War I inadequate technology meant that some wells blew wild for years because the means to bring them under control was not available. Accidental and flare fires also consumed large quantities of gas. In 1928, a joint Dominion-Alberta Commission concluded that the amount of natural gas being wasted equaled the 72.5 million cubic feet harnessed during the year. The U.F.A. Convention had produced several resolutions demanding conservation of the resource and legislation to prevent the waste but the Government moved slowly, finding that stringent technological parameters for development favoured the large corporations as against the small independent drillers. Also, it was argued, waste controls would drive up costs to consumers, a possibility which concerned Calgary and its City operated natural gas utility. Brownlee's attempt to work out a programme of voluntary conservation failed to win much support among the gas companies. He then introduced the Turner Valley Gas Conservation Act, setting up a three man commission with power to determine the volume and regulate the flow of any well or field in the Province. This legislation was immediately challenged by some of the companies operating under Dominion leases as a move by the Province to interfere with leasehold rights protected by the natural resources transfer agreement.

Brownlee, hoping to circumvent this objection, immediately sent his most trusted litigation counsel, A. L. Smith, a Conservative, to Ottawa to ask Bennett to pass federal legislation which would validate the Provincial Act. Simultaneously, because of Brownlee's influence, Ray Milner, Bennett's closest political advisor in Alberta, wrote to the Prime Minister urging the same action. Brownlee had pulled all the strings at his command but Bennett declined to act, citing constitutional difficulties and adding a personal note to Brownlee: "Knowing you as I do, I cannot but think that if you will look into the matter carefully you will at once realize how impossible it was for the Government to take the action suggested." This may have been an oblique reference to the strong representations Bennett had received from the companies operating under Dominion leases, reinforced by telephone calls from his Calgary law partners who acted on behalf of several of the major oil companies. Brownlee had been out-gunned. Natural gas continued to escape into the clear southern Alberta skies at a prodigious rate.

* * *

As economic conditions in the West worsened, more and more individuals advanced solutions. Secession of the western provinces was one idea but a scheme for amalgamating the three prairie provinces into one enjoyed more popularity, being broached on an official level by Premier Bracken. Brownlee coolly pointed out that:

Manitoba has no Separate School; Alberta and Saskatchewan have ... a bill would have to go through the Dominion House setting up the constitution of the new Province ... and anyone who has followed the history of the Dominion House can appreciate at once that no Dominion Government is likely to throw any bill into the House that will again raise the school question as a political issue.

Another solution was to encourage American tourists who it was argued, would be especially attracted to Alberta's mountain scenery. Brownlee weighed the suggestion with characteristic pragmatism and concluded, "With conditions as bad as they are in the United States, I doubt if the return would be worth the effort." Joe Clarke, colourful Liberal partisan and sometime Mayor of Edmonton, proposed a new major stadium to revitalize the economy of that city and Brownlee introduced an amendment to the City Charters Act to allow the Council to appoint a stadium commission. In short, ideas came from those in all walks of life and, at first, Brownlee weighed them carefully and often replied personally at some length.

One writer, for example, suggested Brownlee was the man to lead Canadians out of their doldrums to a vastly reformed society. His modest reply revealed that he was studying all the current literature "by such men as Sir Arthur Salter, Sir Josiah Stamp and J. Maynard Keynes." He had noted that all the experts agreed the depression was a world wide phenomenon, not to be solved by local or even national policy decisions, and that there was something fundamentally wrong with the financial system, but they could offer "no clear-cut idea of the reorganization in finance which should take place to improve conditions."

Alberta's main problem, he went on, was that Canada had to find export markets for over 300,000,000 bushels of wheat. "I have yet to find anyone," he commented, "who can satisfactorily answer the question of how a change in our financial system within the four walls of Canada will greatly change the basic problem that we cannot compel any foreign country to take our wheat or pay more for it than a competitive price." As for the question of monetary reform, the experts were divided as to whether "an inflation of our currency" would be beneficial, in the long run.

Nonetheless, he concluded, "I shall be only too glad to take any action which would in any way improve the position of our people, provided always I am able to see my way through sufficiently clearly to be sure that our financial position would not be worse than at present."

Later, he was equally analytical when dissecting the argument that to ignore any potential solution out of concern for constitutional difficulties was a type of legalistic nit-picking which could easily be swept aside if a leader really wished to act. "I would like you to candidly face the question of the position of one Province attempting to defy the Constitution by itself," he wrote to one such critic. First, neither the Courts nor the federal Government would allow such a move. If the financial and physical force of the rest of the country were mobilized to crush the attempt, Albertans would be much worse off. Secondly, even if Alberta was allowed to do what it liked, it could not create external markets for its products. It could inflate its currency, but, he noted, "the history of the past records more than one example in different nations of the calamity resulting from undue and ill-considered inflation. "In the last analysis," he concluded, "there are only two well defined courses of action open, first, is by revolutionary methods. History has yet to record a single instance of the revolutionary method that has not resulted in a welter of discord and misery for a very considerable time. Secondly, the organizing of popular thought to face the problem candidly and fairly to work out the necessary reforms with an eye to preserving the integrity of our trade."

Eventually though, Brownlee became impatient with those who continued to advocate what he judged to be irresponsible, half-baked schemes. "As a matter of fact," he told one amateur theorist, "I have sometimes felt that. if the results were not so tragical, I would like to see Canada put under the most extreme form of socialistic or communistic Government in order that our people could have the actual experience of what would happen and learn for themselves the lesson that in our present day world situation, one nation cannot fashion for itself any level of prosperity regardless of the position of the rest of the world."

While Brownlee appeared to have an explanation of why everyone else's remedy for the depression was unwise, he was in the unenviable position of having no convincing solution of his own, other than the rigorous economies and cautious debt adjustment which had seemingly been so ineffectual. As an example of the degree of spending cuts already made, government advertising, which had reached a high of $36,000 in 1929, had been slashed, largely under Brownlee's personal supervision, to below $8,000. Now, all those on government pay-rolls who earned more than $100 monthly took ten percent cuts. Brownlee, with a premier's salary of $10,624 and a Sessional indemnity of $4,000 saw his take home pay reduced by about $1,500. He argued that such cuts accomplished little for the amount lost to the Province in income and other taxes almost off-set the savings, but he reluctantly supported them for their symbolic effect and because they were being loudly called for by many of his backbenchers who represented constituencies where Brownlee's salary was more than the combined income of an entire district. Coincidentally, it was at this same time that his private income ended when he sold his Calgary law firm to his partner, M. M. Porter. This move was necessitated largely by the need to avoid a conflict of interest when the Province took action against a U.G.G. agent represented by Brownlee's firm.

Perhaps the most noticeable economy measure was disbanding the Alberta Provincial Police (A.P.P.) and turning over the provincial police work to the Royal Canadian Mounted Police (R.C.M.P.). This had been suggested seriously as early as 1928 but Brownlee resisted, arguing that there was a place for a force responsible for provincial statutes and also that the savings would not be as great as most predicted. However, by 1932, every economy was a necessity and, with a certain blow to Albertan pride, the proud history and tradition of the A.P.P. was traded for fixed police costs, greater Dominion cost sharing and some uncertain savings.

As for debtors, Brownlee remained convinced that his Debt Adjustment Act was the most effective means, within the legislative competence of the Province, to ease the severe problems of debt. This view was strengthened when other jurisdictions began examining the Act and passing legislation modeled upon it. Even envoys of United States' presidential candidate, Franklin Roosevelt, interviewed Brownlee about the Act. The crowning recognition came when his measure served as a model for the federal Farmers' Creditors Arrangement Act. He regarded this as one of his most important contributions to Western farmers for, as he later observed, "there is no doubt at all that literally hundreds, if not thousands, of farmers in the prairie provinces remain on their land today and are successfully carrying on their businesses who would have been put off that land if it had not been for that legislation."

As record low commodity prices continued, the need became apparent for greater legislative strength behind the request for money lenders to be lenient. Some of the most vexatious creditor demands involved loans secured on crop shares. The common practice was for the lender to be guaranteed one-third of the farmers' crop. When prices had been above $1.00 per bushel, the lenders' share could be taken entirely out of the return above the cost of production. Now, though, with farm-gate prices less than one-half the cost of production, the one-third share must come entirely from what was needed for the farmer and his family to survive.

An actual, though not uncommon, case illustrates the situation. A Morinville area farmer owed a total of $9,760. In 1931 he sold his entire crop of 830 bushels of wheat and 1,730 bushels of oats. Because of the extremely low prices, the total return from the sale was $457. His threshing bill, a first charge, was $176 leaving a total gross income for the year of $281. The Debt Adjustment Bureau determined that he could pay his mortgage holder $60, a purely token amount considering the 8% interest, but that the remaining $221 was necessary to support the farmer, his wife and five children for the next year and finance the following year's farming operations. Had this farmer had a one-third crop share agreement and had the creditor enforced that agreement, as he was legally in a position to do, the farmer's net income would have been only $129 or little more than $10 per month.

Such cases existed in the thousands across the West and Brownlee found mortgage companies reluctant to accept anything less than what the contracts provided, regardless of how penurious such action would leave the farm family. He therefore armed himself with a draft bill which would limit crop shares to a maximum of one-quarter. This, as Brownlee intended, disposed the

203

lenders to discuss what voluntary limits might be worked out short of such legislation. He further suggested that his was a voice of moderation to which they would be well advised to listen in order to defuse more radical proposals.

Of course, some mortgage lenders were more reasonable than others and Brownlee bluntly informed the manager of the Canada Permanent Mortgage Corporation that, "certain letters sent out by your own Company have primarily been the cause of this recommendation. Some of these letters, held by our Members, are addressed to farmers in the areas where with the very small crop yield of the last year and the present price per bushel, the return could not possibly take care of the living expenses until the next crop. Notwithstanding these apparent conditions the letters asserted the complete ownership of one-third of the crop and demanded the delivery of same." Through such plain spokenness, Brownlee was able to bring the mortgage companies to the conference table and in early June he met their representatives at the Banff Springs Hotel. For almost a week, in the lavishly appointed suites and over sumptuous banquets, the money lenders considered their attitude toward the tattered, care-worn farm families of Alberta.

The result was that the Mortgage Loans Association agreed, "they will not commence foreclosure proceedings this year without first giving the Debt Adjustment Board three or four week's notice to give the Board an opportunity of working out a satisfactory adjustment. Secondly, that foreclosures will not be brought for principal only, that is if interest and taxes are paid the Companies will be satisfied." As for the crop share issue, the province was divided into zones and it was agreed that within each zone crop yields would be considered. In high yield areas the full one-third share would be allowed, while in areas of low yield the maximum share might be limited to one-quarter or less, by general agreement of the mortgage companies. In view of the disastrously low prices and the fact that the farmers' fate was still entirely in the hands of the money lenders, the agreements received only very grudging support. They were better than rampant foreclosures but to most, not a satisfactory solution.

The 1932 crop was excellent in quantity and especially in quality. The bins were bulging, cattle were sleek in the fields, but the people were haggard and anxious. It was the summer of 1932 which underlined the truth in the soon popular slogan, "poverty in the midst of plenty". As one writer told Brownlee, "there was a feeling of absolute, hopeless discouragement at seeing a vast volume of grain melt away, and no return, no indebtedness paid, not even taxes." The utterly depressed prices of farm commodities and the consequent lack of purchasing power, aggravated by large debt charges which siphoned out of Western Canada much of what little cash income farmers received, pointed Albertans in the direction of economic reforms -- a direction for which there was a solid cultural base in the popularity of previously advanced schemes.

One suggestion was that creditors be forced to accept payments in grain at a certain fixed price. This, it was argued, would "compel creditor interests to take some of the loss", and "give some reasonable value to the grain of this province." The idea reflected a major theme born of the great depression in Western Canada -- that the hardships of the times were not being shared equitably. There was a strong feeling, for example, that it was fundamentally unfair for the interest income of lenders to continue unabated, enabling them to live in increased luxury thanks to undiminished income during a period of deflation. while the harsh burdens of a world depression were visited with a vengeance on farm families who could not afford proper food or clothing.

Perhaps it was not unexpected then, that the summer of 1932 should spawn a countervailing ideology. In any case, it was this summer that saw the emergence of popular radio evangelist and respected high school principal, William Aberhart, as the leader of such an ideology, built mainly from indigenous modifications of several reform theories and known popularly as "Social Credit". Brownlee had confronted Social Credit economic theorists such as George Bevington for more than a decade. For Brownlee, whatever merits the theory might have, it was obvious that to implement it in any practical way was beyond the constitutional capability of a province. For him, that ended the discussion. For a growing number of Albertans, however, Brownlee's constitutional concerns evaporated before the stark necessity of doing something.

If Social Credit was the answer, it must be tried regardless of constitutional niceties. If the rest of Canada remained unconvinced, Alberta would have to go it alone. To Brownlee such a prospect was nonsense but, again, to Albertans staring hunger in the face while their bins overflowed, it became more and more appealing. Aberhart argued that Social Credit was the answer and that it could be applied, if necessary, in Alberta alone. He declared this, not with pedantic convolutions or legalistic qualifications, but straightforwardly with utter certainty bolstered by an emphasis on applied Christianity, the prophecies of Scripture, and topped off with good humour and rousing hymns. The walls of Jericho were not breached by constitutional amendments or economic retrenchment but by faith in God and the implementation of His will.

Just as Aberhart was introducing Social Credit into his weekly radio sermons, some, such as William Irvine, once a leading, advocate of Social Credit economic theory, were meeting in Calgary to organize what would be called the Cooperative Commonwealth Federation. The C.C.F. Manifesto shared with Social Credit such notions as the nationalization of banks and other credit institutions, but it went far beyond monetary reform to a more thorough going programme which had an indigenous element but also included the basically foreign accretions of the League for Social Reconstruction and the European Socialism of the leaders of organized labour. The new U.F.A. leaders were actively involved in the formation of the C.C.F., Norman Priestly becoming its first secretary, but H.W. Wood proved to be still a more authentic spokesman for the Alberta farmers when he declared the "farmers' movement [had been] turned back forty years by the U.F.A.-Labor combination." Brownlee, too, was very cool toward the C.C.F. group, frankly telling Norman Lambert, a backroom organizer for the national Liberals, that he would be unable "to follow Farmer-Labor proposals if applied to the provincial field."

Lambert had been sent to see Brownlee by King who was again promoting his idea of a fusion of all those opposed to the Conservatives. Brownlee was not interested. "He said his policy had been to treat equally with Liberals and Conservatives at Ottawa," Lambert recorded. "[He] had tried union tactics with Liberals but could get nowhere in Alberta." Lambert next took his arguments to the Alberta Liberals but he got nowhere either. "Met Chas. Stewart, McLaughlin & Howson in pm and discussed possibility of union but strong antipathy expressed to J.E.B.," he wrote in his diary. "Met group at night ... very militant and stupid with one or two exceptions ... Feeling strong vs. any relations with Brownlee, U.F.A. or anybody else."

It was evident that the provincial Liberals sensed the new vulnerability of the Brownlee Government which, only two years before, had appeared invincible. Now that the depression was seriously harming all Governments, the local Liberals smelled political blood and were not to be distracted by talk of union or cooperation. As Lambert noted, there was particular hostility to Brownlee, who more than anyone else was responsible for the Liberals' lengthy sojourn in the political wilderness. In October, they chose one of their most militant members, W.R. Howson, as the new provincial leader. Howson was to pursue an aggressive style, focusing particularly on potential scandals, in order to hasten the demise of the Brownlee administration. His attacks were aided by two of his closest friends, Peter Campbell, publisher of the Edmonton Bulletin, and Neil MacLean, prominent courtroom lawyer and a member of the same law firm as Howson. Increasingly, this aggressive rump, and various shadowy associates they attracted, would aim at destroying Brownlee himself to clear the field for their own ascendancy

The first tilts at scandal mongering were not long in coming. MacLean emerged as legal counsel for the disgruntled former head of the Liquor Investigation Bureau who had some bitter charges against Attorney General John Lymburn following the phasing out of the Bureau as an economy measure. Little of embarrassment to the Government emerged but there was a strong rumour campaign that the Deputy Attorney General frequented a premises which sold liquor illegally. MacLean was behind another rumour campaign alleging that Brownlee had intervened to quash charges against one of H.W. Wood's sons. Such rumours and the suspicions they generated had a surprisingly telling effect, primarily because the loyalty of the grassroots U.F.A. supporter had been seriously eroded over the years. As one commentator has noted, to many rural people, Brownlee and his Cabinet were, by this time, "indistinguishable from the distrusted old line parties. As the

Cabinet Ministers and certain other influential Members returned year after year to the Legislature, an increasing urbanization of their lives and outlook became apparent, a metamorphosis that did not go unnoticed by the constituents." It was also noticed that Brownlee and his Ministers were not suffering any personal financial hardships because of the depression. Like others on comfortable salaries, they could afford maids, new cars, and fine clothes while farmers patched their rags for another year and worried about how they were going to feed their children.

Perhaps the most graphic illustration of the estrangement between the Government and the less fortunate segments of society came at the so-called Hunger March, in December. The March brought together elements of the three most disadvantaged groups in the Province. First, the sizable number of unemployed, especially single unemployed men of whom there were estimated to be over 2,000 of in Edmonton. Communist organizers were active among this group and undercover police reported to Brownlee that these organizers were promising, "If we get enough men here, we will parade whether the police like it or not, and they won't stop us." A second group consisted of representatives of unemployed coal miners. Under-production at the mines meant numerous lay-offs, a condition which precipitated strikes. These were long, bitter and sometimes violent and when finally settled, many strikers found themselves laid-off. The miners' unions were often led by active Communists, as was the third element to organize the Hunger March, the Farmers' Unity League. This organization was growing in popularity in the northeast section of the Province where it had held a number of meetings, all passing the same resolutions protesting capitalist exploitation of farmers and demanding exemption from taxes, cancellation of interest on all debts, abolition of seizures by creditors, and relief payments of twenty dollars per month per family plus two dollars per month per child. Brownlee had repeated to them, somewhat sadly but firmly, his explanation that,

> "the Provincial Government has no jurisdiction whatever over banks or banking, nor over the issuing currency and our power to spend depends upon: 1) revenue received from our own people in the nature of taxes, 2) ability to borrow in the market of the world. As both these sources

of revenue in these times have been very seriously restricted we are accordingly restricted in what we can do ... It would, therefore, be utterly impossible for us to comply with the spirit of this resolution even if we felt it was sound in other respects."

Now, however, he advised Lymburn that the Farmers' Unity League was "undoubtedly an extremely Communistic Organization ... doing a very great deal in working up the people in the Ukrainian districts."

The organizers of the Hunger March planned a mass meeting of as many as 5,000 people at the Edmonton Market Square, to be followed by a march to the Legislature where they would demand an appearance by Brownlee. For his part, the Premier steadfastly refused to grant permission for the march, asked for special assistance from the R.C.M.P. in controlling the demonstration, and announced he would be willing to meet a small delegation at any time but that he would not respond to any mass gathering. The organizers went ahead with their plans, perhaps as many as 1,000 gathered, they marched toward the Legislative Building despite not having permission but were met by a squad of mounted police and easily dispersed. As one participant recalled, "it was no good, Premier Brownlee didn't even come out to meet us. That's what most defeated us. I mean, a lot of us understood that he couldn't do too much but we figured since it's a farmers' government, least he can do is come out and explain. But they wouldn't let us near the Parliament Building."

Brownlee was certain he had made the only sensible decision. "It was almost inevitable that in any such gathering there would be those who were emotional and not in control of themselves under pressure." He recalled, "I made it quite clear that at any time of day on the shortest notice I was prepared to meet any delegation from the unemployed ... But the Government would simply not permit this gathering with the danger of violence which is always present if you get a large number of people led by irresponsible men in a march such as was organized. On the whole we received the support of the press and most of, I think, the better thinking people of the Province."

Unfortunately, the strength of Brownlee's position was undermined by the coincidence that on the day of the march,

December 20, 1932, the price of Number 1 wheat, in store, fell below 40 cents per bushel, which meant the lowest farm price for wheat in over 400 years. Brownlee was fully alive to the seriousness of the situation. In drafting his traditional New Year's Day message, he wrote, "The people of our Western Provinces are facing the future with undiminished courage, fortitude and faith in the ultimate well being of our country." In the final text, he crossed out the word "undiminished".

Chapter 16: The Royal Commission on Banking

"What we, as a Government, will have to aim at," Brownlee wrote at the beginning, of 1933, "is some line of action that will give the necessary relief to the debtor interests in view of the disastrously low prices of farm products, while at the same time not unreasonably injuring the creditor class." He was still attempting to cling, at least in principle, to his basic idea that government should act as an impartial mediator in the ordinary operations of existing institutions. By doggedly maintaining this position, he was becoming increasingly isolated. The U.F.A. Convention was busy reaffirming their support for a slate of sweeping "C.C.F. principles" for which the Premier had slight sympathy. Elsewhere, former U.F.A. members were trooping to join William Aberhart's Social Credit study groups modeled on his very successful Bible study groups.

However, while in Alberta Brownlee was seen as a staid, fiscal conservative, outside the West he was viewed as a representative of the unorthodox reformers, a perception reinforced at the Dominion-Provincial Conference in Ottawa in mid-January. There, he threw cold water on the "back to the farm" schemes touted by some Eastern leaders to relieve urban unemployment. New settlers could hardly be expected to succeed, he pointed out, when present farmers were experiencing such difficulty. Neither could farmers "hire help with farm products at their present prices." Thus, since unemployment was likely to remain a serious problem for several years, he suggested considering such permanent policies as unemployment insurance. He thought special attention should be given the growing number of high school and university graduates unable to secure employment.

He made the controversial suggestion that the practice of delivering relief in kind be amended to allow as much as ten percent to be paid in cash. Another controversial suggestion of his was that Canadians holding provincial bonds payable in United States funds should not receive the large, unanticipated bonus of the foreign exchange premium. Alberta had had to pay over $740,000 more on its debt because of the exchange factor and much of this had gone to Canadian bond holders. Perhaps most responsible for

Brownlee's reputation with the other Premiers as a spokesman for the unorthodox was his advocacy of banking reforms, especially his suggestion that the Dominion should act to lower interest rates, and his plea that something be done in the direction of debt adjustment. He suggested amending the Bankruptcy Act to enlarge the role of such bodies as his own Debt Adjustment Bureau.

He also returned to a point he had raised at earlier Dominion-Provincial Conferences: that while provincial sources of revenue were severely restricted, the services for which they were responsible were continually expanding. "Unquestionably the present division of jurisdiction is out of date," he told the press, "anything that will help clear up these confusions and overlappings will be almost as important as the original framing of the [B.N.A.] Act." The Western Premiers recommended that the Dominion assume a greater share of the cost of programmes, and were willing in return that some provincial jurisdictions be curtailed so necessary national policies, such as unemployment insurance, might be implemented. By the time the Conference had concluded, Brownlee had impressed everyone as the strongest voice from the West and, as Bennett confided to friends, the "ablest mind" in attendance.

The bleak economic prospects and the harsh budgetary realities of the three prairie governments led them to a joint request to the federal Government for thoroughgoing financial relief. With the existing prices of agricultural commodities, they argued, tax increases would be counter-productive, leading to "wide-spread default in tax and debt payments." They described the extreme rigour of the economies they had already taken and the large uncontrollable expenditures imposed by the depression on the provinces; such as, direct relief and foreign exchange payments. From the predicament, they maintained, there were only two ways out: "To very seriously reduce our expenditures for schools, health institutions, old age pensions and mothers' allowances; or; to default on payments of either exchange premiums, or interest, or both." The first alternative would lead to "grave social disturbances" while the economic implications of the second would be equally severe.

All of this led to the request that the Dominion loan the Provinces all the money necessary to pay "for Unemployment

Relief, at least until such time as our securities can be sold on a reasonable basis" and that, "the Dominion proportion of direct relief costs should be at least 50% rather than 33-1/3% as at present." It was concluded that with such assistance, the prairie provinces could carry on without further requests for aid.

Early in March, Bennett responded with a letter berating each of the four Western Premiers for showing "no convincing evidence ... that every possible effort is being made ... to adjust your affairs and work into a position of self-reliance." Each Government must pledge itself to bring in a balanced budget or, if it could prove that such was impossible, limit its deficit to under one million dollars. In the event that any Government was unable or unwilling to comply with those terms, no further financial assistance from the Dominion would be forthcoming unless that Province agreed that its financial affairs should come entirely under the supervision of "a financial controller who may be nominated by your Government but who must be satisfactory to the Government of Canada."

Such an ultimatum was a shock to Brownlee who had struggled so hard and done so much, to the extent of seriously compromising his own and his Government's position, in order to follow a policy of strict economy and strive for a balanced budget. The blow was softened a little by a confidential covering letter from Bennett recognizing that, "you have dealt with conditions better than any one of the Western Provinces, but in order that there may be no cause for complaint by the other Provinces I am sending a letter to you in exactly the same terms as to the other Provinces."

The fact was though, that Alberta was now absolutely dependent on Ottawa for loans with which to meet the situation. Fortunately, Bennett's confidence in Brownlee spared Alberta some of the humiliation of the other provinces forced into a cap-in-hand attitude while Ottawa intruded into their economic autonomy. Brownlee, in turn, had a general admiration for Bennett and his handling of depression problems, especially his promptness and decisiveness. Despite the private relationship and understanding, however, Brownlee took care to put his position clearly on the record, rejecting the need for any financial controller and pointing out that the entire $5,782,000 the Dominion had so far loaned Alberta had been spent on direct relief costs and had not gone into general revenues. He concluded his case forcefully, declaring: "With respect to the total amount of these loans, your Government, of course, holds the Treasury Bills of this Province which should be regarded as perfectly good security unless all confidence in the future of Western Canada has been lost."

* * *

During 1933, the Alberta political situation became even more volatile. Howson vigorously attacked O.L. McPherson and his administration of the Public Works Department, prompting a Legislative inquiry which revealed that almost two-thirds of 1932's sixty road construction contracts had been let without a call to tender. McPherson defended this practice as necessary considering the make-work nature of many of the projects. The inquiry raised concerns about cost over-runs in only one case but, embarrassingly for McPherson, that contract had been let in his home constituency. Howson's attacks were bitter, sustained and personal to the degree that George Webster, former Liberal House leader, formally disassociated himself from the remarks.

McPherson was particularly vulnerable to attack at this time because of a plethora of rumours, fraught with salacious details, about his divorce and re-marriage. Most of these details became public in May when his former wife, through her counsel -- Neil MacLean -- petitioned the courts to annul their divorce. The grounds cited were that McPherson had conspired with the former husband of his second wife (a woman McPherson had allegedly flaunted as his mistress) to entice the first Mrs. McPherson into an adulterous act which provided the basis for the divorce. While the Court grappled with the intricacies of this action, the Liberals took full advantage of its political implications by focusing public attention on McPherson. The Liberal Edmonton Bulletin published the spicy details of the testimony and, even more pointedly, copies of these editions were circulated free of charge in McPherson's southern Alberta constituency.

The case was eventually dismissed but the "McPherson scandal" was obviously damaging to the Government. The Liberals' over-zealous efforts to capitalize on the situation sparked some expressions of support for McPherson from U.F.A. leaders but for many rank-and-file members, and their neighbours, such a scandal helped them to rationalize their already seriously eroded loyalty to the Government and reinforced their rapidly growing feeling that the personnel of the Government were not authentic representatives of rural Albertans.

Brownlee was aware that tensions created by severe economic restraint made the public much more than usually critical of questionable conduct. For example, he reprimanded the President of the University about an unwise choice of counsel to defend against a suit. "It seems to me that ... there is bound to be a very considerable amount of public criticism that the son of the Chairman of the Board and the son-in-law and law-partner of the Chancellor have been retained. While I do not think that I have been prone to pay too much attention to the "jumpiness" of public feeling in these days, on the other hand there is a question as to whether it is wise for bodies that are looked upon as governmental, to deliberately take action that is certain to arouse public suspicion and wide-spread criticism."

Despite this characteristic caution, by July rumours were being widely circulated that Brownlee himself was the central figure in a scandal. As early as May, Howson had visited Ottawa with "reports that Brownlee involved in a triangular affair with stenographer in his Attorney General's office." The stenographer was Vivian MacMillan. The case broke open, so to speak, on the night of July 5, 1933. Brownlee returned from a speaking engagement in Vermilion about 9:45 that evening and immediately telephoned MacMillan, a close friend of the Brownlee family for almost three years. There had been earlier discussions about her joining the family at the Brownlee's rented cottage at Sylvan Lake for her summer holidays. According to Brownlee, the purpose of his call was to see if she had gotten the necessary days off from work to enable her to go to the lake, as he planned on leaving the next morning to join his family, all of whom were already there. MacMillan told him she had not made up her mind and had several other problems bothering her. She asked Brownlee to come and pick her up that night and take her for a drive so she could discuss things with him. This Brownlee readily agreed to do, later describing his relationship with her as that of an uncle with a favourite niece. Soon after picking her up at her lodgings just north of the Legislative Building, he noticed he was being followed closely by another car. There began one of the most bizarre episodes of his life as he sped about the streets of Edmonton at high speeds making completely unpredictable turns and switch-backs; first to confirm that the car was purposely following them, and then in a vain attempt to lose it.

The wild chase of "hounds and hare" finally ended with Brownlee depositing MacMillan back at her lodgings and returning home alone, shaken by the experience and expecting some further consequences. The next day, he joined his family at Sylvan Lake but nothing further developed until the first week of August when he received a rather cryptic letter.

We have been instructed to commence action against you for damages for the seduction of Miss Vivian MacMillan.

We see by the newspapers that you are about to leave the Province for three months and would be glad, therefore, if you would let us have the name of your solicitor who will accept service on your behalf of the Statement of Claim which we will be issuing within the next few days.

The letter was from Neil MacLean.

* * *

In fact, no Statement was forthcoming for seven weeks. In the meantime, Brownlee was serving on the Dominion Royal Commission on Banking and Currency. The appointment of the Commission was in response to a rising current of public opinion that government should be playing a more direct role in economic and monetary management. The example of the Bank of England and the United States Federal Reserve Bank were both used to argue the need for a similar institution in Canada. Given the growing popularity of other more revolutionary reform schemes, astute political observers anticipated the Commission would recommend creation of a central bank.

Bennett wanted Brownlee to act on the commission as the representative of both Western and unorthodox viewpoints. Brownlee was hesitant, as Sir George Perley advised Bennett in England, "he would like to know the names of the other members of the commission as he might be embarrassed if he found them of a stand pat type and dice loaded against any new ideas. Says that Englishman named in the press and correctly named would be satisfactory to him and suggests that man for other appointments be somebody like Keynes. He evidently is rather bothered because two other Canadians suggested are both banking men." Finally, though, Brownlee had agreed to serve, despite lingering reservations about the other members.

On the last day of July, 1933, the Order in Council appointing the Commission was passed and a lengthy press notice was issued describing its members. The Chairman was to be Lord Macmillan, an "eminent British jurist" and "well-known as the Chairman of the so-called Macmillan Committee appointed ... to inquire into finance and industry in the United Kingdom." The second British member was Sir Charles Addis, "a director of the Bank of England" as well as of "a number of important shipping and banking concerns." Of the Canadians appointed, Sir Thomas White had been Minister of Finance from 1911 to 1919 and later Vice-President of the Canadian Bank of Commerce, while Beaudry Leman was the General Manager and Director of Banque Canadienne of Montreal. Brownlee, the only non-banker, was described as having "a wide knowledge of conditions in western Canada." The Commission was to examine the operations of the Bank Act and related legislation, as well as "recommend measures to promote revival of trade and enterprise and to facilitate intra-Imperial and international cooperation for the purpose of raising the level of commodity prices and to increase domestic employment and stability of the economic, financial and social institutions."

The first meeting of the Commission was in Ottawa on August 8, a date which gave Brownlee very little notice and for which he was hurriedly preparing to leave when the special delivery letter about the MacMillan suit arrived. He barely had time to meet his lawyer, M. M. Porter, before catching the train for Ottawa. Later evidence would reveal that MacMillan had consulted MacLean and Howson as early as the twenty-fourth of May. The lapse of time gave credence to later charges by Brownlee's supporters that the timing of the unfolding of the case was calculated to have the most damaging effect possible on his political position.

Following the Ottawa meetings, the Commission adjourned for five days to travel to Victoria. Brownlee broke his journey at Edmonton and he and Florence drove to Edson to interview the parents of Vivian MacMillan, ostensibly to clarify the nature of the action which was being brought against him. According to later testimony, A. D. MacMillan and his son, Harry, avoided the Brownlees who had only a short meeting with Mrs. MacMillan while standing on her doorstep. Brownlee told her that pursuing the action might ruin Vivian's future, to which her mother retorted coolly, "What about you?" Florence attempted to entreat on behalf of her home and boys but Brownlee, seeing nothing was being gained by the conversation, led her away.

Rejoining the Banking Commission, he gradually took a more active part. He showed particular interest in how much the decline in purchasing power on the prairies had contributed to the slowdown in such British Columbia industries as salmon packing and lumbering. He also asked the extent to which banks had local or regional autonomy in granting credit. It was revealed that any loan for more than $5,000 had to be approved by the head office in Eastern Canada. As well, he inquired closely as to the banks' relationship with the various cooperatives in B.C.

When the Commission reached the prairies, he became even more active, frequently questioning witnesses in detail so as to help them bring out clearly the roots of their concerns.

For example, he questioned a Calgary cattle dealer:

Hon. J.E. Brownlee: When you speak about over-expansion, is my information accurate that the expansion following the war was very largely incurred as a national proposition ... ?

Mr. Layzell: Yes, absolutely.

[B] That is with the whole nation behind it?

[L]: Yes.

B: And therefore the over-expansion was not so much the outburst of enthusiasm on the part of the farmers as their response to a national appeal.

L: Yes, to buy cattle and things like that. That was encouraged -- hogs and everything.

B: There is no doubt that many of the difficulties subsequently experienced by the farmers were the result of that expansion which came as a result of the combination of high prices and a national appeal.

L: Yes, advertising -- that was the cause of it.

B: In your position as a livestock dealer, you would be in a position to give us some expert evidence on the livestock situation in this Province?

L: Yes.

B: And Alberta is possibly the best situated of any province in Western Canada for the raising of livestock?

L: I do not think there is any place in the world as good.

B: And that business, which developed from the old ranching business in Western Canada, has practically failed?

L: Yes.

B: And can you give us some relative figures of the depreciation in livestock since 1925 down to the present time?

L: I think, roughly, 75 percent.

B: From your position as an expert in that business, would you venture to suggest some of the reasons contributing to that failure? Had the Fordney Tariff in the United States anything to do with it?

L: Yes, it stopped the market in Chicago

Thus, he led the inarticulate witness to demolish such common Eastern arguments as: the West's troubles resulted from "frontier" conditions; farmers were the authors of their own problems through poor management; and the problems were in areas unsuited for agriculture. As well, Brownlee brought out the point that the West had contributed fully to the national effort in the World War but now was being left to shoulder the sacrifices of a world depression on its own. All these points and counter-points were made while the witness struggled with mono-syllables and simplicities. It was a fine example, though only a small one, of the kind of contribution John Brownlee made for the Western farmer and, indeed, for the entire West.

Also at the Calgary hearing, held in the Palliser Hotel, Robert Gardiner presented a major submission on behalf of the U.F.A. It explained the over-riding concern for economic and monetary reform in Alberta by declaring that such farm prices as "25 cents per bushel for # 1 wheat, 9 cents per pound for # 1 cream, 3 cents per dozen for eggs, and 2 cents per pound for hogs, compelled the farmer to recognize that the financial system is the dominant factor governing his economic welfare" and forced him "to make an intensive study of monetary problems." The brief emphasized that "the depression was not due to Acts of God but to Acts of Man," a point which future commentators would overlook almost entirely as they increasingly equated "drought" and "depression". In point of fact, by 1933 a very small minority of Albertans had suffered any severe drought while a very large majority suffered acutely because of the record low prices of primary products.

The U.F.A. brief also criticized the existing interest rates to farmers of 8 to 12 percent when the Bank Act set the maximum at 7, as well as the sharp restriction of bank credit, asserting, "there has been no attempt ... to maintain a correct relationship between the volume of credit and the needs of production and consumption, and thus maintain price stability." A fundamental cause of the depression, the brief claimed, was that a system had developed "in which money and credit are regarded and treated as commodities to be bought and sold in the same manner as real wealth." It concluded starkly, "the monetary system has failed" and called for a government owned central bank and for more effective controls on interest rates, two points which Brownlee supported.

He also supported the U.F.A.'s concern about the difficulties farmers had had over the years in getting financing for binder twine. It was a sore point with him for he was convinced the banks were shirking their legitimate function and attempting to have governments assume the losses while they reaped the benefits. At the Edmonton hearing, the official submission of the Alberta Government cited actual case records and statistics of binder twine loans. For example, in 1931, 5,353 such loans were made and within six months 4,812 were fully repaid. The conclusion was that "these figures show conclusively that the Banks could have, without undue risk, made ninety percent of these loans without Government guarantee." Details of an actual case were presented to show excessive bank charges on such loans. The loan, for $37, at simple interest would have cost $3.16 but the actual charges were $8.40 due mainly to the practice of compounding interest every three months and so-called "renewal charges". It was mainly thanks to Brownlee's urging, and sometimes his considerable efforts, that actual case details and statistics were presented to the Commission to substantiate what otherwise would have been expressed simply as "interest rates are too high". Of course, the precise data were more effective and for this, and other reasons, Westerners owed a debt to Brownlee for getting their case effectively before the Commission.

The official Alberta brief, prepared by Brownlee but presented by Acting Premier George Hoadley, discussed five general subjects: 1) high interest rates, 2) lack of agricultural credit, 3) creation of a Central Bank, 4) control of foreign exchange rates, and 5) the failure of Banks to treat Eastern and Western Canada equally; either in agriculture or business. Echoing the ideas of the "provincial bankers" of a decade earlier, the brief was highly critical of the fact that "while the Province is unable to sell debentures at less than 6.76 percent, Banks are able to borrow under the Finance Act from the Dominion Government at 3 percent. We urge the Commission recommend the extension of the provisions of the Finance Act to Provincial Governments, or set up other facilities through a National Bank." Similar points were made at other hearings across the prairies.

At these hearings, Brownlee showed himself capable of questioning representatives of Banks closely and tellingly, laying bare the attitudes farmers faced and the twin oppression of short term notes and high interest rates. He became particularly heated in his criticism of the Banks' contention that restrictive legislation was responsible for restrictive credit. At one point, he even found himself defending the Debt Adjustment Act from the completely gratuitous opinion of fellow Commissioner Lord Macmillan that it affected "the law of contract in a very grave way" and was "an interference with the ordinary flow of credit." Brownlee, who had written the Act and administered it for more than a decade, rejoined:

> the principle of the Act, as I understand it, and you will correct me if I am wrong, was simply to give a breathing space to debtors who incurred debt when wheat was selling at $1.25 or $1.50 a bushel and who were having extreme

difficulty in paying off their debts when wheat was down to 40 cents a bushel. The principle was simply to set up an impartial board before which a creditor must go and get the permission of the board before he takes the normal action in court.

Brownlee was fifty years old August 27, 1933, while traveling by train with the rest of the Commission from Winnipeg to Halifax where the hearings resumed two days later. He took little part in the Maritime or Quebec sittings, returning, to his previous style only in Toronto where he attempted to clarify a submission by W..C. Good on behalf of Ontario farmers. Good's vague non-answers and deferential generalities made his contribution almost worthless. The hearings concluded in Ottawa with a series of rebuttals by head officers of the Banks. Jackson Dodds, for example, defended many of the criticized banking practices as "customary" which led Brownlee to chide, "I suppose you discount, Mr. Dodds, because of your custom and tradition and not in order to get the higher rate of interest?" He was alluding to the Banks' practice of charging more than the legal maximum rate of interest by deducting a fee from the principal loaned and asking the borrower if he agreed to the charge. The borrower could say "No" and be refused the loan, or accept and pay the higher charge which, to the Banks' satisfaction was not "a higher interest charge." The publicity given this shady practice confirmed many negative opinions about Banks.

The Banking Commission concluded hearings on September 15 and set about writing their report. Brownlee's work was sensationally interrupted when, on September 22, Neil MacLean filed a Statement of Claim in the Supreme Court of Alberta before Mr. Justice Boyle (the former Liberal leader), on behalf of A. D. MacMillan and his daughter, Vivian. The Statement alleged that Brownlee had arranged to have the girl move from Edson to Edmonton, had secured employment for her with the provincial government, had seduced her in the fall of 1930 when she was eighteen years old, and had had ongoing sexual relations with her in various locations including his automobile, his office and his home during an ensuing period of almost three years. Brownlee immediately privately offered to resign from the Commission (an offer which both Bennett and Lord Macmillan refused) and issued a short statement to the press:

> I have received by long distance the contents of the Statement of Claim. While one regrets to have to face a case of this kind, still it will enable me to come to grips with rumours that have been spread abroad through the Province for some weeks. There is not a word of truth in the allegations against me and I will defend the action to the limit and hope to show before I am through, the real cause behind it.

It was a testimony to Brownlee's powers of concentration that with such an action pending, he was able to return to his Commission work and a week later deliver his contributions to the report. There were two major recommendations: the first, "that a central bank for Canada be forthwith established" was opposed by White and Leman, while the second, "that an inquiry be instituted... to investigate the existing organizations for the provision of rural credit with a view to the preparation of a scheme for the consideration of Parliament," was unanimous.

Brownlee attached a separate memorandum to the Report. He expressed concern about interest rates on bank loans to Western provincial governments, municipalities and school boards being 1/4 to 1/2 percent higher than similar loans in the East. He recommended that the Banks take a lead in ending discrimination against the West by placing "the rates of interest on loans to public bodies on a basis uniform with those of the other Provinces." As for general interest rates, he was the only Commissioner to recommend that a statutory maximum be maintained and he argued strongly that a reduction in interest rates was absolutely vital in order to encourage a revival of business. He also called for a closer examination of Bank profits and of bank directorates interlocking with those of major corporations.

However, his most important recommendation was his suggested constitution of a Canadian Central Bank.

> I ... recommend that the capital be subscribed by the Government of Canada, and that all directors and executive officers be appointed by that Government, each appointment to be for a fixed number of years.

The source of capital is in itself of little significance. The control of the bank is of great significance. The election of directors by private shareholders means private control, and notwithstanding the limitation of the rate of dividends, this control might place earning capacity as a first consideration. The only reason advanced in favour of private, as against national, control is the fear of political influence. I am not impressed by this argument. ... In times of stress the policies of the State must prevail, whatever may be the constitution of such a bank. ... It is suggested, in the plan in the Appendix that the Government should exercise partial authority in the selection of the executive officers of the bank. In my judgment it should exercise full authority.

The Bank of Canada. subsequently created, was at first a mixture of government and private capitalization and control but within a few years it was reorganized as an entirely government owned institution. Brownlee regarded the eventual structure of the Bank of Canada as a clear vindication of his recommendation.

He had enjoyed his association with the Commission and the intellectual stimulation it had afforded. His contribution had been a major one, especially in bringing out the concerns of the West and of farmers. The fact that he had been the only Canadian Commissioner to recommend in favour of a Central Bank and the only Commissioner to recommend that it be Government owned would have, under most circumstances, been enough to earn Brownlee at least a small place in Canadian history. However, this major achievement, together with the many others that dotted his career, would soon be largely and lastingly obliterated from the public mind by the allegations of Vivian MacMillan. John Brownlee's reputation was on trial.

Chapter 17: Scandal Charges

Publication of the allegations against Brownlee immediately altered the political equation in Alberta and sent ripples across the national scene as well. Bennett was soon advised that the action might force Brownlee's resignation, while to King, the development could only assist the "real Liberal revival in Alberta." The rumoured prospect of Brownlee joining Bennett's Cabinet was quickly shelved as the Premier began a dogged fight for his reputation, his career, and the life of his Government. His contribution to the Banking Commission, pronouncements on the economy, and indeed his entire leadership, were seriously undermined. The tension of the times heightened the impact of the charges. Immediately most people formed their conclusions on the basis of gossip. In general, those who knew Brownlee least were readiest to accept the charges at face value, while those closest to him found it most difficult to believe he had been living a double life.

On November 13, a counter claim was filed, alleging that Vivian MacMillan and John Caldwell, a third-year medical student at the University of Alberta, had conspired together and "with others, at present unknown, with intent to obtain money." Caldwell, it was charged, was to be paid by "political opponents" for bringing Brownlee's character into disrepute. Counter damages were asked because the MacMillan claim had caused Brownlee to be "much injured in his public profession and personal reputation."

The counter claim was not made out of whole cloth. Investigations had begun well before the issuance of the Statement of Claim. Lymburn authorized Harry Brace, the detective who had done so well on the George Smith case, to investigate a charge by a Mrs. Schwantze that she had been approached by Neil MacLean and offered rewards to "put Mr. Brownlee in such a position that Mrs. Brownlee could get a divorce." This story took on more plausibility when combined with a widely circulated rumour that MacLean had vowed to wreak vengeance upon Brownlee. Supposedly, years before, MacLean had been involved in a motor vehicle mishap while drunk. Another motorist had pulled his car from the ditch but before the chains could be disconnected

MacLean tried to drive away causing damage and injury for which he was subsequently charged. As the story ran, MacLean approached Brownlee, then Attorney General, to have the charges quietly dropped. Brownlee refused, whereupon MacLean was said to have vowed to "get Brownlee".

According to Brownlee and his supporters there were three elements which created the so-called "Brownlee Scandal". First, the continuing personal animosity of Neil MacLean. Second, the militant, aggressive tactics of Howson and his Liberal rump who sought to destroy Brownlee by any means so as to open the way to their own ascent to political power. Third, the greed for money of John Caldwell and Vivian MacMillan who he had somehow convinced to support him in an assault upon the family who had befriended her.

Brace's investigation was designed to link together these elements. Several witnesses, he reported, were ready to testify that Howson had been among several individuals alerted to the fact that Brownlee would pick up MacMillan on the night of July fifth. Some declared that Howson had watched the meeting from a parked car while Neil MacLean and Caldwell were in the car that had given chase. As for other Liberals involved, the Edmonton Bulletin published the complete text of the Statement of Claim in its noon edition, despite MacLean's not having filed it with the Court until after eleven o'clock, a collusion that, while not unexpected, was, to say the least, unethical.

The most promising potential evidence, to the Brownlee camp, seemed to be the activities of John Caldwell. According to Brace's reports to Attorney General Lymburn, at least three people were prepared to testify that Caldwell had talked about soon coming into a large sum of money from someone "high up in political life." The most interesting account came from one of Brace's operatives who, posing as a loan shark, interviewed Caldwell in a hotel room about a possible loan. According to that agent's report:

> I made arrangements to have Special Constable Allen present as a stenographer. He was hidden in the closet and later under the bed. Caldwell returned at 10:45 pm. Talked about a loan and he said hc would be in a position to pay me back in December when he gets his money from the

Brownlee case. ... He related what Vivian had told him about Brownlee and herself. He said, "I hate Brownlee and am out to get him and the innocent must suffer with him -- he is sewn up so tight he'll never get out of this -- I deliberately set out to frame him -- Mind you there are no politics in this thing as far as I am concerned. They are incidental to the case and crept in afterwards. Of course I was smart enough not to go to a Conservative lawyer like Milner -- I went to a Liberal lawyer Neil MacLean and told him my story. I didn't tell Vivian I was going to see a lawyer about it. It was entirely my own idea ...

From there, Caldwell's reported story became even more bizarre.

I got some fellows, members of a secret order I belong to in town and we followed Brownlee and Vivian another night -- there are thirteen of us in it, all sworn to stick by each other -- Politics have come into this thing, you can't keep them out. But I won't be the loser by it. Of course this is all under the hat but I have been promised that if the Liberal Party get in, as they sure will now, there is nothing I want I won't be able to get. ... I expect to get $20,000 or $25,000 out of this." Johnnie [Caldwell] also said that they had given B.[rownlee] ten or twenty days to settle out of court but he refused.

Most disappointing for the defense was that the investigation uncovered no evidence which refuted or denied the charges of a sexual liaison. On the contrary, both Caldwell's reported remarks and the possible testimony of one C. H. Snell tended to confirm such a relationship. According to Brace:

Snell will testify that Vivian MacMillan told him in 1932 that she was having a sexual relationship with J.E. Brownlee but did not at that time suggest that it was in any way against her will or ever had been. At the same time she stated to him that she could put J.E. Brownlee any place she wanted because there was nothing that his political opponents would not give to get from her the information she had just given Snell.

While the investigations were going on and his lawyers were preparing his case, Brownlee was in an emotional turmoil, discussing the "conspiracy" at length with close friends and torn between his desire to resign and spare his family and colleagues from further embarrassment, and his determination to fight to the last ditch in order to prove his innocence. Richard Reid often found him in "the depths of despair" and spent hours with him, talking him out of resigning "hundreds of times."

However, despite the circumstances, Brownlee was never away long from the routine demands of his office. By mid-January he was, as usual, the capable voice of Alberta at yet another Dominion-Provincial Conference. He spoke firmly, yet with his characteristic even-handedness against high interest rates, and supplied one of the Conference highlights when he lashed out angrily at the charge by some Eastern premiers that Western Provinces were showing deficits because of "extravagant" spending. Alberta's expenditures, he protested, aside from relief costs, were now under $8,000,000, a 50 percent reduction from 1929 figures. Suddenly, though, he was called away from the Conference by news that his father was critically ill.

He arrived in Sarnia by train on a cold, windy winter afternoon. The next evening, January 21, 1934, William Brownlee died, at the age of seventy-seven. A "quiet, inassumingl [sic] man and very highly respected", he had continued as Clerk-Treasurer of Moore Township until just before the end. He was never more than a small town merchant but he communicated an interest in politics which his son had developed to the fullest. He also supplied an example of hard work, patience and meticulous attention to detail which, together with the covert ambition and firmness of Christina, characterized John's approach to the duties of his office. William and Christina had always had a quiet but deep pride in their son's achievements and the MacMillan allegations shook the family deeply. William's death while the case was still pending removed him from the situation but John's mother and sister were left in a state of perpetual embarrassment verging on Victorian mortification.

Brownlee's reversals continued when the Legislative Assembly opened in February, on a day suitably visited with a raging blizzard. In a move which emphasized the rapid erosion of his support, P. A. Miskew (U.F.A. - Victoria) refused the honour of moving the address in reply to the Speech from the Throne. Instead he launched into a harsh denunciation of Brownlee's failure "to reorganize and supplement the personnel of his Cabinet which has been the chief underlying cause for many of the failures in the administration of the affairs of this Province." Miskew was especially critical of the increases in the public debt and the failure of the Government to take a stand against the Convention decisions to link the U.F.A. formally to the C.C.F. and its "socialistic" policies, such as the nationalization of all industries and land. He concluded by announcing that he was crossing the floor to join the Liberal Party of Alberta. 0. St. Germain (U.F.A. - St. Albert) followed suit, citing Brownlee's failure to demand the resignation of the scandal stained O. L. McPherson and to disavow the "socialistic" statements of Chester Ronning (U.F.A. - Camrose).

The two defections highlighted the impact of both the McPherson and Brownlee scandals in many rural communities, and graphically illustrated the serious fracturing of the U.F.A. by the Convention resolution to support the fledgling C.C.F. Both "philandering" and "socialism" were foreign to the values, cultural roots and character of the farm movement and combined they speeded the mass exodus of members. Most of these found a new and much more acceptable home in the Social Credit study groups sprouting up across the Province. There, as they had in 1921, they became part of a zealous movement led by an obviously practicing Christian. That William Aberhart, while preaching the undiluted fundamentals of the Gospel, was also unreservedly advocating the familiar theories of Social Credit as a remedy for the depression made his appeal very strong.

While Aberhart's indigenous brand of Social Credit was developing its political appeal, enough attention had been attracted to it as an economic theory to force a closer examination. The Legislature held a series of hearings at which numerous witnesses were questioned, including Aberhart and eventually even Major C.H. Douglas, the Scottish originator of the theory. Aberhart, in his appearance on March 19 and 20, 1934, began by describing the abundance of foodstuffs and other resources in Alberta while at the same time there was widespread poverty and privation due to a shortage of purchasing power. From this he went on to discuss what would soon be the familiar elements of Social Credit: the "A + B theorem", the "blood stream of the state", and the "just price". Brownlee wanted to know exactly how a farmer in Alberta, possessed of only non-negotiable Alberta credit certificates, could purchase a farm machine from Massey-Harris Company in Toronto. Aberhart's replies were indefinite and circular. The exchange illustrated the complete antithesis in the thinking of the two men. Aberhart was fuzzy and indefinite about details, content to leave them to the "experts", but he had a clear and compelling vision of the principles involved. He advocated more purchasing power in the hands of the average citizen, state intervention to guarantee a just price for all goods and services, and a break up of the bankers' monopoly on the issuance of credit. In short, he promised with the certitude of unimpaired faith, a reformed system in which the practices of democracy and the morality of Christianity would be applied to end privation and lead to prosperity. Brownlee, on the other hand, could not pass by the technical details and pragmatic considerations. He could make no leap of faith but must subject every proposal to the most rigorous rational examination.

He subjected Major Douglas to the same sort of questioning when he appeared the following month but it was apparent from his tone that he had a greater regard for Douglas than for Aberhart. He asked Douglas to define Social Credit in one or two sentences. The Major replied:

Social Credit in its essence is a correct estimate of the productive capacity of a given unit based upon that which is the real social credit of the unit. You have something which we call financial credit which can also be made to be a reflection of this real social credit, and that I should say can be defined as the power of monetizing, to any extent desirable, the real wealth of the unit so it can be freely exchanged.

Brownlee led Douglas from this position to an eventual admission that the actual credit value of a commodity such as coal or wheat, depended on markets outside Alberta. Douglas was no more successful than Aberhart in explaining how changing the credit granting practices in Alberta could command greater markets or higher prices for the primary products upon whose export the province was so dependent.

In the orthodox view of Brownlee, relief was not to be found in such novel and basically vague concepts as the "compensated price" but in such traditional beliefs as the "law of supply and demand". This explained his support for a federally sponsored wheat acreage reduction scheme, worked out as part of the world's first international wheat agreement. The London Agreement committed participants to reduce production and control exports of wheat. Its intent, to reduce the world glut of wheat, was soon nullified by such countries as the Argentine resuming dumping, however, it was to be the precursor of other international wheat agreements with which Brownlee would be more closely involved.

A wheat acreage reduction scheme was, to say the least, politically unpopular on the prairies where for most farmers, the only hope seemed to be to plant and pray for a price increase. Brownlee was willing to take these political risks because he believed that only by solving the world over-production problem would the price rise. He was prepared to join the other prairie Premiers in a series of radio broadcasts during seeding season to "educate farmers" to the need for reducing production. The series was dropped when Bracken was forced by some of his supporters to abandon the scheme. His difficulties had been expected but some Conservatives in Ottawa thought Brownlee was still strong enough to "handle the situation." In fact, some of Bennett's Calgary friends saw Brownlee as the logical leader of the Alberta Conservative forces after a political realignment. One wrote:

> Brownlee is the biggest man in the West today as far as Provincial Governments are concerned. Howson has overplayed his hand as far as persecution is concerned and whether John is guilty, as far as the young lady is concerned, it is going to be hard to prove and they have so many things on her that he will come out of the racket clean.

Ray Milner had a series of long talks with Brownlee, exploring the possibility of forming a Union Government of moderate U.F.A. Members, Conservatives and Independents against an Opposition divided between Liberals and C.C.F. advocates. However, Brownlee never took the final step of publicly calling for such a realignment. As Milner recognized in a penetrating report to Bennett:

> ... in any novel or unusual situation he is inevitably timid and vacillating. However, he realizes that the present Government cannot very long survive. The disrepute into which some of its Members have fallen, the internal dissension's of the U.F.A. and the lack of any aggressive policy is rapidly breaking up his Party. ... if an election were to be called this year ... he would inevitably be defeated.

Brownlee's procrastination and political embarrassments had, by now, radically changed the regard in which he was held by the Prime Minister who replied to Milner tersely,

> So far as our relations with the Premier are concerned, I think you will agree that we have not reason to assume that he is either sincere or anything else, other than a time server whose one object, apparently, is to retain office.

The Liberals, for their part, were tremendously encouraged. Howson thought the unfolding developments were a vindication of his aggressive tactics and was adamant that the federal wing should use the same approach. He advised King on how to handle the U.F.A. federal M.P.s:

> We believe that we have the Provincial U.F.A. members fairly well silenced and even broken in spirit. Are Gardiner, Garland, Irvine, Speakman, Coote, etc., not being opposed? ... if a real drive is made against each one of them we will remove for a good many years the real enemies of the Liberal party. The Conservatives are not our opposition in this Province and these C.C.F. disturbers can be removed if they are gone after.

Against this background of rising optimism by his opponents about his imminent political demise, Brownlee continued with his moderate, orthodox steps. These did nothing to arrest the erosion of his support. The ever lingering skepticism, the feeling that he was not really a part of the farmers' movement and did not really understand or feel its resentments and desires, now blossomed into widespread cynicism and criticism of his efforts. He was judged too well off and too close to the city businessmen and bankers to legitimately represent depression ravaged farmers.

On the other hand, his ability to act as an intermediary on behalf of those farmers whom he thought were meritorious was being undermined by increasingly uncompromising bankers who now showed themselves, for the first time, prepared to disregard his interventions. In one such case, when repeated appeals to a Toronto based general manager were disregarded, he was forced to conclude lamely, "it does seem to me rather strange that a man should be penalized for all time because, through force of circumstances, he was obliged to make a certain compromise in the past, entirely regardless of the merits of his position today. However, I presume there is nothing further to be done."

The result underlined what had always been the central weakness of Brownlee's reliance on personal persuasion and reasonableness. If and when the force of these was lost, the debtors of Alberta, whom he had hoped to defend with such means, would be left without effective economic, political or even legal power with which to defend themselves. At bottom, the persistent demand over the years for legislation to provide such protection, and the distrust of Brownlee's voluntary creditor restraints, stemmed from a clear realization that only in law was there any hope, and even then an uncertain hope, of justice being done the less powerful and influential elements of society. The undermining of Brownlee's personal and political stature left most of those who had supported him in two previous elections entirely exposed, as they had long feared, and thus they turned to yet another movement that promised justice for them. While Brownlee was writing private letters filled with an air of dejection and futility, Aberhart was glibly promising laws to insure a "just price" and an end to gouging and exploitation. Aberhart promised the state would act to make certain everyone could buy food and clothing for their family. He promised to force the "fifty big-shots of Bay Street" to take their share of the hardship right along with the quarter-section farmer.

In fact, to a degree greater than he realized, Brownlee was now a "lame duck premier". His trial on the seduction charges, twice delayed, was finally set for the last week of June, 1934, and as it approached there was a rising current of rumour and innuendo. Off colour "jokes" made the rounds and his sons came home with black eyes after "discussing" the case on high school playing fields. They were soon sent East to stay with their grandmother for the duration. Brownlee continued attending to his duties even while the trial was imminent. There was even some political maneuvering when, for the first time in eight years, he made a change in his Cabinet. The appointment of Frank Grisdale (U.F.A. - Olds) as Minister of Agriculture shifted George Hoadley out of a portfolio where he had become unpopular. However, it was much too little and far too late. Brownlee was not one to make radical changes. In one of the last letters he wrote before appearing in Court, he summarized and reaffirmed the approach he had taken throughout his political life. "I can only repeat what I have said on many occasions that the Government has acted as it believes right and with a clear conscience from our viewpoint of the Province as a whole. I ... of course, will have to take the full responsibility before the people for any stand which I have taken." The next week, John Brownlee's trial began.

* * *

The basis of the action against him was a tort of some 200 years standing in British law whereby a master could claim damages against any man who "seduced" a female servant. While the term "seduction" was used, the defense argued that under British practice, with no clear case of any exception, damages consisted of the loss of service resulting from the impregnation and subsequent confinement of the female servant. Later, but still consistent with the legal attitude that women were chattels who could be "interfered with", the right of action was extended to the girl's father. Again the precedents involved impregnation, confinement and the delivery of an illegitimate child. This law was transferred to Canada and continued unchanged until 1903 when the Northwest Territories Council, in response to a growing demand for "women's rights", tacked on one more class of persons who had right of action under the law -- the woman herself. It was not until the Brownlee case that the courts came to grips with the problem thus created of how a woman might claim damages for events in which she might have willingly participated.

Neil MacLean recognized this difficulty and took care to enter the action on behalf of both A. D. MacMillan and his daughter. He also attempted to show that the alleged sexual relationship was initially and continued to be against Vivian's will. Despite these points of law, in the popular mind, including that of the jury, the question was a simple one of whether or not John Brownlee had had sexual intercourse with Vivian MacMillan. On June 25, 1934, MacLean presented his star witness. Sensationalized by the press, especially the Edmonton Bulletin, her three days of allegations were the exciting topic of adult only conversation throughout Alberta and beyond. Early morning crowds jostled for the few public seats in the courtroom and craned to read the expressions on the faces of the principals as they entered and left the Alberta Supreme Court.

Vivian MacMillan appeared in the witness box, a modestly attractive young woman, somewhat older looking than many observers expected. She was carefully dressed and groomed with the well-scrubbed air of the girl-next-door become career woman. In response to MacLean's guiding questions she sketched her background as a small town high school girl who taught Sunday School and played the organ in the Edson Baptist Church. She described at length meeting Brownlee in June 1930, near her eighteenth birthday, and how, as they traveled by car to his rural campaign meeting, he had asked about her future plans. When told that she was debating between music and nursing, he advised that coming to Edmonton and training for a business career would be more practical. When the parents demurred, Brownlee allegedly said, "I can assure you that if she comes to Edmonton she will be very welcome to come to my home and make it her home and I will act as a guardian to her and see that she doesn't get into any trouble and she just won't be alone in a strange city."

Vivian implied that Brownlee had been much taken with her but admitted he had had no further contact until after she enrolled in a business course in Alberta College and, accompanied by her mother, had moved to Edmonton and taken up residence for the term in the Y.W.C.A. Supposedly, almost immediately following her mother's departure, Brownlee telephoned saying, "a birdie told me you were in here and I thought I would 'phone you up. I would like to have you come over to my home Sunday afternoon and meet Mrs. Brownlee and the boys." According to MacMillan, the next day, September 7, 1930, she did visit the Brownlee home and soon was visiting there two or three times per week. "I became very fond of Mrs. Brownlee and had a big respect for Mr. Brownlee," she told the court.

However, on the first Sunday in October while driving Vivian home, Brownlee, she alleged,

> took a hold of my hand and said he hoped I was liking Edmonton, that I felt at home in his home and he asked me what I knew about life ... I told him I did not exactly know what he meant but I probably knew as much as any other girl of eighteen did and he suggested that I come out with him and he would tell me and I thought that rather strange and I remembered he had said he would act as my guardian and I thought probably he wanted to give me some advice.

The advice she received the next evening, she testified, was that she should have sexual relations with Brownlee because: he was madly in love with her and had been from the start, he was very lonely and badly needed a "pal and confidant," he and Mrs. Brownlee had not lived together as man and wife for years as a pregnancy would endanger her life, and in sum because,

> he could not be Premier of the Province of Alberta any longer if I did not give in to him. He asked me what I thought of Mrs. Brownlee and I told him I was very fond of her and he said: "Well this is one way that you can show your gratitude to Mrs. Brownlee and myself.." And I told him if there was any other way... I would gladly do it and he told me this was the only way.

The next week, she alleged, they again drove out in the country and a similar discussion ensued, only this time,

> he forced me down on the back seat of the car and I fought against him but on this occasion he gained partial entrance and because I resisted so much he flew into a rage and got back in the front seat of the car and drove back into Edmonton and down to the government garage.

There followed a lengthy account of the complexities of changing from the large eight cylinder Studebaker to a smaller government car. In the ensuing public uproar, outrage was divided almost equally between the activities alleged and the use of a taxpayers funded car in which to conduct them.

MacMillan continued with an account of virtually the same episode, two weeks later, on yet another country side road. This time, she claimed, there was complete sexual intercourse.

> after he had been sexually satisfied he sat on the back seat of the car and took me in his arms and told me how wonderful I was and that it seemed strange that he should have to wait until he was almost an old man before he met the woman he loved. [He spoke of] plans for the future, [how he would] retire from public life [and] spend all his days making me happy. He asked me why I was trembling and I told him I was afraid of becoming pregnant and he told me I need not worry because he knew of some pills that he would give me and if I took them at the end of each month before I menstruated that they would be very safe and there would not be any danger of me becoming pregnant.

The public was shocked by such testimony, reported in what was regarded as outrageous and tasteless detail by the Bulletin. For many, the mere fact that a young woman could describe such sexual matters proved she was recounting what actually happened, while for Brownlee's most adamant supporters her vague descriptions of a little known abortive capsule suggested coaching by her medical student boyfriend, John Caldwell. They were prepared to admit sexual familiarity on MacMillan's part but not that it had been with Brownlee.

There were even more sensational allegations ahead. After outlining how she had quickly secured a job for herself as a stenographer in the Attorney General's office, only to be told by Brownlee that it had all been arranged for her in advance, she went on with the testimony that began the elaborate explanations of the Brownlee family's sleeping arrangements. Both sides agreed that the second story of the home was divided into four quarters with a hallway running along the east-west centre line. In the south-east

237

quarter there was a bathroom and stairwell while across the hall to the north was the maid's room. Next to it, in the north-west quarter, was a bedroom in which Brownlee and the elder son, Jack, occupied twin beds and across the hall to the south of this was the master bedroom in which Mrs. Brownlee and Alan normally slept. According to MacMillan, in September of 1931 she stayed at the Brownlee home for three days while her mother accompanied Mrs. Brownlee to Vancouver. While Florence was away, Alan was, over his vigorous protests, put in the bedroom with his brother while Brownlee occupied the master bedroom. MacMillan alleged he demanded she come to him from the maid's room and that they "had connection" the two nights he was in Edmonton.

In the spring of 1932, Vivian filled in for an absent maid. During this time the Brownlee's were distributed as usual but, she alleged, Brownlee insisted she come to his bed. Supposedly this was accomplished by him going to the bathroom and running the water to cover the noise of Vivian getting out of bed as both the floor and the bed in the maid's room squeaked. According to her account, when Brownlee returned to his bedroom she would fall into step immediately behind him so that it would sound like one person walking. Arriving at his bedside he would spread his bathrobe wide while Vivian got into bed, then, after turning out the lights, they would have "connection" in the bed beside that of the sleeping son. After this, Brownlee would again go to the bathroom, with Vivian in lock step behind, and again run the water to cover the sound of her getting back into bed in the maid's room. She claimed this went on every night for almost six weeks.

Later that summer she collapsed on the way to work and contacted Mrs. Brownlee who had her admitted to hospital and wrote a cheque to cover the stay. According to MacMillan, she was diagnosed as having "stomach trouble brought on by nerves" and "a nervous breakdown." After a short hospitalization, she was sent home to Edson for seven weeks of complete rest. However, that autumn, she returned to her job in Edmonton and resumed her liaison with Brownlee, having sex with him on more or less regular drives out to the same one or two country back roads and on other occasions as opportunity presented.

Then, Vivian met and fell in love with John Caldwell. This, she declared, strengthened her resolve to leave Brownlee but when she told him, he flew into a rage and said it would mean his wife's death and threatened to have Vivian fired and barred from any other job "in the Province of Alberta." Supposedly, he returned her to her lodgings, pushed her from the car, and told her not to bother going to work the next day. She ran to her room where the landlady's daughter discovered her sobbing. MacMillan told her everything and determined to break off with Brownlee by writing a letter as when she was with him, "He seemed to have a kind of influence over me. His will power was just so much stronger than mine." However, she reconsidered.

> I started to think what probably my breaking off with Mr. Brownlee would mean to Mrs. Brownlee and Mrs. Brownlee had been as a mother to me. And then I thought about losing my position and having no work and I knew it was impossible almost for a young girl to get a position and ... I tore the letter up and threw it in the waste paper basket.

The next incident allegedly occurred on Hallowe'en with Mrs. Brownlee in the East. Vivian went to have dinner with the boys and also visited Brownlee who was confined to bed with illness. She claimed he insisted she have intercourse with him and despite her protest that she was on her way to a party with Caldwell, he remained adamant. So, after telephoning Caldwell that she would be late, they had intercourse about eight in the evening. It was one of her most specific allegations but there were others. On the morning of January 2, 1933, she claimed, Brownlee telephoned.

> I told him Mother was with me ... he said, "Well just tell your mother you are going back to work for a while ..." ... Mr. Brownlee picked me up ... and we went over to the Parliament Buildings and I had intercourse with Mr. Brownlee and then we went for a short drive and then he drove me home.

By the end of January, Caldwell proposed, whereupon, she testified, she broke down and told him everything. Caldwell said,

> he would still come around but that the question of marriage would naturally have to be dropped. He told me he would

do anything to help me find my feet and start living again the right kind of life.

In May, at Caldwell's urging, she consulted a lawyer but, by her own account the affair continued until the night of the wild car chase. Finally, court adjourned for the day leaving an amazed audience. The amazement soon spread when the next day's Bulletin carried several pages of testimony, only briefly edited and introduced with the sensational headlines and stock phrases of yellow journalism. MacMillan was described as having,

pictured the Premier of Alberta as a love torn, sex crazed victim of passion and jealousy ... flying into passions of rage when she attempted to deny him ... a lonely, sex-starved man, and that she owed it as a sacred duty to the public and to the wife of the Premier to submit lest he throw up the reins of office or send his wife to death as the victim of childbed agonies.

At another place, the Bulletin gratuitously explained to its readers that MacMillan had recounted how Brownlee had "defiled his wife's sanctum with his lawless desire." To those who knew dour, cautious John Brownlee, it seemed utterly incredible that such purple prose should be applied to him.

Figure 7

Brownlee's home while Premier of Alberta: 11151 - 88th Ave., Edmonton. To the Brownlee family it was a pleasant, modest home where they raised their two sons and a series of large dogs. To Vivian MacMillan, it was the scene of some of the most bizarre episodes in "The Scandal". The orchestration of her story by Brownlee's political enemies ended his political career and blighted his deserved place as a major figure in Alberta's and Canada's history.

(Photo courtesy of Glenbow Archives
ND-3-6475)

Chapter 18: On Trial

A. L. Smith had a rotund figure and a reputation as an excellent courtroom lawyer and devastating cross examiner. The line of defense he chose was to examine MacMillan's account closely, attempting where ever possible to discredit it. He faced a dilemma. He had to be aggressive enough to shake, if not break MacMillan, but he had to be careful for if an attack failed, he would have shifted the jury's sentiment strongly in her favour.

He began slowly, touching only briefly on the Edson meeting before going on to show that MacMillan had several acquaintances in Edmonton and a C.N.R. pass enabling her to visit home frequently. She had been accompanied to the city by her mother, had decided on her own not to live in College residence because the evening restrictions were too close, and on all subsequent choices of residence she had had no advice from Brownlee. He then produced a letter she had written, prior to meeting Brownlee, requesting information from Alberta College. Smith challenged her:

Q: You told me a moment ago until Brownlee came you had not communicated with anybody. And you were wrong, weren't you?

A: Yes.

...

Q: So that we stand with this spectacle, that after a conversation of an hour or less there was no communication of any kind between your parents or yourself with Mr. Brownlee or Mrs. Brownlee?

A: No.

Q: ... yet you still come back and say that you believe that in that hour he made up his mind to entice you from your home to seduce you. You don't believe that do you? You don't believe it? It is too silly isn't it?

A: After what happened when I came to Edmonton I do believe he had some idea.

Smith next adopted the dubious tack of suggesting the physical impossibility of sex in a car's back seat.

Q: So that in getting into the back seat that night it is still the fact that you had no idea he wanted to have intercourse with you?

A: I did not think he could have intercourse with me in the back seat of a car.

Q: I do not think so yet. You were lying flat, were you, parallel with the back of the seat?

A: Yes.

Q: And how tall are you?

A: Five feet seven inches.

Q: And how tall is he?

A: Over six feet.

...

Q: That a man whose wife you had known just for a month should put a proposition to you that you should have intercourse with him to save the life of that wife whom you had known that length of time? Didn't that strike you as a staggering proposition?

A: Yes, it was staggering.

Q: Did you believe it?

A: Yes.

Q: And you fought as hard as you could?

A: Yes.

Q: What did you weigh at that time?

A: About one hundred fifty pounds.

Q: So we find him with one arm around your shoulder and the other raising your clothes and getting on top of you and you a one hundred fifty pound girl fighting your best in that back seat to save your honor. Is that the situation?

A: Yes, sir.

Q: Did you put a mark on him?

A: No, sir.

Q: Eh?

A: Not that I know of.

Smith then examined the story of changing cars and forced MacMillan to admit she was wrong by showing the smaller car she claimed Brownlee had used in October, 1930, had not been purchased by the government until June, 1932. He attempted to cast doubt on the probability of her story at every turn. Looking at her account of her motives, he asked:

> Q: So that in this City of eighty or ninety thousand people, here you were, and your parents in Edmonton occasionally and a long distance telephone which you used frequently ... having intercourse with this man from terror. Is that your story?
>
> A: From terror and because he told me it was my duty to do it and he seemed to have an influence over me which I could not break.
>
> Q: ... did he hypnotize you?
>
> A: No.

As to the extent and nature of the alleged sexual activity, he asked:

> Q: ... after the first six months this intercourse went on as a matter of course?
>
> A: Yes, it became a habit.
>
> Q: And this was always physically painful to you?
>
> A: Yes.
>
> Q: An average of three times a week for three years ... hundreds of times in other words?
>
> A: Yes.
>
> Q: Always physically painful?
>
> A: Yes.
>
> Q: And no love in it?
>
> A: No.

Turning to the alleged sexual relations in Mrs. Brownlee's bed, Smith pressed harder but MacMillan was unshaken, adding new shocking details to her account.

> A: Mr. Brownlee had intercourse with me, I would say, on many occasions that I was menstruating.
>
> Q: And on this occasion he had intercourse with you twice?
>
> A: Yes.
>
> Q: Disgusting?
>
> A: Yes.

Q: And there was a bolt on the inside of Mrs. Brownlee's
    door? Why didn't you use it when you were sick?
A: Because I just did as Mr. Brownlee said.
    ...
Q: And under those circumstances this man Brownlee
    stayed with you in his wife's bed for hours?
A: Yes.
Q: And are you swearing to that are you?
A: Yes, I am swearing to it.

Here Smith introduced a letter Vivian had written to Florence
Brownlee the day after this alleged episode. It was a friendly, child-
like letter detailing the activities of the family and describing baking
a cake which the boys pronounced "tasted like Lysol." Smith
described it to the court as a "Happy, chatty letter to Mrs.
Brownlee on the day after having intercourse with her husband in
her bed while menstruating."

Next, the alleged sexual activities while Vivian replaced the
maid were examined. The Bulletin told its readers that Brownlee
was accused of ravaging MacMillan every night for a period of
nearly seven weeks at this time. Under Smith's cutting questions
the period Vivian had been at the Brownlee home was reduced to
five weeks -- from April 6 to May 10, 1932. Then, using
Brownlee's appointment calendar, Smith showed that the Premier
had been in the East from April 6 to 24 and had taken several rural
speaking dates upon his return. He had been home only about ten
nights during the period. Asked about this, MacMillan replied:

A: Well as far as my memory serves me it was more than
    ten days.
Q: You are accusing this man of some terrible things and I
    want to have your memory right about it
    occasionally ... How long was it? For whatever
    your memory is worth, how long was it?

Despite such thrusts, Smith was unable to "break" the
witness. Once, only, a single tear rolled down her cheek. Cynical
young lawyers watching speculated that that one tear should be
worth at least $5,000 from the jury. All day the questions came.
Why had Mrs. Brownlee, a notoriously light sleeper, not noticed

and taken an interest in her husband's great use of the bathroom during Vivian's visit? What specific pills had he given her? Why had she come back from her rest in Edson and resumed her affair with Brownlee? Why hadn't she broken free after revealing everything to Caldwell, or to the lawyers? Sometimes she would admit errors in detail, saying her memory had failed, but she clung to the basic outline of her story. For example, she stuck to her claim of intercourse in Brownlee's sick-bed on Hallowe'en even while admitting that the maid had been in, both boys were continually in and out of the house "trick-or-treating", the doctor had been in to see Brownlee, and the bedroom door, only five steps from the bathroom, had been open the entire time.

The cross examination concluded with questions about her motives and her relationship with Mrs. Brownlee.

Q: Why couldn't you break free?

A: Because I was saving Mrs. Brownlee's life and Mr. Brownlee would just refuse to hear tell of me breaking off with him and I did not want to hurt Mrs. Brownlee in any way because I had a much deeper love for her than ever ... [there were] threats about losing my position and I did not want Mrs. Brownlee to know that this had been going on.

Q: You have let her know pretty well [now], haven't you?

A: Yes.

...

Q: You made out affidavits on the twenty-fourth of May and after ... making out these affidavits with the solicitor you went to the house of the woman whose husband you are suing now and you kissed her good-bye on the twenty-ninth of June and she was leaving with her youngsters for the lake on the same day?

A: Yes.

This last point was one of several calculated to show that, on her own testimony, she was capable of carrying off the most bold-faced of deceptions.

Neil MacLean used some rebuttal questions to have Vivian explain in greater detail the logistics of back seat sexual intercourse, to dispel any doubt that it was physically possible. Then, finally, after parts of three days on the stand, Vivian MacMillan stepped down. MacLean called a series of other witnesses. A former Brownlee maid testified that she had once seen Brownlee pick up MacMillan late at night. When she volunteered that she recognized the car because she had been out in it herself, the Court disallowed further questions. Mrs. MacMillan described the family background and Brownlee's initial meeting with Vivian. Dorothy Mackay, a daughter of one of MacMillan's landladies, told of finding Vivian in her room one night sobbing, but the Court disallowed an account of the conversation. The landlady herself appeared with what were ostensibly scraps of the letter Vivian had written breaking off with Brownlee but the Court ruled them inadmissible. The doctor who examined MacMillan during her hospitalization was called and her medical records were introduced. They did nothing to substantiate sexual intercourse but rather suggested examination of several intestinal complaints which amounted to chronic constipation.

Then, just before adjournment for the day, Judge Ives delivered a stern admonition to the <u>Edmonton Bulletin</u> and removed its press privileges at the trial. Publisher Peter Campbell was fined $300 or ten days at hard labour and reporter J. S. Cowper $100 or three days for contempt of Court and publication of material "likely to inflame public opinion and interfere with the even-handed course of justice." It was one of the stiffest of such fines dispensed in Alberta and reflected general disgust at the paper's sensationalist tactics and poor taste.

June 28, 1934, was John Brownlee's day in court. Under Smith's questioning he sketched his background briefly and dealt with his wife's illness which, he declared, began about three months before Alan's birth and was serious for some three or four years. After this, "she seemed to be fearsome for some two or three years following of any little pain -- which I considered was possibly more mental than real." However, the Mayo Clinic had pronounced her "organically sound in every way ... That seemed to be the one thing needed. She came back and since that day has lived a normal life." Under questioning he declared that his sexual relations with his wife were, what he would consider, normal.

Turning to the fateful meeting with Vivian MacMillan in Edson, Brownlee described it as;

> ... a very casual conversation, as I recall, in the same way as I have done on hundreds of occasions.
>
> Q: Did you at any time promise to act as her guardian?
> A: I never said anything of the kind and would never contemplate saying anything of the kind.
> Q: Did you promise that you would get Miss MacMillan a position after she had finished her business course?
> A: In the thirteen years I have been in public life I have never promised any person in this Province a position.

He then described his summer of activity in the East in 1930, working on the problems of the Pools. The family had spent "two or three weeks driving around our old familiar places in Ontario" before driving home in an eight cylinder Studebaker being delivered to the government. Asked if he had used it personally during that fall he declared he had not but instead had driven a five passenger Hupmobile which he purchased shortly after his return.

Smith's questions then turned to the specific dates as MacMillan had described them. On September 6, 1930, the day alleged as the day of the first telephone call, Brownlee had not reached Edmonton with his family until three in the morning. However, he admitted going to his office in the afternoon for about twenty minutes. MacMillan, he testified, had not visited the next day. He recalled, instead, that the boys had spent the whole of that Sunday building a miniature golf course in the backyard. Indeed, he alleged, it was not until a week later that Christopher Pattinson, the Member for Edson, had informed him that MacMillan was in Edmonton. On his suggestion, Florence had gone to the Y.W.C.A. and invited Vivian to join the family on an outing to the Edmonton Air Show on September 17.

As for Sunday, October 5, the day of the alleged first drive home alone, Brownlee testified he left Edmonton on Friday for Winnipeg and had not returned until late Monday morning. With regard to Tuesday, October 28, the alleged date of the first full intercourse, he described leaving Edmonton about noon and speaking to the Stettler Chamber of Commerce at seven that evening. almost exactly the time when MacMillan alleged she was fighting him unsuccessfully in the back seat.

Next, Brownlee's appointment book was introduced to show his typically hectic schedule. In November, 1930, for example, he was out of Edmonton on at least twenty nights, while in January 1931, he was home only seven days. Through February and March the Legislative Assembly was in session and he briefly suggested his tremendous work load by stating simply, "I am responsible for the working of the Legislature and for approximately two weeks before I am engaged night and day from say nine A.M. to twelve P.M." All of this was to call into question MacMillan's claim that she had been ravished two or three times a week during the first six months of the alleged affair.

Brownlee challenged MacMillan's veracity on several points including her claim that her mother had been invited to go to Vancouver because Florence was afraid to travel alone. He dismissed this contention declaring, "Mrs. Brownlee left home as a girl and traveled West to teach and since that time has traveled by herself on all occasions." Asked to describe the sleeping arrangements during Vivian's visit, he maintained that, as a guest, she had been given the use of his wife's room; Alan had been put in the maid's room; and Jack and he had occupied their usual places. As for her more extended stay the following spring, he confirmed that he had indeed been absent from April 6 to 24, had been in Calgary on two nights and on another had attended, with Florence, a dinner for former Governor-General Byng from which they returned very late.

Asked to comment on the alleged bathroom strategy, he outlined the background of Florence's light sleeping.

Alan has always, from very early childhood, walked in his sleep -- her care for him has developed in her a subconscious attitude of her mind that she is always listening for him ... the slightest movement around the house wakens her up.

He disputed the alleged intercourse in his office on January 2, 1933, by recalling he had been meeting at that time with O. H. Snow of Raymond to discuss that town's financial difficulties.

Next he was asked how he spent his non-working time. He said that he was very fond of driving and that for both his wife and himself it was a favourite relaxation. In winter, the family went skating occasionally and a few times MacMillan had joined them. In the summer of 1930 and 1931 he had played a good deal of golf, usually leaving the office early on Saturday "to get on the course before the rush." In the following years the pressure of work had meant less golf but he "tried to be with the family on Saturday afternoon as much as possible." He subscribed to a number of New York and Toronto papers and he and Florence often spent Sunday mornings reading these.

He was then asked:

Q: What was Miss MacMillan's position in your house?

A: Well it was just as near being a member of the family as a person not being a natural son or daughter could be. I would say like a niece. As a matter of fact she was there and came at odd intervals whenever she wanted to without any arrangements whatever and as far as we knew was always very happy in that home.

It was against this background, he claimed, that Vivian had talked of trying to change her scheduled September holidays to July to allow her to spend time at Sylvan Lake with the Brownlees. She wanted to go on the Dominion Day weekend but Florence had demurred, not knowing exactly what the accommodation would be in the rented cottage. Brownlee claimed he had contacted Vivian that fateful July 5 because, "I had promised her the previous evening that I would get in touch with her before I went to the lake to see if she had made any arrangements as to when she could go down so I could let Mrs. Brownlee know." He then described the various events leading up to the publication of the Statement of Claim.

Asked if he had ever kissed MacMillan, he admitted that he "may have done" a few times if she was at the house when he was leaving for a long journey. It would have been strictly a goodbye kiss, he claimed, never a kiss of passion. Smith then left him with one final question:

Q: Did you, on your solemn oath, at any time have sexual intercourse with Vivian MacMillan?

A: I did not.

The next day, MacLean's cross examination went directly to the reason for the late visit on July 5. He asked:

Q: It could have been done over the 'phone?

A: Yes.

Q: And instead of that the Premier of Alberta in these distressing times takes an evening off to go out into the country to discuss a girl's vacation?

A: With a girl I had complete confidence in and who was a close intimate of our home, yes.

He also admitted driving out with Vivian on July 3 about six miles west and following the common Western practice of turning off on a side road to go around the square.

Q: Did you stop for a cigarette or anything like that?

A: I do not smoke cigarettes when I am out, Mr. MacLean.

Q: Is it a fact, Mr. Brownlee, you are one of the strongest men in town?

A: I never thought so.

Referring to the investigative work on the counter claim, MacLean jibed:

Q: ... the Government spent $1400 before you put a nickel into this case?

A: If you wish to put it that way, yes.

This admission was soon on the lips of Liberal speakers across Alberta and finally prompted a statement from Lymburn that his Department had investigated a claim by a young woman that an "Edmonton lawyer" had offered her money to put Brownlee in a compromising position. It was his duty to investigate these charges, Lymburn explained, since it was a criminal offense to solicit any person to have unlawful relations. However, because it was a criminal charge and thus required corroborating evidence, no prosecution had followed. "Over my head and in spite of my protest," Lymburn went on, "Mr. Brownlee insisted on refunding these moneys to the Department ... to place himself absolutely above even an innuendo in connection with the matter."

MacLean next tried to show Brownlee's persuasive powers.

Q: Before 1921 you were a lawyer at Calgary? ... So you were quite used to preparing evidence for cases and getting witnesses ready for the witness box?

A: No, sir, because I did not take court cases at all. I did not like them and only took two in my life. I specialized in commercial law.

Not content to let the point escape, he turned to Brownlee's reputation in the Assembly, describing him as,

... indulging at all times in arguments, debates ... and able to hold your own on the floor of the House at all times with anybody?

A: I would not say that. I don't know.

Q: ... in 1930 when Vivian MacMillan came here you were Premier, a lawyer and King's Council and forty-six years of age ... and she was eighteen, a country girl without previous city experience?

A: She was eighteen. She came from Edson and was a girl I think who could take her place in any company. She was not a poor country girl ....

Asked to describe his feelings toward MacMillan, he replied. "We undoubtedly formed a very high opinion of Vivian MacMillan and liked to have her in our house." In response to the query of why he had been so willing, even at personal inconvenience, to drive her home he replied, "I would be very tired or very ill before I would refuse a guest the ordinary courtesies ... Mr. MacLean."

The defense next called Florence Brownlee who testified to her recovery of health and declared she had lived a normal life in every way, "including sex matters," since 1928. She had discussed her health history with MacMillan on several occasions. She "remembered vividly" her first meeting with the girl, at the Y.W.C.A., because "She was a much smarter looking girl than I had expected to see -- rather more traveled looking." She denied that MacMillan had begun immediately visiting frequently, explaining, "anyone who knows me knows that I am rather slow making friends. I had another friend staying there and I had nieces at the time staying with me and I had a pretty full house."

Asked to comment on her feelings for Vivian, she testified:

... she was like a daughter to me ... I was annoyed with her at times ... I was very happy with her at times. She was careless around the house ... just one of the family ... she played with the boys and the dog ... she was just a bit of sunshine in the house.

As an example of how much a part of the family MacMillan was, she recalled an incident, probably Bennett's offer to Brownlee to join the Tariff Board, in November 1932.

... my husband received a very nice offer from Ottawa for a permanent position with a salary -- a good salary -- and we discussed the advisability of going to Ottawa to live, I remember, in the morning up in my bedroom. Miss MacMillan was there and she said: "What will become of me if you go to Ottawa?"

Court resumed the next day with Mrs. Brownlee still on the stand. Asked if she was ever suspicious of Brownlee's driving MacMillan home, she described her habit of looking at her watch when he left and fixing in her mind the time when he would be back. He was, she declared, "very seldom late." She also described the weekend activities of newspaper reading and, together with her husband, working out the crossword puzzle in the New York Herald Tribune or doing jigsaw puzzles on a tray. In all, she said, her household had been "very, very happy and very informal."

MacLean attempted to discredit her testimony very simply by suggesting that, as a wife,

... whether he was right or wrong you would have gone to his defense?

A: No, scarcely.

Q: Oh, now?

A: Do you think any woman could countenance a thing like that?

Next, a succession of other witnesses appeared for the defense. Miss E.A. Brown, Brownlee's personal secretary for seventeen years, gave what amounted to a character reference for him. Frederick Smailes, the Civil Service Commissioner, explained how MacMillan had come to be hired in July, 1931. He admitted he was aware she was acquainted with the Brownlees but he denied that there had been any intervention on her part by Brownlee. He described MacMillan as a "bright, cheerful and conscientious" worker and a very "fine type of girl." Jean McCloy, the maid, confirmed Brownlee's testimony about the circumstances of the home at Hallowe'en, 1932. Four janitors in the Legislative Building described their routine and testified that they had never seen any young woman entering or leaving the Premier's office.

Following the noon adjournment, A. L. Smith startled everyone by suggesting that the Court and jury inspect the Brownlee house. MacLean, apparently taken aback, at first said he could see "no good purpose in it." However, when the jury was asked the response was:

A Juryman: I think it would be well, My Lord. We were speaking amongst ourselves and we thought if we did have a chance we would like to see this road out in the country -- if we did have a chance. I am only speaking of it and possibly it would not be necessary?

The Court: Inspect this what?

A Juryman: This road out here -- out west ....

Mr. MacLean: ... possibly on the return trip they could go to the Brownlee house, if that is convenient ... I would suggest that the plaintiff go out and pick out, and point out the road. If Your Lordship would come in the car with counsel we would ask the plaintiff to go ahead and pick out the road in another car.

The last week of June is typically a time of heavy showers across the parklands of Alberta and 1934 was no exception. When the impromptu entourage of Chryslers, Studebakers and Hupmobiles turned down a sideroad near Winterburn, the hard narrow tires slipped and skidded on the muddy surface. More than once jurors and counsel had to join forces to push bemired automobiles out of giant potholes. Had it not been for the seriousness of their purpose, the whole episode might well be regarded as a ludicrous mad-cap adventure. A road answering MacMillan's description of a deep ditch on one side and trees on the other was observed but in a well settled district. According to later analysis, two significant pieces of non-verbal evidence resulted from the excursion. Brownlee denied his claim that he did not smoke when he "was out" by chain smoking through the entire outing, and the jury supposedly took note of the substantial bolt on the inside of Florence's bedroom door.

Court resumed on Saturday morning with yet another surprise announcement by Smith.

I am calling no further evidence. I say that because we have now a very clear cut issue - seduction or no seduction, and I do not intend to complicate it by the counter claim in respect to conspiracy ....

He then began his final address to the jury. Interrupted by the noon adjournment, it lasted a total of two hours and fifteen minutes, while MacLean's was a comparatively short forty minutes.

Small, distinguished looking, silver-haired Acting Chief Justice Ives then began his charge to the jury.

The issue is clear cut and easily defined. It is a question of seduction and that alone is the issue. "Seduction" ... means this: inducing a woman to part with her virtue ... the inducement or persuasion may be by deception or bribe or flattery -- any artful device that brings about her consent ... the presence of force does not necessarily prevent it being seduction but if force alone is used it would be rape.

Brownlee himself had raised this point, astounding the junior lawyers on the case with his detachment. He asserted that on MacMillan's testimony he should have more correctly been charged with rape. Smith, too, had touched on it in his address and the Bulletin had predictably headlined "Defense lawyer says Brownlee should have been charged with rape."

Justice Ives continued with his charge, instructing the jury on how to approach its task.

... you must weigh the evidence -- bring to your aid your experience as men of affairs in your daily lives. ... Defense counsel asked you if it was reasonable to suppose that the Prime Minister would take the risk of parking on a road which bears evidence of being used considerably in a thickly settled district, with a conspicuous car. ... You do not find a verdict upon possibilities, you balance probabilities, what is probably so, and it is upon probabilities that you come to a conclusion as to truth.

The story of the female plaintiff ... is wholly and entirely unsupported by any other evidence. If this were the subject of a criminal inquiry, a jury would be prohibited from bringing in a verdict because of the absence of corroboration ...

The evidence, on the other hand, of the defendant is supported in many instances by that of other witnesses ... there is no evidence of ... sexual intercourse ... It is quite clear that the female plaintiff is out and wrong in her dates, in a measure ... If no damage follows the seduction the action is not maintainable. There must be damage accruing. Without it the action cannot be maintained.

Then, at four in the afternoon, the jury retired to consider the questions they had been given. Some had wondered, in light of the pre-trial publicity, if an unbiased jury could be found but at length the six had been selected. They were all males and included a clothier and an art shop proprietor from Edmonton, a merchant and a pool room operator from Wainwright, a merchant from Athabasca and a farmer from Stony Plain. It was rumoured that at least two had daughters of Vivian's age.

After they retired, MacLean immediately challenged two points of the charge. He objected to the statement there had been no corroboration but the Court maintained there had been "corroboration of opportunity perhaps, not the corroboration of misconduct." The second objection was to the comment that the Court was "astounded there was no suspicion" on the part of those close to Brownlee. MacLean protested he had not been "entitled to bring evidence before this Court on mere suspicion." However, the jury was not recalled. Despite the six days of testimony and the addresses of counsel and the Court, it was basically a question of one person's word against another's. Vivian MacMillan maintained that John Brownlee had had sexual relations with her and Brownlee denied it.

Four hours and forty minutes later the jury returned and informed a stunned courtroom of their answers:

Q. 1: Did this defendant seduce the plaintiff, Vivian MacMillan?

A: Yes.

Q. 2: If so, when?

A: At the time when Mr. Brownlee gained only partial entrance, as stated by Vivian Macmillan.

Q. 3: If so, did she suffer damages and in what amount?

A: Yes, $10,000.

Q. 4: If so, did the male plaintiff suffer damages and in what amount?

A: Yes, $5,000.

Instantly there began the debate which possibly will never be resolved: had the jury arrived at the correct verdict? Justice Ives was the first to record his opinion.

Gentlemen of the Jury, you are excused and you may go, I think I should say openly and publicly while you are present that I strongly disagree with your answers. The evidence does not warrant them. You may go.

It was obvious from this comment that the standard conflicting motions by counsel following the jury's verdict would not be simply a routine. Consequently M. M. Porter was allowed to elaborate on the defense motion that the court dismiss the action:

Mr. Porter: ... mere seduction in itself has never been a cause of action. ... even in cases where the action is brought by the girl herself she must suffer the kind of damage that would give her parent or master the right of action ... there was no loss of wares and no evidence that she was in any way damaged....

Mr. MacLean: I submit, with great respect, this Court cannot render a verdict contrary to the decision of the jury.

The Court: Oh yes it can. I have done it before now on two different occasions and been upheld by the Court of Appeal.

MacLean protested that A. D. MacMillan was out $500 for jury fees for which he had mortgaged his home but Ives retorted that that was irrelevant and, declaring that he would write a judgment later, he adjourned the Court.

* * *

Those who were there report general amazement at the jury's verdict. Supposedly, the main reason the counter claim was withdrawn was complete confidence that MacMillan's case had been destroyed. It was later contended that had the counter claim been proceeded with, Brownlee would have been completely vindicated. The evidence for the counter claim, only recently come to light, does not substantiate this. It suggests that there was a conspiracy but what little additional information it provides on the question of whether or not there was a sexual relationship indicates there was, but not as characterized by MacMillan. If there was, however, some other evidence, withdrawing the counter claim was a colossal blunder on the part of the defense. Clearly the withdrawal deflated Brownlee's case and its manner and timing may well have prejudiced the jury and left the impression that the counter claim was nothing more than a bluff.

Another common explanation for the decision was the sensationalized and prejudicial coverage by the press, especially the Edmonton Bulletin. It was argued that such coverage made it impossible for Brownlee to receive a fair trial in Alberta. While it is clear that the Bulletin sensationalized the reporting of the case in an effort to build sales and maximize the political effects of Brownlee's embarrassment, it must also be admitted that below the sensational and calculated headlines there was a practically verbatim report of the testimony.

What cannot be overlooked in any consideration of the outcome are the attitudes of the day. It was then the common wisdom that in sexual relations the woman should always be thought of, even by herself, as a victim. This post-Victorian assumption accounts for what was for many the most telling argument, that a young woman who could go into such detail and talk so knowledgeably about somewhat bizarre sexual encounters must be telling the truth. Others would maintain that Vivian MacMillan, both before and after the Brownlee episode, "wasn't what she should have been."

The most perplexing enigma in the case is Brownlee himself. For many who knew him well, the contentions of MacMillan were so outrageous as to be almost inconceivable. The idea of passionless, remote, cautious and calculating John Brownlee behaving like a love torn teenager discovering sex was ludicrous. That the man who lived in his briefcase, who virtually was the Government of Alberta, with all the work load that that entailed, went out two or three nights a week for quickie sex on district backroads seemed, to say the least, improbable. Yet for some, even those close to him, there was a lingering doubt. There was his capacity for indirection, his calculating not to say manipulative manner of influencing people behind the scenes, a sense that he was never completely open or entirely what he presented himself as being.

In the final analysis, the question remains today much as it did when it was sent to the jury, a question of Macmillan's word against Brownlee's. A later generation would have laughed out of court an attempt to seek redress for a three year affair on the ground of "seduction" or wondered who had seduced whom. In one perceptive comment, Chief Justice Harvey, in a later judgment characterized MacMillan's action, accepting her testimony at face value, as an application to the courts for retroactive compensation for fornication. Even if one accepts her story, Brownlee, compared to some of today's recycled politicians, paid a very heavy price for a discreet affair. If on the other hand, he was entirely innocent, as he continued to maintain, then what happened was a piece of political and personal chicanery as dastardly as any in Canadian history -- a character assassination of the first order.

Between the two extremes is the easier, but somehow less satisfying, interpretation that there was a sexual relationship of some description which was eventually exploited by those with personal or political motives to see Brownlee's standing destroyed. There are those who still maintain that one or more persons got some sort of mysterious "hold" over MacMillan that accounted for her testimony against a man and a family she had once regarded as almost her own. This view is less satisfying than it first seems because from either point of view half measures are not enough. If MacMillan was capable of bold-faced fabrication of one incident, she was capable of the same in her entire testimony; while for Brownlee, coming from the background, position and era of intense regard for character he did, one small incident would have been just as damaging to his reputation as the lustful adventures MacMillan attributed to him. Perhaps that was why he contested the case so doggedly as it wound its way through the courts for the next six years.

In any event, on July 2, 1934, Justice Ives delivered his formal judgment dismissing the action with costs charged to the plaintiffs. In thus overturning the jury's verdict, he cited the fact that MacMillan had left home with the consent and approval of her parents, and that there was no evidence of illness or other damages from the alleged "seduction". "In my opinion," he wrote, "the law is well settled that damage is the gist of the action. In the absence of any evidence of such damage," he concluded, "the action must be dismissed with costs."

Immediately there was a howl of outrage from the Edmonton Bulletin about the attack on the sanctity of jury verdicts and the plight of MacMillan seeing a favourable verdict overturned, Brownlee exonerated by the judge, and she and her father left with all the costs to bear. The Bulletin opened a much advertised fund for public subscriptions by those who wanted to help defray those costs and finance an appeal. Eventually over $2,000 were collected.

For Brownlee, however, and for his family, the future discussion was largely academic. He recognized that the decision of the jury had ended his political career. He immediately announced that he planned to resign as premier as soon as a successor could be chosen.

Four years earlier there had been predictions that he might be Premier for another twenty years and that his major accomplishments, such as the transfer of the control of the natural resources, would guarantee him a prominent place in the memory of Albertans forever. Yet well before those twenty years had passed, the name of Brownlee was largely forgotten and when remembered at all it was usually because of the so-called "Brownlee scandal". However, his career was not over. He was still to make an important contribution to Western Canada in the years ahead although that could not have been predicted when, on July 10, 1934, John Brownlee's career as Premier of Alberta ended.

Chapter 19: A Career Resumed

Brownlee's replacement as premier was Richard Reid, a quietly competent, gentle man who spoke with a soft Scots burr. Reid merited the confidence of his colleagues but as the leader of an embattled group under impassioned attack from all directions, he was distinctly out of his element. Some had expected that U.F.A. president, Robert Gardiner, would be approached to lead a new government but the Ministers and most M.L.A.'s were strongly opposed to his C.C.F. advocacy. Reid described the link with the C.C.F. as an "unholy amalgamation" and Gardiner as a "far left" radical who "got much more notice than the solid chaps." Only O. L. McPherson was dropped from the old Cabinet, while Hugh Allen, J.J. MacLellan and J. Russell Love were added. The first act of the new Cabinet was to issue a statement, drafted by John Lymburn, reaffirming their support of Brownlee and their confidence in his integrity, although regretting that with regard to the events of July 5, 1933, he had allowed himself to be put in a position in which suspicions could not be totally dismissed.

While Brownlee and the Reid Government were reorganizing to repair the torpedoed ship of state, their political opponents were hastily adjusting to the new circumstances. The Conservatives, for the most part, regretted the turn of events while recognizing the new opportunities it afforded. Meanwhile, Howson and his gang were in a veritable frenzy to take advantage of their sudden good fortune. Convinced that his forces would now sweep to power, he began a steady stream of advice to King as to how the federal campaign should be organized. He proposed a conference "for the purpose of formulating a Western Canada Policy" and persisted with the idea even after King threw cold water on it by pointing out, "there is nothing which can prevent victory to the Liberal cause between now and the time of a general election but possible cleavages or divisions in our own party." Eventually Howson had to be content with a mere provincial conference but he assured King, "we so-called 'irresponsibles' did not go off the deep end." However, he went on to explain again why it was so vital the federal Liberals also sweep to victory. "This province, as you are aware, has been the breeding ground of new movements, all of which have been detrimental to Liberalism. We originated the U.F.A., the C.C.F., the Farmers' Unity League, and are protagonists in no small way of Socialism, Communism and Social Credit. It is necessary to have an outstanding Liberal victory in both fields to cure this situation."

The platform passed by the Alberta Liberal Convention was an obvious attempt to appeal to every strain of thought. It promised action on virtually every solution that had been put forward including a pledge, "when returned to power to employ three of the most expert Social Credit Advocates." The Liberals would continue to underestimate the potential of Social Credit as a political force in its own right.

* * *

Outside Calgary's Central United Church, newsboys stamped their feet to keep warm in the biting mid-January, 1935, cold as they hawked papers replete with the latest headlines of the "Brownlee Case", then before the Appellate Division of the Alberta Supreme Court. Inside the church, delegates to the U.F.A. Convention deserted the afternoon session to make their way to the basement where the U.F.W.A. were meeting. Soon the hall was crammed, every available place to stand taken and even the entrance corridors packed with expectant people. Soon a heavy set man wearing thick glasses and a rumpled suit and towering above the onlookers maneuvered his way through the crowd and toward the platform. After a period of virtual seclusion, John E. Brownlee was making a dramatic return to the public stage. He had spoken to these people many times in the past but now they strained and jostled for a better view of the man who had been so much the topic of conversation in the last several months. His appearance took courage. He admitted, "It was not an easy matter to speak at all to you this afternoon." However, he went on to deliver a stinging critique of Social Credit and Aberhart's contention that it could be introduced on a provincial basis alone. "If it is the last word I speak in public," he implored, "I would impress you that nothing but disillusionment, loss of hope and additional despair can follow any attempt to inaugurate a system of that kind, because the Province has no jurisdiction in these matters."

264

The U.F.A. Convention to which Brownlee spoke was a turbulent and decisive one. In part due to his intense pronouncements, several resolutions calling for the adoption of so-called "Aberhart Social Credit" were rejected, even though Aberhart himself spoke to the gathering. The U.F.A. leadership held the control of the Convention, supported Brownlee's contentions, rejected Aberhart, reaffirmed the link with the C.C.F., and lost virtually the entire base of their support. The support of the scandal-stained Brownlee, the rejection of the views of one of the most respected Christian evangelists of the day, and the attempt to foist upon Alberta the godless, materialist doctrines of European socialism under the guise of the C.C.F., all were fundamentally distasteful to most of those who once had filled the zealous ranks of the U.F.A. These people responded, not with detailed briefs or letters to the editor, but by quietly ceasing to attend U.F.A. meetings and instead tuning in their radios to Aberhart's immensely popular "Back to the Bible Hour".

What most commentators have not fully realized is that the religiosity of the U.F.A. and Social Credit in their early periods of spectacular growth was not simply a frill of local colour but the very essence of the movements. When Brownlee had observed in 1921 that "the U.F.A. was something of a religion to many of its members," he had been closer to the actual well-springs of its support than with all his subsequent rational arguments about competent administration and judicious financial control. In its heyday, the U.F.A. had been a movement responding to a Christian infused moral critique of social, economic and political injustice, and advocating policies based fundamentally on the application of Christian ethics. H. W. Wood had been one of the inspirational leaders, correctly recognizing that there was often more of active Christianity in the meetings of the early U. F. A. or Alberta Wheat Pool Locals than in the traditional churches. After an hiatus of relative affluence, Aberhart represented a return to the evangelical advocacy of applied Christianity as the basic remedy for social and economic injustice. Thus, he was not assuming Brownlee's role as the competent business administrator, but Wood's mantle as the inspirational leader of a Christian revival. Therefore, Brownlee's attempt to refute Aberhart by pointing out the weaknesses of his economic theory failed because it was fundamentally irrelevant.

During the next months, Brownlee was in an anomalous position. On the one hand he was now a simple backbencher who sometimes found himself on the losing side as, for example, when he opposed a resolution for the Crown to be represented in "a less expensive and simpler way" and the official residence of the Lieutenant-Governor to be turned into a "Tubercular Sanitarium." On the other hand, he emerged as the chief Government strategist and spokesman in the struggle to combat the swelling tide of Social Credit support.

On the personal front, on February 2, 1935, the Appellate Division, by a margin of three to two, sustained Justice Ives' dismissal of the MacMillan action. In a lengthy judgment, Chief Justice Harvey commented:

... in every other case there was a birth or pregnancy to prove sexual intercourse. The pills she alleged using were unknown to her physician or to dictionaries and no specimen was provided. Her whole story is quite unsupported by other evidence and is of an impossible not to say incredible character ... in cross-examination she showed a readiness to admit that she may have been mistaken as regards very positive statements previously made when by the questions it appeared there may be independent evidence she was wrong.

As for her claim that she did not know that she and Brownlee were being followed, he commented sharply, "It looks much more as though it was a deliberate attempt, with her connivance if not more, to trap the defendant in some compromising situation."

He admitted that, "It seems almost as incredible that a girl could concoct such a story as that it can be true." However, he referred to one bit of revealing evidence on that count, a question as to why she had realized, some time into the alleged affair, that Brownlee must have planned her seduction from the very first meeting. MacMillan had replied, "Well, I was older and I would hear girls talking about men and then I was working in the Attorney General's Department and there were always all kinds of files to read about young girls getting into trouble." Clearly the implication was that she had had ample source material from which she might have concocted such a story.

The Chief Justice then turned to "circumstances indicating that the jury may have been swayed by something other than the evidence given in Court" and referred to "newspaper reports and comments so unfair and prejudicial" as to remove the possibility of a fair trial. He concluded, "There being no proper evidence of damages which could support a verdict, it was the right and duty of the Judge to dismiss the action as he did." Within days the Edmonton Bulletin had kicked off another "Seduction Appeal Fund" to finance an appeal to the Supreme Court of Canada.

* * *

The first phase of the attack on Aberhart was an attempt to argue that his was an "incorrect" interpretation of Social Credit. This line was fully developed by Brownlee in speeches across southern Alberta. Central to this effort was a series of letters to Major Douglas, attempting to have him contradict Aberhart's claims. Premier Reid offered to appoint Douglas as Chief Reconstruction Adviser of Alberta at a fee of $7,000 per year. The Major, after haggling to insure he would not have to spend more than three weeks annually on the job in the Province and that his fee would be paid in advance, agreed to arrive "by May". Aberhart was also invited to come to Edmonton where, it was promised, he would be given every assistance necessary to prepare a comprehensive Social Credit plan for Alberta. The two moves were attempts to force both Douglas and Aberhart to make specific proposals which could then be subjected to detailed criticism and contrasted to show that Aberhart did not correctly "understand" Social Credit. The attempt failed as both Douglas and Aberhart, each in his own quite different way, were remarkably adept at avoiding specifics and moving the argument back to virtually invulnerable generalities and principles.

In April, Brownlee was the major figure in the Government's attempt to meet Aberhart on his own ground and counter his immensely popular radio broadcasts with a radio series of their own. Brownlee's talks were hard-hitting and, strangely, some of the most relaxed of his long public speaking career. He followed essentially the same line as in his personal appearances, defending the orthodox approaches of his Government and criticizing the impracticality of Aberhart's proposals. As it became increasingly obvious that such appeals to reason and the record were futile, he stepped up his personal attacks, accusing Aberhart of using "through the looking glass logic" and of being a Pied Piper leading Albertans astray. When Aberhart retorted that he did not mind being compared to the Pied Piper since he had "rid the capitol of all the rats," Brownlee rejoined; "unfortunately his memory of the legend is, like his economic proposals, rather vague" and went on to remind his listeners that ultimately the Pied Piper had led all the children of Hamelin to their destruction. The exchange underlined Brownlee's importance to the Government for he was one of the few who could get the last word on Aberhart.

Finally, in May, the Social Credit League abandoned what it had insisted was a purely educative role and decided to field candidates in the next provincial election. Brownlee remarked wryly on the procedure of Aberhart interviewing and selecting, but not announcing these candidates. "All these would be candidates are now being chosen, four in each constituency and wrapped in cellophane and carefully hidden away so they will not dry out on him, until the day he calls out the fittest and discards the rest. That day will be like the Judgment Day in one respect at least. I venture there will be much weeping and wailing and gnashing of teeth." The closing allusion foreshadowed the last line of attack when all else failed. Aberhart would be ridiculed for his "unethical" combination of religion and politics. Such ridicule of an obviously sincere, practicing and possibly inspired Christian evangelist did nothing but intensify the loyalty of Aberhart's following.

As if to confirm his contempt for Aberhart, Brownlee took the lead in wining and dining Major Douglas when he finally arrived. The two had lengthy private chats as they toured the carefully groomed fairways of the Edmonton Golf and Country Club or relaxed after a match in the exclusive club house. Douglas delicately avoided becoming embroiled in the controversy. Finally, John Lymburn asked him to prepare a critique of an Aberhart radio broadcast and, when the Major demurred, informed him he had been "engaged to advise and the Government wished his advice on Aberhart's proposals." Douglas pointed out some "technical errors" but cautioned that "political speeches" should not be taken with too much seriousness. After more vague comments of dubious usefulness, Douglas collected his fees and left, as it turned out, for good.

Far from Douglas eroding Aberhart's support, as Brownlee and his colleagues had hoped, his comments merely confirmed for many that Aberhart was by far the abler exponent of Social Credit. Of no small importance in creating this impression was Aberhart's presentation of Social Credit as one aspect of a deeply rooted cultural response through which applied Christianity would transform society. Such a touchstone elicited a deep and resonant reaction from the majority, while Douglas' pompous utterances, related only to a vague conception of a materialist and technocratic society, left Albertans cold.

All attempts to reverse the Social Credit tide had failed but the election could no longer be delayed. It was called for August 22, 1935. Brownlee remained the Government's most effective campaigner although it was obvious his influence had been seriously undermined. Interestingly, Vivian MacMillan, whose charges had destroyed his reputation, now overcame the alleged damages to her marriage opportunities and wed Henry Sorenson, an Edson confectioner described as "several years her senior."

Meanwhile, Brownlee was concentrating on trying to win his seat in Ponoka. Indeed his phenomenal powers of concentration now became a hazard. One night Florence, deeply concerned about his late return from an election meeting, tried to telephone Ponoka but the lines were down. Eventually he limped in saying he had "fallen asleep at the wheel" and his car had run off the road, knocking down the telephone lines. Another such incident indicates that rather than "falling asleep", his condition, which persisted for several years, was a case of his mind becoming riveted on his thoughts to the exclusion of all else. In this second incident, he became so involved in a discussion that he turned to the back seat to rummage through his briefcase to find a file. Only the alertness of his passenger grabbing the steering wheel avoided yet another tour through the ditch. Likely, the major problems of the day and MacMillan's accusations, helped create such a mental state. The election campaign was not a pleasant one. For Brownlee who had been acclaimed in 1921 and 1930, it was only his second personal contest. Social Creditors were so fanatical in some places it took real courage for him to appear but he refused to be intimidated. In one hostile district the packed hall was quiet and outwardly attentive until he turned to Social Credit.

A group of big fellows near the door then left the hall, slamming the door violently as they went out. Some of them got into cars and started to blow horns. Others got logs and began pounding the walls and doors ... from outside, while they hooted and yelled. Some of my supporters went outside and the rough stuff stopped. But the meeting inside was a tumultuous uproar.

Years later, he reflected on the significance of a similar reaction. I had the best attention possible until the question period. ... one man got up and said, "Mr. Brownlee, we have listened to you with a great deal of attention and the answers you have given seem pretty hard to meet. But I have one more question ... I'm selling my wheat at 25 cents a bushel. If I tried to sell a steer tomorrow I'd probably hardly get enough to pay the freight. I get 3 cents a dozen for eggs. I'm lucky to get a dollar for a can of cream. Will you tell me what I've got to lose?" and a cheer went over the audience. I knew then what the result of the election was going to be. But I think that is an indication that that election was influenced by the effect of the depression on the farmers. I don't believe that it was influenced by any widespread conversion to a new theory. You must remember that ... monetary reform was not new.

The Social Credit forces campaigned strenuously against Brownlee. Their candidate in Ponoka was Edith Rogers, a dynamic and compelling speaker and organizer. Aside from Aberhart himself, they could not have fielded a stronger candidate. The choice of Mrs. Rogers, a woman, to oppose Brownlee, the "sober faced seducer", was an additional bit of shrewdness. Brownlee had "an active group of faithful workers." Later, he remembered, "they assured me I would come out with a majority, particularly around Rimbey. ... Well we didn't have it," he recalled with a laugh, "As a matter of fact, we lost Rimbey by quite a decided majority."

Rogers scored an overwhelming win with 2,295 votes. It was a testimony to Brownlee that despite all the factors that conspired against him, he still received 879 votes while the Liberal trailed with 696. Provincially, not one U.F.A. Member survived as Social Credit swept 56 of the 63 seats. It was an ironic footnote to the demise of the most politically successful farmers' group in history that the one U.F.A. candidate who came closest to re-election was lawyer John Lymburn in the City of Edmonton.

Yet the upset was not simply a rural revolt. Social credit had swept the villages and towns as well as the farms and had destroyed more hopes than those of the U.F.A. and the few forlorn U.F.A.- C.C.F. candidates. The Conservatives, realistically, had expected little and won two seats but the Liberal's confident expectations of filling the vacuum created by their destruction of Brownlee and sweeping to power, were utterly dashed. Despite previous wins in Saskatchewan, Ontario and New Brunswick; imported campaigners such as hockey star Eddie Shore; strong press support; and Howson's predictions of at least forty-five seats, they lost ground and were reduced to only five. They could only conclude that the Alberta electorate was irrational and turn their hopes to filling the vacuum once Social Credit was discredited. This they turned their attention to accomplishing. The Edmonton Bulletin was soon leading a vendetta against William Aberhart.

For his part, Brownlee's oft' professed desire to leave public life was fulfilled, although not in the way he would have hoped. His political career was over.

* * *

Never one to be idle, he soon re-established a law firm, taking a small office on one of the upper floors of the Imperial Bank in downtown Edmonton. In building his legal practice he was greatly assisted by the continuing loyalty and friendship of many who were influential in farmer organizations and businesses. While publisher Norman Smith's comment that Brownlee "didn't lose a friend worth having" over the MacMillan episode is overly generous, there is no doubt that it was because of his long association with several United Grain Growers directors that he was soon, again, General Counsel of that firm.

On the U.G.G. Board, three veterans: F.J. Collyer, John Morrison and J.J. MacLellan (late of the U.F.A. Cabinet), had shared in Brownlee's work on the amalgamation in 1917. Four others had joined the Board in the early Twenties and one of these, Snow Sears, an archetypal southern Alberta rancher, was one of Brownlee's strongest supporters. Sears had had a large role in Brownlee's early involvement in the Alberta Wheat Pool and the two had worked together on both its formation and that of the Alberta Livestock Cooperative. It was Sears' voice, powerful enough to hush a stormy convention hall, that was raised the loudest in support of Brownlee's expanding role with the U.G.G. Also instrumental in his advancement was the firm's president, R. S. Law. He had joined the Board in 1929 to replace T. A. Crerar who was resigning after twenty-three years as president in order to join the King Cabinet. Law had been the Company's secretary for years and his association went back at least twenty years to the time when both he and Brownlee were involved in the early days of the old Alberta Farmers' Cooperative Elevator Company. It was fortunate for Brownlee that Law was now the president for Crerar was noticeably cool to Brownlee after this period.

Perhaps Crerar's coolness stemmed from the MacMillan charges. In any event, the Supreme Court of Canada, on March 1, 1937, upheld her appeal, the first court decision unfavourable to Brownlee. The majority concentrated on the construction of the Act contending that its framers could not have intended that the character of the damages to the woman should be the same as that for a master or father. Justice Davis, who believed the appeal should be dismissed, looked more at the evidence and the validity of the verdict than the construction of the Act. It was his opinion that there must be damages as in the earlier sections or "some negation of choice."

However, the majority decision meant that Brownlee had to pay $10,000 in damages plus the costs of all trials. He settled with the Court for these amounts on April 7, 1937, but ultimately decided to pursue the matter further. On July 1, 1937, the federal Cabinet passed an Order-in-Council granting him leave to appeal to the then highest court of all -- the Judicial Committee of the Privy Council in Britain. That Court did not hear the arguments until March 11 and 12, 1940, when Frank Gahan of the British firm of Charles Russell and Company appeared on Brownlee's behalf. Gahan "invited their Lordships to review the evidence and the summing up of the trial judge, with a view to disturbing the verdict of the jury but their Lordships were not disposed to take this course." Gahan then argued that "to give a woman damages for the voluntary loss of her chastity" was a "radical departure" from English law. The Judicial Committee, however, concentrated on the construction of the statute and concluded "the appeal should be dismissed." John Brownlee's final attempt at formal vindication had failed.

By this time he had re-built his career to almost exactly what it had been twenty years earlier. There was his solid and growing legal practice with a number of agricultural concerns as clients. There was his major work of representing, defending and assisting the Board of Directors of the U.G.G. There was even his legal advice column in Norman Smith's new publication, the Western Leader.

His interest in political and economic developments continued but he expressed his opinions only confidentially to his closest associates. He resented the Social Credit contention that they had come to office with the provincial treasury bankrupt. He claimed instead Alberta had been left with a solid credit rating and a firm basis for economic recovery after the depression, including the control of the natural resources. He also regarded each of the several disallowances of Social Credit legislation as confirmation of his long held contention that any serious attempt to implement the theory was beyond the legal competence of the Province. However, he did provide some little known, but important advice and assistance to the new Government, even to the point of drafting some sections of the famous, The Case for Alberta. This served as Alberta's submission to the Rowell-Sirois Commission, which was reviewing Dominion-Provincial relations in light of the Depression. It forcefully presented the Alberta viewpoint. Clearly, Brownlee agreed to contribute to this brief as a contribution to illuminating Western insights into how Canada had failed to respond adequately, both before and during the Great Depression. Thus, despite his antipathy toward Social Credit and especially toward Aberhart's "propagandist" approach to politics, Brownlee remained a thoroughly committed Westerner and Albertan.

Figure 8

Through the support of those who knew him and still valued his expertise, Brownlee (seated at the far left) was able to rebuild his career; first in law and later, again, as a major figure in Western Canada's agricultural organizations. Here he continues his contribution to the co-operative movement by serving on the 1944 Alberta Cooperation Advisory Board.

(Photo courtesy of the Provincial Archives of Alberta A3978)

Chapter 20: Reorganization

In 1936 and 1937 serious drought was, for the first time, more accountable than low commodity prices for depressed farm incomes in Alberta. For the two years combined average wheat yield was about nine bushels per acre, one-half the long term average. It was not until 1942 that record yields, combined with 1928 level prices, produced the first substantial profit for wheat growers in thirteen years. By then, Brownlee had joined the Board of United Grain Growers Limited.

His promotion was due to both the personal contacts he had in the Company and his achievements in two complex areas: the capital re-organization of the U.G.G., and a long controversy involving the taxability of the U.G.G. and the Pools. These two issues occupied centre stage during the difficult transition period in which Western agriculture recovered from the depression and entered a new era after World War II. The U.G.G. was singularly successful in weathering the catastrophe of the depression. In fact, it emerged from the 1930's in a strong business and financial condition. This was explained as a result of,

> The old, old story of the virtue of thrift ... In the fat years surpluses had been built up as a bulwark against the lean ones. They were consolidated and used for their intended purposes, to meet losses and bolster dividends when earnings were reduced.

Obviously, such management policies could not have been more compatible with Brownlee's views. Thrift, the development of large reserves even in the face of some shareholder discontent, and the retention of sufficient working capital to meet unexpected heavy expenditures were all policies he had strongly recommended and attempted to follow as "business manager" of Alberta. There, "shareholder" pressure had ultimately proved impossible to restrain. Now, both his management philosophy and financial conservatism would find a more welcome home at the U.G.G.; and his skill in handling the annual meeting would virtually insure that neither would be seriously challenged.

His first important, opportunity to demonstrate his expertise came when he was given the responsibility for remodeling the Company's capital structure. The existing structure was limited by the stipulation that only farmers could buy shares from the Company. Given depression conditions, few farmers could afford shares. On the contrary, many were anxious to dispose of them for some ready cash and this, along with farmer deaths and retirements meant that many shares had passed into the hands of non-farmers. Thus the basic principle of a farmer controlled company was threatened and the Company was capitally under-nourished as well.

The problem had been recognized but it was not until the Directors, with considerable assistance from Brownlee, advanced a proposal that any progress was made. The plan was to recall the old $25 shares and in their place issue shares of two types: a "Class A" or preferred investment share with a par value of $20, and a "Class B" or voting share with a par value of $5. Class A shares could be purchased or held by anyone, subject to a limit of 250 shares per holder, but Class B shares, to a maximum of 25, could only be held by *bona fide* farmers on the basis of one man - one vote. There was an additional rider that anyone registered as a shareholder before the new structure came into effect was entitled to hold Class B shares. Whether Brownlee added that rider to meet his own situation or not, it certainly had that effect. Never a *bona fide* farmer, he acquired 26 old shares just before the Directors' by-law brought the new structure officially into effect. He was thus entitled to hold the necessary Class B shares to allow him to participate in annual meetings and become a Director.

The capital restructuring was the major topic of the 1939, 1940 and 1941 annual meetings. On each occasion, "Mr. J.E. Brownlee, K.C., ... made a very full and complete explanation of the plan, after which questions were invited. He then made careful and complete answers to all questions." He also drafted the necessary by-laws and resolutions to effect the change and played a large part in handling the complications around the securing of the required Parliamentary approval for the charter amendments. When the restructuring was finally completed in 1942, the paid up capital was represented by 144,739 Class A shares and 63,065 Class B shares. More important, the new structure, especially the new class of investment shares, provided scope for a financial foundation vital to the Company's future. Without it, the necessary massive expansion of the next two decades would not have been possible. Brownlee played a major role in laying this groundwork.

Partly in recognition of this, when Director and First Vice-President, D. G. McKenzie, resigned to become Chairman of the Board of Grain Commissioners, the Board named Brownlee to succeed him in both functions. This appointment was confirmed at the 1942 Annual Meeting when the delegates elected him to a three year term as Director. The promotion meant a full-time commitment to the U.G.G. so, after an absence of twenty years, John and Florence returned to Calgary. They moved into Suite 4 of Donegal Mansions, then one of the more prestigious apartment buildings in the city, located on the fashionable north bank of the Bow River.

There were many changes in the Brownlee family during these years. Son John was for a time a clerk and bookkeeper in his father's law office before leaving for Los Angeles to study photography. He returned at the war's end and found employment with McDermid Studios. Son Alan enrolled in the University of Alberta and graduated in law. Following a period with the Canadian Armed Forces, he became a partner in his father's firm, which then became Brownlee, Baldwin and Brownlee. On April 15, 1941, Christina died in Brigden at the age of eighty. Brownlee returned for the funeral of the woman who had stood beside him when he had been baptized in the little church in Port Ryerse, over half a century before. She had provided an example of seriousness of purpose, unrelenting industry, and of reserve approaching aloofness, which had characterized much of his life. Ironically, in view of Brownlee's repeated talks to the U.F.W.A. over the years about the importance of everyone having a will, she died intestate. However, the estate was valued at only $1,507. There was still $100 outstanding on the mortgage on the brick cottage purchased in the summer of 1904 just before John started university. Brownlee immediately surrendered his claim on the estate in favour of his sister, Maude. During the latter years she had cared for her mother who had, at least twice, refused her permission to marry. Maude quickly sold the property and on August 12, 1941, married her childhood friend, Carl Smith, a widower with one grown daughter.

As both First Vice-President and General Counsel for U.G.G., Brownlee could both advise and speak for the Company. This combination proved of great value in confronting the first major challenge of his period on the executive -- a long and complex struggle with the Income Tax Department. Historically the U.G.G. and its ancestors were among the earliest to advocate the graduated income tax as the most just way of raising governmental revenue and re-distributing wealth. In light of this, after the introduction of income tax in 1917, the Company paid it without objection. However, when, during World War II, corporate income tax rates were raised to first 20 and later 40 percent of net revenue, the U.G.G. had to re-evaluate its position, especially when the Turgeon Grain Commission revealed, supposedly to the surprise of the U.G.G., that the Pools were exempt from income tax. The Pools' claim was that they were acting simply as agents for their members and that any net revenue should be taxed not as corporate income but as personal income when it reached the member in the form of a patronage dividend. The U.G.G. argued that since the end of contract pooling in 1931, the Pools had been, in structure, organization and operation, identical with itself. Therefore, taxing one farmer owned grain company and exempting others was inequitable.

Brownlee went to Ottawa in the spring of 1941 to put the U.G.G.'s case before officials of the Income Tax Department and the Minister of National Revenue. Also in Ottawa was O. M. Biggar, familiar to Brownlee as the Dominion's lawyer in the transfer of control over Alberta's natural resources. Now Biggar was acting for the private grain corporations, grouped together as the North-West Line Elevators Association, also protesting the Pools' exemption by arguing that it gave them an unfair competitive advantage. Since the position of the U.G.G. and the N.L.E.A. on the issue was similar, Brownlee and Biggar collaborated on a joint brief.

To complicate things, the Pools were alert to the possible re-classification of their taxable status and had their lawyers in Ottawa. The Alberta Wheat Pool was, of course, represented by M. M. Porter, Brownlee's former partner and more lately his personal lawyer. The Pools claimed that their tax status was protected by a statute exempting all cooperatives and on April 22,

1941, they presented their case to officials of the Justice Department against any re-interpretation of the exempting clause. The U.G.G. Directors advised Brownlee to stay in Ottawa and "present argument to Justice Department to refute [Pools] case presented yesterday ... our interest so strong that we should suffer great injustice if matter should be dropped at this stage without at least reference to Exchequer Court."

Brownlee did not agree with the Directors in Winnipeg that an appeal to the Exchequer Court was the route to take. His experience told him that the ultimate decision would be made at the political level and he proceeded in that direction. Recognizing, very belatedly, that a furor would result if it became known that the U.G.G. had collaborated with the N.L.E.A., he decided not to file the joint brief with the Commissioner of Income Tax where it might become part of the official record and thus possibly available to Pool officials. He suggested it be filed with the Minister of National Revenue but was advised that in that case it might become part of the Parliamentary record. He then prepared a separate brief on behalf of the U.G.G. which he filed with the Commissioner of Income Tax on June 19, 1941. By then the Department of Justice had decided that the Pools were taxable and the Income Tax Department had issued them tax assessments. The Pools appealed these assessments and the case went to the Exchequer Court in 1943.

The eventual decision was against the Pools but by then, as Brownlee had anticipated, the issue was a political controversy. The federal Government, in a move to offset the criticism of Pool supporters, announced that all cooperatives who had reason to believe they were exempt "were to be completely free of tax up to 1941, although they were to pay taxes after that date." To make the taxation more palatable, cooperatives would be taxed as a separate class and be eligible for rather generous exemptions, the most important of which was the right to deduct patronage dividends. This move recognized the Pools, claim that they were agents handling their members' income, at least with regard to patronage dividends, while also responding to the concern of the U.G.G. and others that the Pools had revenues beside that returned to members – revenue used for capital expansion and in other ways which improved their competitive position.

Brownlee, by this time, was the U.G.G.'s leading spokesman. He enhanced this role by publishing several wide-ranging statements advocating specific government policies. The first, typical of those to come, he delivered to the 1942 Annual Meeting before it was widely circulated in pamphlet form under the title, Statement of Agricultural Policy 1942 - 1943. It began with the expected optimistic references to the war effort before focusing on the problem of the huge surplus of 600,000,000 bushels of unsold wheat. By 1943, all wheat sales were under the Canadian Wheat Board and farm deliveries were controlled by a quota and permit system. Brownlee pointed out that the guaranteed minimum price for wheat of 90 cents per bushel was ineffective if the farmer was unable to deliver his grain because of slow Wheat Board sales. He was soon among the first to urge federal cash advances to farmers against the security of farm stored grain, a proposal that spent more than a decade as a political issue before it was eventually implemented. He also recommended strong government action to expand markets through encouraging such varied uses of grain as in the production of industrial alcohol, and through a much more vigorous development of exports. The promising United States market for feed grain, he thought, should be guaranteed a supply even if that meant temporary Canadian shortages in those short crop years which, he warned, would inevitably come.

He went on to urge that agriculture be classified as an essential industry in the allocation of manpower for the war effort. Showing his characteristic foresight, he recommended that planning begin immediately for the post-war era, including the staging of agricultural reserves to assist countries as they were liberated. In conclusion, he advised the federal government to consider agriculture's role in the post-war economy and to be prepared to use Canada's place at the peace tables to attempt to secure free international trade in agricultural commodities. It was a brief but thorough consideration of the issues and showed a foresight few other Canadian leaders could equal. Such displays confirmed, for both the Directors and the delegates to the Annual Meeting, that they had not made a mistake in promoting John Brownlee to a leading position in their Company.

As the controversy with the Pools over the question of taxation became more heated, U.G.G. officials felt forced to defend their Company's place in the constellation of Western agriculture. Many Pool advocates denied that the U.G.G. was a cooperative and claimed instead that it was just another line elevator company. The U.G.G. Directors were impatient at this as they were proud of the Grain Growers' tradition as the oldest and most successful farmer cooperative in Canada, the one most closely modeled on the founding Rochdale principles of co-operativism. To put their case before the public, they assigned staff member L. P. Bancroft to compile a short history of the Company. Brownlee edited the draft and wrote several sections, including the chapter on the Alberta Farmers' Cooperative Elevator Company. However, with typical modesty, he did not have his name attached to <u>The Grain Growers' Record 1906 - 1943</u> which was widely circulated.

The Pools, meanwhile, led by the Saskatchewan Pool, solicited the support of all members of the Canadian Federation of Agriculture for a concerted effort to force the federal Government to suspend attempts to tax the income of cooperatives. Brownlee, replacing the ailing Law as the U.G.G.'s delegate, advised that the time was definitely not right to make such demands on Parliament. There was litigation pending, he pointed out, and moreover, such a demand would open cooperatives to criticism of self-interest in the face of a crucial need for all out financial support of the war effort. There would also be strong criticism from the heavily taxed private corporations who were already "jealous of cooperative exemptions and who would strongly oppose further exemptions or even the continuation of existing ones."

Brownlee's position was opposed by some members of the C.F.A. and the issue flared at the Annual Meeting in Ottawa, just before the customary meeting with the federal Cabinet. There were some strong objections to Brownlee's innocuous resolution on the taxation matter. After a heated exchange, his position prevailed but just one-half hour before meeting the Cabinet, W. C. Good arrived with a prepared submission urging "freedom for the cooperatives from income tax." The Saskatchewan Pool representatives insisted Good be allowed to join the delegation while Brownlee and the Alberta Pool representatives objected. Good withdrew and the interview with the Cabinet passed without incident but when the

C.F.A. Board reassembled there was further argument about Good's paper. Brownlee, "after obtaining Good's admission that the submission was his own, stated the U.G.G. could not endorse it."

When "printing and circulating, the statement as endorsed by the cooperatives" was suggested, Brownlee took umbrage and warmly rebuked the implication that the U.G.G. was not a cooperative. Then, "Mr. Good withdrew the statement and the incident closed."

Good's hopeless naiveté and bullish pursuit of his objective stood in sharp contrast to Brownlee's tactful recognition of the political and personal considerations in presenting what was at bottom simply one more special interest competing for the attention of federal decision makers. Indeed Brownlee's political skills were such an obvious asset to the U.G.G. and to Western agriculture that they prompted periodic rumours that he might re-enter political life. One such rumour he started himself when he fell into conversation with M. J. Coldwell, the new national C.C.F. leader, on the train. Coldwell reported to some of his Alberta lieutenants that Brownlee,

> would be prepared, if he were invited, to consider a nomination on our behalf. ... He told me that because of his connections with the Cooperative Movement and the importance of that Movement in the federal field, he would prefer to seek a federal seat rather than re-enter the Provincial Legislature. I have, of course, known Mr. Brownlee for some years and ... the part he played in bringing about the Nationally-owned Bank of Canada. Personally I would welcome his adhesion to our Movement.

Elmer Roper, the Alberta C.C.F. leader, proved more familiar with Brownlee than was Coldwell. "Knowing him I questioned how definite he would be as soon as I received your letter," he countered, "but I was prepared to get in touch with him making a special trip to Calgary if necessary." However, any slim prospects of Brownlee embarking on a C.C.F. candidature were totally quashed when an incautious and over-bearing C.C.F. organizer simply telephoned Brownlee to verify his intentions. Such an undiplomatic move put Brownlee off and Coldwell was forced to send an apologetic letter regretting his disclosure.

Nothing more was heard of Brownlee as a possible C.C.F. standard bearer.

Despite eschewing direct political involvement, Brownlee remained a leading Western spokesman and his major pronouncements, such as an address to the 1944 U.F.A. Convention on "Post-War Reconstruction", were widely reported. Typically, he dealt with a wide range of issues. He "frankly dreaded the early post-war years" because of a danger of the return of the unemployment levels of the Thirties. Full employment as part of an overall planned economic effort must prevail, he maintained, and it must be meaningful work. "I, personally, have never been able to see that it is economical or good to put men to work building roads like coolies in China when machines can do it better."

The government would never again be allowed to let commodity prices fall to the lows of 1932, he predicted, and warned that there was still considerable resentment among those who had suffered so severely because of depressed prices. This resentment had been intensified by the fact that the Winnipeg Grain Exchange had not been closed in response to farmer demands during the depression but had been closed during the war at a time of rising prices. The war-time ceiling of $1.25 per bushel for wheat meant that again farmers had borne a disproportionate share of the costs of a so-called national effort. An adequate floor price for wheat and other commodities was, he declared, imperative.

In preparing such comprehensive statements, he drew heavily on his wide ranging files of newspaper clippings, some of which he obtained through a clipping service. In addition to the expected agricultural topics he also kept organized files on such topics as Banks, Education, and Foreign Policy. He even began to be involved at the international level.

Late in 1945 a delegation from the National Farmers' Union of Great Britain visited Western Canada as part of an international tour of farmer organizations. In the spring of 1946, representatives of such organizations in thirty-one countries met in London. Brownlee accompanied the Canadian delegation as an alternate. The party arrived in Southhampton on May 9 on board the Aguitania and were met "by the Mayor in his robes of office." There followed tours of some of the larger English farms, including

Windsor Estates where Brownlee was among those introduced to the King and Queen and the Princesses Elizabeth and Margaret. The actual conference was a series of speeches and sumptuous banquets at the Savoy Hotel. Everyone supported the principle of an international farmers' organization. When it came time to draft agreements and otherwise get down to the practical implementation of the statements of principle, Brownlee's involvement increased. He was uniquely experienced in creating the framework of agricultural organizations and his practiced hand lent important aid to the creation of the International Federation of Agricultural Producers.

* * *

In the immediate post-war period, the major issue before Brownlee was the question of taxation and the fierce controversy sparked by the Pools' appeal against the decision to tax their income. The federal Government appointed the Royal Commission on Taxation of Cooperatives to explore the many complex issues. Brownlee presented the lengthy U.G.G. brief to the Commission on April 30, 1945. He began with an exhaustive review of the Company's history to show that it was truly a cooperative. He pointed out that it had never tried to avoid paying taxes, including income tax, but that it objected to the discrimination implicit in its being taxed while the Pools, organized along similar lines, were not taxed prior to 1942 and were taxed much more leniently thereafter. He concluded with several suggestions for the Commission's recommendations including exempting patronage dividends and share dividends of up to 5 percent.

The Royal Commission's report was very favourable to the U.G.G., perhaps as a result of the quality and effectiveness of Brownlee's brief and its presentation. The U.G.G. contention that it was a true cooperative was fully accepted and the Commission recommended exemptions for patronage dividends and for share dividends up to 3 percent. Brownlee thought the report fully confirmed his position that there should be complete equality in the taxation of the U.G.G. and the Pools. However, late in 1945 the U.G.G. received tax assessments for 1940 and 1941. Immediately he launched an appeal on the ground that since the Pools were exempt for those years, taxing the U.G.G. was inequitable. It remained for Parliament to clarify the situation in 1946 by amending the legislation regarding taxation of cooperatives by defining such bodies more clearly and stating more precisely how they would be taxed. The amendments established. a clear set of ground rules for the years after 1946 but the complexities of the 1940 to 1945 period had to be worked out through the normal appeal channels.

Naturally the Pools resented being subject to, what was for them, a new tax and such provisions as a 3 percent tax on employed capital. They had pioneered the practice of deferring patronage dividends and applying the money to capital reserve accounts. This practice was approved by the Annual Meeting but it reflected management's perspective more than that of the members. Nevertheless it allowed the build up of substantial reserves which, though ultimately still payable to individual farmers, could be employed to expand or improve the business operation. However, although the new tax rules exempted patronage dividends, the exemption did not include such dividends when in the form of capital reserve certificates. At the peak of resentment about the new tax situation, the eyes of Pool supporters fell with increasing suspicion on the U.G.G.

Finally the Alberta Wheat Pool published a pamphlet entitled, A History of Events Leading to Taxation of Cooperatives. In it were charges that the entire effort to tax the Pools could be traced to an address by R. S. Law to the Turgeon Grain Inquiry Commission in 1937 pointing out that the Pools were paying no income tax. It was further charged that the U.G.G. had allied with the North-West Line Elevators Association "to enforce taxation of the Wheat Pools." In defending against such attacks, Brownlee was on shaky ground because the joint brief he had prepared with the N.L.E.A. now came back like an embarrassing ghost from the past. He was unsure of exactly what information the Pool officials had. As he told Law a conversation he had in Alberta suggested that Pool officials knew about the joint brief.

> ... the most disquieting information I received from him was when I mentioned that the Company had filed no brief on May 31, 1941, as stated by the North-West Line Elevators. He questioned that statement very directly and said that the Wheat Pool claimed to have a copy of a brief signed by us

and North-West Line Elevators and they said "it was a dandy." ... Just how much attention should be paid to this comment I do not know, but from the way he acted it did appear to me that the Wheat Pool either had a copy of Biggar's joint brief, or had seen a copy on the file of the Income Tax Department.

Brownlee's denial of a brief "as stated by the North-West Line Elevators," implied no brief had been submitted. In fact, only the technicality of the date mentioned could be denied. Brownlee feared he had been caught in this a legalistic subterfuge. Two weeks later, at the U.G.G. Annual Meeting, the shareholders were demanding answers to the Pool charges. Brownlee delivered a hard-hitting defense but his denials were much less categorical than they must have seemed to the delegates. He told them,

> ... in answer to the charge that Mr. Law started this whole thing, I say that it is not true in substance, nor true in fact ... I say in reply to the other charge of an unholy alliance with the North-West Line Elevators Association, that right from the time that this question was raised, it has been known in important quarters that our position was different from that of the Association. In all of the official submissions we never once asked that other cooperatives be taxed. ... We asked that patronage dividends be exempt and the North-West Line Elevators Association took exactly the opposite position.

Brownlee's very judicious selection of points to admit was an attempt to defuse the threat of an acrimonious division among farmer organizations. In large measure though, he had contributed to the controversy. In his pragmatic view, it was entirely reasonable that two lawyers preparing similar briefs should collaborate, even to the point of preparing a joint brief if there was no serious difference on the specific issue at hand. In the legal fraternity such collegial cooperation went on despite animosity between respective clients. Brownlee was aware that such collaboration, if known, would be unpopular with many farmers but the impact of the controversy provides yet another illustration of his underestimating the emotional element of the farmers' movement.

There were many staunch Pool supporters who regarded anyone who consorted with the line elevator companies as a traitor to the farmers' cause. John Brownlee never experienced such feelings and only partly understood their existence.

However, the delegates accepted his defense and a series of radio broadcasts he made in each of the three prairie provinces largely ended the controversy. Doubtless, his explanations were assisted by his emphasis on the U.G.G.'s effort to achieve the exemption of patronage dividends. Now that that exemption had been granted, he was able to announce that almost $2,500,000 in dividend reserves would soon be streaming through the mails.

While there was good news about the patronage dividend question, the appeal of the U.G.G. from taxation for 1940 and 1941 still had to be settled. In February 1947, Brownlee was in Ottawa for a series of interviews and the presentation of a brief on a number of tax claims by the Company to bring its treatment into line with that accorded the Pools. Brownlee's approach revealed his mastery of the proper forms of the political process. He did not participate in the preliminary discussions, leaving his assistants, Steer and Griffin, to prepare the agenda along with the Deputy-Minister of Finance, Dr. Clark, and his assistant, Mitchell Sharp. The next day Brownlee joined the group for a discussion on the best approach to the Minister himself, Douglas Abbott. On February 12, that meeting took place and Brownlee reported how it was handled.

> We presented a completely revised brief which, however, was not handed in until Mr. Steer had made a verbal presentation of the case. ... The Minister gave us the closest possible attention, and, although the case was new to him, grasped our position very quickly. We felt we had not only the support of Dr. Clark but also the sympathy of the Minister. The latter subsequently told Mr. Steer at a social gathering that a magnificent presentation of our case had been made.

The U.G.G. Board agreed with the Minister's assessment. There was no doubt that Brownlee's competence and style were major factors in the eventual favourable decision which saved the Company hundreds of thousands of dollars. His effectiveness confirmed the U.G.G.'s place as a major voice on agricultural policy with effective access to federal government decision makers. As he had while Premier, he took care to remain on good terms with influential people in both major parties. For example, while the taxation question was before Parliament, he lobbied not only the members of the Liberal Government but saw to it that there was a quiet canvass of opposition Conservatives as well. This was eased by his close association with such figures as the new, unlikely Conservative leader, John Bracken, and the Member for Calgary West, his former lawyer, A. L. Smith. As his chat with Coldwell had shown, he even took time to keep channels open to C.C.F. leaders, as well, since the C.C.F. was riding high in the public opinion polls in the mid-forties..

Brownlee recognized the Pools had considerable political influence but his ability largely off-set their initial advantages of larger numbers and a more aggressive tone. Thanks largely to his efforts, the U.G.G. achieved its objective of complete equality of taxation between itself and the Pools. On the other hand, the Pools, although receiving some further concessions, failed in their attempt to retain their tax exempt status. The most important concession was the enlargement of the tax exemption on patronage dividends to include even those deferred and retained as capital reserves. Brownlee was to use that exemption to introduce a system of financing which was to provide the U.G.G. with a solid basis for capital expansion and a modernization programme unprecedented in the Company's history.

At the 1947 Annual Meeting, he moved two resolutions:

Resolved that the Directors be and they are hereby authorized to distribute to customers the amount set aside on the balance sheet for patronage dividends by issuing in lieu of cash Class A or Class B shares or Certificates of Indebtedness in such form as the directors may approve, and
...
That the Board of Directors be authorized to issue additional shares of stock, either "A" or "B" shares at the par value of each to a maximum amount of $500,000 ...

The effect of the change was that, instead of disbursing $250,000 in patronage dividends each year, the Company could divert these funds into paid-up capital. It was a dependable, economical method of financing and while many might complain about expropriation of their dividends and involuntary purchase of capital stock, the majority at the annual meeting supported Brownlee's plan. As he had while Premier, he believed strongly that the financial strength of the over-all organization was vastly more important than individual short term income benefit. The new policy resulted in an immediate and dramatic broadening of the number of stockholders and in the size of the investment by each. As well, increased business volume would now translate into both higher revenues and, automatically, parallel increases in capital stock sales.

By this time, Brownlee was closely involved in all aspects of the Company's operation. In February 1947, he was named Acting General Manager and, in light of R. S. Law's continuing failing health, on January 1, 1948, became General Manager. He signed a revolving eight year contract which provided that even in the unlikely event he was not re-elected as a Director, he would continue as General Manager. Later, Law was forced by illness to resign his role completely and on May 1, 1948, at the age of sixty-four, John Brownlee became President and General Manager of United Grain Growers Limited.

Figure 9

John Brownlee as "Grand Old Man" regales his friends and supporters just prior to becoming President and General Manager of United Grain Growers Limited, in 1948. He would guide the company through the difficult post-World War II era, positioning it for the future where it still ranks in the top 100 of Canada's businesses. Brownlee relinquished his responsibilities less than one month before he died - July 15, 1961.

(Photo courtesy of Glenbow Archives - NA-4338-17)

Chapter 21: President of United Grain Growers Ltd.

John Brownlee was now the head of one of Canada's largest business organizations. The U.G.G. operated 114 grain elevators in Manitoba, 206 in Saskatchewan, 308 in Alberta, as well as a 5.5 million bushel terminal elevator in Port Arthur and another terminal in Vancouver. In addition to being a major grain handler, the Company's extensive network of farm supply centres sold binder twine, coal, the newly introduced agricultural chemicals and the U.G.G.'s own line of "Money Maker" livestock feeds. Among the subsidiary companies, the Public Press published The Country Guide whose over 200,000 subscribers made it the largest farmer oriented magazine in Canada, while U.G.G. Securities was a major underwriter of fire and accident insurance.

Also, the U.G.G. supported, with both dollars and delegates, the various provincial farmers' organizations, the Canadian Federation of Agriculture, and the International Association of Agricultural Producers. Brownlee served on the C.F.A. executive for many years and attended numerous international meetings on agricultural policy. In Canada, he appeared frequently before a wide variety of governmental and other bodies, on behalf of his Company, farmers, and Western Canada. However, he was never parochial and his suggestions were always presented as ones which, if heeded, would benefit all Canadians.

To supervise this vast responsibility, he maintained offices both in Winnipeg, at the Hamilton Building, and in Calgary where he occupied the same third floor room in the Lougheed Building as he had when he first joined the Company as General Counsel in 1917. In both places he was provided with a full staff. He spent about forty percent of his time in Winnipeg where his home away from home was Suite 298 at the Royal Alexandra Hotel. There, sometimes accompanied by Florence, he would host informal business meetings. However, mainly his suite was simply an office away from the office. His proclivity for work continued and, if possible, increased. One of the early executives to use the Dictaphone extensively, he frequently arrived on Monday morning with a briefcase full of spools which kept two or three secretaries busy all day typing letters he had dictated during the weekend. In fact, he was known by his staff as a man whose life was his work, who lived in his briefcase, and whose only recreation seemed to be changing from one job to another. However, he did have a family life. He was proud of son Alan who had taken over the law firm in Edmonton, now Brownlee and Brownlee. It was a successful and growing practice with several large agricultural and commercial clients. Son John now managed his own photography studio in Edmonton and both sons were married and soon presenting Brownlee with grandchildren. In Calgary, the Brownlees enjoyed a quiet life in their small one bedroom apartment in Donegal Mansions. They could often be seen going for walks along the river bank on a summer evening but otherwise they lived a secluded existence, entertaining infrequently and confining their social life to family and a few old friends.

In the fold of his family, Brownlee was a different man from the austere executive known to business acquaintances, although in these later years he mellowed considerably, especially toward his "U.G.G. family". However, with his own family he was more relaxed, actively participating in the domestic routine and given to a puckish sense of humour, sometimes at his own expense. On one occasion, his son John made arrangements to buy a car being retired from the U.G.G. fleet. Brownlee was to drive it from Winnipeg to Calgary where his son would take delivery. A midsummer heat wave was in full course as he made the drive through the hot, open prairie between Winnipeg and Calgary. The car, however, was equipped with a primitive air-conditioner which worked in conjunction with the heater. He turned on this new device but it seemed to give little relief from the intense heat, despite his turning it higher and higher. Finally he arrived in Calgary complaining about his uncomfortable journey and the unusually severe heat. It took his son only a moment to determine that Brownlee, never mechanically inclined, had had on, not the air-conditioner but the heater. He often retold the story over the years, chuckling at his own expense, about driving over 900 miles through the blistering heat of the southern prairies with the car's heater on full blast.

Curiously, in these immediate post-war years, the woman whose accusations had destroyed Brownlee's political career also moved to Calgary after being widowed by the Edson confectioner she had married in 1935. By 1950, she (now Vivian Sorenson) was working only a few blocks away from Donegal Mansions as a secretary and bookkeeper for Howie Construction Company. Frank Howie, a former plasterer on his way to the top of a large and diversified construction company, lived with his wife Elizabeth in a suite above the office. Five years later, Vivian was Mrs. Frank Howie and lived with her new husband on a prestige acreage on Calgary's outskirts.

* * *

As President and General Manager of the U.G.G., Brownlee faced some formidable tasks. Expansion was necessary to handle another large prairie grain surplus and to meet stiff competition, especially from the Pools. Modernization was needed because rapidly improving farm technology meant larger deliveries arriving more quickly than in the days of real horse power. Also, inflation was putting a premium on business efficiency.

The key to both expansion and modernization was the financial strength, especially the capital position, of the Company. Brownlee's restructuring of the shares opened the way for much larger capital investment than ever before, while the tax exemption for patronage dividends paid in capital shares or debentures provided an avenue for capitalization in amounts which even a decade before would have been inconceivable. Brownlee designed and piloted through the Annual Meeting a series of policy changes creating large new issues of stock subscribed mainly by the automatic issuance of investment shares, rather than cash, as patronage dividends. Thus, well over $3,000,000 was subscribed during his first three years as President. Even this amount was not sufficient for the ambitious expansion under way and, in 1950, the bonded indebtedness was refunded and expanded by issuing $6,000,000 in debentures through the traditional bond markets. There is no doubt Brownlee used the financial expertise he had gained while Premier, in meeting his new responsibilities.

Expansion meant a large building programme of annexes and new elevators. As well, elevators were purchased, usually from smaller privately owned companies. One of the largest deals was the purchase of the entire Reliance Grain Company which included 110 elevators, mainly in Saskatchewan. Such acquisitions greatly increased the U.G.G.'s total capacity and spread its business presence more uniformly over the grain growing region so as to protect from losses resulting from local or regional crop failures.

There was more than caution behind such a move. The key to success in grain handling is volume. The more delivery points, the more volume coming into the system. However, in some cases, the cost of operating an elevator was greater than the revenue generated by the volume it contributed. Brownlee was one of the first grain industry executives to face this problem head on. He was also one of the first to recognize the pervasive and potentially devastating impact of inflation on the grain handling business. As early as 1952, he ordered a study of the operating cost and volume handle of every delivery point in the Company's system. The results showed that below a handle of about 35,000 bushels annually, the costs of operating an elevator were greater than the revenue it generated. Only about a dozen elevators were in a loss position but it was evident that with continuing inflation of operating costs, such delivery points would either have to be expanded or abandoned. Once again, Brownlee had to weigh the pragmatic considerations of the entire Company against local concerns in the communities affected. Some localities would never produce enough volume to continue to support a local elevator. Others with three competing elevators might have only enough volume to make one viable. In such cases, prudence urged that one or more companies withdraw rather than all remain to operate losing concerns. The U.G.G. explored possible trade-offs, achieving most success with the Manitoba and Alberta Pools.

The study also revealed that the U.G.G. was over represented in small delivery points with no growth potential while it was under represented or completely absent from such centres as Regina, Brandon and Winnipeg. Brownlee was fully aware of the pressing need to rectify this situation and several future purchases of elevators aimed at doing so. Such pragmatic analysis and long range planning were characteristic of Brownlee and were a large factor in keeping the Company abreast of, and in some cases ahead of, major changes in the farming and grain handling operations of Western Canada. His expertise was given additional recognition when, in 1951, he was appointed to the Board of Catelli Food Products Limited where he made meaningful contributions to the policies and management of that major firm.

He also put his stamp on the internal operations of the U.G.G., fostering communication among employees to keep alive a traditional team spirit. One method of achieving this was the U.G.G. News, an in-house publication which he was mainly responsible for introducing. Never the bedraggled mimeographed newsletter common to many organizations, the News quickly developed into an attractive glossy magazine full of Company events, profiles of employees, and articles designed to encourage pride, involvement and a sense of the Company's history and tradition. Some of the features he directly sponsored were straightforwardly educational, such as an essay contest for agents on the best way to prevent fires in elevators.

However, the main way he encouraged his "U.G.G. family" was through personal contact. His schedule was always busy, from attending staff picnics in summer to New Year's parties. His always impressive presence was given added impact by the fact that it was still an age when deference to position was shown. Food would not be served until he arrived and when he did, senior employees would rush to welcome him while more junior staff members waited deferentially for the honour of being spoken to. Here, Brownlee's political experience was again valuable for he impressed with his ability to go to an agent at even the remotest point and call him and his family by name.

Another challenge was his work with the various agricultural organizations. On the executive of the Canadian Federation of Agriculture, for example, he had to do his part to overcome rivalries and animosities and attempt to unify the voice of agriculture so that it might better be heard. One of the sharpest differences was over the British Wheat Agreement.

The Pools, especially the Saskatchewan Pool, initially favoured the agreement to sell large quantities of wheat to Britain over a four year period at a fixed price. This deal promised to insure continuing sales and hedge against the expected price decline after World War II. However, throughout the four years of the agreement, world prices were above those of the contract. The terms of the Agreement provided that the price in the final two years would be reviewed "having regard to" existing world prices but when Canadian negotiators attempted to offset losses by asking, for a higher price over the final two years, they were met by stubborn refusal by their British counterparts. The British were prepared to "have regard to" the world price but they steadfastly refused to amend the terms of the contract and it was quickly apparent there was nothing in the Agreement to compel any other action. As a result, Western Canadian farmers were out upwards of $350,000,000.

By this time, there was a hue and cry over who was responsible for these losses. The Pools admitted they had initially favoured the Agreement but blamed government negotiators and federal Cabinet Ministers for being out-negotiated to the point farmers ended up being fleeced. There was also negative feeling generated toward the British, especially when it was learned that they had resold much of the Canadian wheat in Europe for up to one dollar per bushel more than they had paid for it. In the West it was felt the British had received millions of dollars which justly belonged to Canadian growers.

However, the British were not about to make any refunds. The Canadian Government was left to face demands for compensation. Those who argued that it should accept the responsibility argued that the losses were the result of the inexperience and ineptitude of the Canadian government as a world trader. Finally the Government announced it would supplement the final payment for the wheat by $65,000,000. This pleased no one. Such a payment would be only a small fraction of what, by even the most conservative estimate, farmers had lost through not receiving the world price. In Eastern Canada, however, there was a storm of protest over even this small payment for it was argued the Government should not accept any responsibility for the loss or provide any "subsidy" payment to prairie farmers.

At this point, Brownlee entered the fray. He had been cautious about the British Wheat Agreement but when the compensation payments were criticized, he authorized full page advertisements in major newspapers across Canada to counter the argument that "subsidies" were being paid to prairie farmers. The advertisement pointed out that since 1941, wheat for domestic milling had sold at 77 cents per bushel. With the world price as high as $2.18, this represented a subsidy to Canadian consumers of at least $100,000,000. This statement was one of the first to publicly identify the real situation in Canada. It was consumers, not growers, who benefited from federal agricultural policy.

Another legacy of the British Wheat Agreement fiasco was a growing maturity among agricultural leaders toward the international situation and a related disillusionment of the pro-British sentiments that had flourished during the war years. The feelings of mutual cooperation seemed to have lingered longer in Canada than in Britain. One evidence was the recent sharp dealing of the Agreement but their was also British isolationism toward the International Wheat Agreements and an apparent disinterest in maintaining Commonwealth ties. As Brownlee commented upon his return from London in 1952, where he had been a Canadian advisor to the drafting of the Second International Wheat Agreement, "Many of us feel that Britain is taking our loyalty to the Commonwealth too much for granted and is unnecessarily diverting much of her purchases of farm products to other countries, to the advantage of her own export trade."

The International Wheat Agreements were attempts to introduce stability, both of supply and price, into the world wheat market. Brownlee had long supported this principle, recognizing that major price influences were outside Canada. At the same time, he was pragmatic enough to realize that such agreements could never be more than guidelines, easily broken due to the lack of any means of forcing nations to honour their agreements. He was also cautious about the benefits to Canadian farmers, believing, as many did, that the security of long term sales might well entail sacrifices of price. That was the case during the first agreement so when negotiations for a second began, in London in the spring of 1952, the exporting countries demanded higher prices. The conference adjourned without a new pact but it reconvened the next year in Washington with Brownlee again one of four advisors to the Canadian delegation. Eventually agreement was reached and maximum prices were set at $2.05 and the minimum at $1.55. In theory, both exporters and importers were protected from price extremes and supply was stabilized by a system of import allotments and export quotas.

By the mid-1950's, the relatively new practice of national governments acting as international traders was in full bloom. The Canadian Wheat Board was the sole buyer and seller of export and milling wheat and operated like the private and cooperative export organizations of the past. The Board thus required considerable expertise in all aspects of the grain trade. To help to supply this, an eleven member Advisory Committee was formed, seven of whom were to represent producers. Brownlee, as the head of one of the world's largest grain handling organizations, was a logical choice for the Committee and served several years on it. There, he had direct input into the formation of Canada's domestic and foreign grain marketing policies.

He also continued to speak out on the important implications of agricultural policies, taking an increasingly international view. He urged the Canadian Government to protest the growing practice of subsidizing agricultural exports. To Brownlee, such policies disrupted the influence of supply and demand and encouraged production of commodities which were already in surplus. He declared:

> Canada has sufficient status in international trade to warrant it in taking the lead in an effort to check this practice of subsidizing exports, but if it is to be attacked the ground will have to be carefully chosen. Certainly there is nothing wrong in subsidizing agriculture as such. Every advanced country does that in one form or another. The practice is justified to assure the health of the country's basic industry and to counter-balance advantages of other industries. The attack ... must be ... limited to subsidized dumping. ...
> Since dumping ... has come to be considered a reprehensible practice by practically all trading nations, dumping when subsidized by the State, must be considered more reprehensible. It may seem a large undertaking to try to bring about a limitation ... but in its own interest Canada should make the attempt.

By 1956 Brownlee was even more involved in international wheat marketing. In March, he was again one of the advisors to the Canadian delegation in Geneva where the Third International Wheat Agreement was concluded. Following the conference, he and Florence spent three weeks touring western Europe. It was a more relaxed and reflective visit than their hurried jaunt of thirty years before. Now that he was approaching his seventy-third birthday, there was the knowledge that this might be their last opportunity to see the sights of Europe. The relaxation was well timed for upon his return he was to embark on the most strenuous year of his presidency -- the celebration of the Grain Growers' fiftieth anniversary.

Throughout the year there was a steady stream of assorted dinners, staff parties, picnics, retirement banquets and Local meetings; all emphasizing the fiftieth anniversary theme and all expecting a visit from the President and a few remarks about the Company's past achievements and its future prospects. It was a schedule as demanding as any election campaign but it was a task Brownlee warmly accepted because he viewed a knowledge of the past as essential to any who were involved in shaping the policies of the Company or any other sphere of activity.

Indeed, there was cause for pride in the Company's record and it was appropriate that Brownlee was the leading figure in its celebrations for no other individual, excepting T. A. Crerar, had a career so closely involved in the entire history of both the Company and the Canadian West in which it had grown. In his many speeches, he traced the achievements of the past and referred frequently to the Rochdale pioneers of co-operativism and connected them directly to the founders of the Grain Growers' Grain Company. This emphasis countered continuing criticism, some of it from U.G.G. members, that the Company was more a joint stock company than a cooperative. In the large volume of anniversary publicity there was continual reference to the U.G.G.'s role as a cooperative -- in fact, the pioneer of Canadian co-operativism. The celebrations also did much to heighten employee pride and public awareness of the U.G.G. both as a successful business and as a distinctive Western Canadian institution.

To maintain this pride and awareness, a Company history was commissioned which in many ways was the centrepiece of the fiftieth anniversary celebrations. Such a publication would record the adversities overcome and the achievements made, show the true cooperative roots of the Company, and detail the generous assistance to various farmer organizations, including the crucial help in the formative years of the Pools.

As early as 1952, R. D. Colquette, a retired editor of The Country Guide, began preparing the history, for a stipend of $100 monthly. Brownlee kept closely in touch with the work, approving such details as the general outline and chapter sequence. Finally, in late 1955, the first draft was ready for his consideration. It arrived when the entire Company was saddened by the death from cancer of veteran Director J. J. MacLellan, the last remaining member of the original U.G.G. Board. As well he had served on the U.F.A. executive and in the Legislative Assembly, both as a Brownlee backbencher and in the short-lived Reid Cabinet. Because of their long association, Brownlee was touched by MacLellan's death. It symbolized the ending of an era and provided additional incentive to complete the history to record the achievements of a generation now passing from the stage. Brownlee asked for a complete re-writing of the manuscript to make it less colloquial and to reduce the number of statistics and biographical details. Colquette had suffered a mild heart attack so a committee of staff was assigned to do the revision but in the end, Brownlee did most of it himself, re-doing whole chapters, including the one dealing with his own presidency. He was embarrassed about appearing to take "advantage of the History to make extensive references to myself. On the other hand, I cannot quite see how references can be left out as, after all, there has been quite a change in the set-up of the Company during the past eight years."

He took over the supervision of virtually every detail of the final product. He chose the title, The First Fifty Years, from a list of 120 suggestions entered in a Country Guide contest. He directed the copyrighting of the book and completely re-vamped a suggested distribution plan. He ordered a first run of 5,000 copies and defended the relatively large number by explaining, "This will be the main book of reference of the Company for the next ten or fifteen years." He was, however, surprised and pleased when it was received, not just as an in-house publicity vehicle, but as a work of both historical and literary merit. As a result, he recommended Colquette receive another $1,000 honoraria for his considerable effort in preparing the book.

All such details were, theoretically, the responsibility of Vice-President R. C. Brown who, nominally at least, was in charge of the subsidiary companies, including Public Press which published the book. There was tension between the two men, stemming from Brownlee's interference in areas which were not his responsibility. Some attributed this to his inability to delegate decision-making, while others referred to incidents where it appeared he had deliberately set out to upstage Brown. The relationship was typical of one reaction to Brownlee's style of leadership. Those who liked considerable structure and direction from the top enjoyed working under him but those who wanted more independence and the opportunity to make their own decisions felt thwarted and confined under his tutelage.

There was also tension between Brownlee and his Assistant General Manager, P.C. Watt. Here again his tendency to involve himself in details of responsibilities which might better have been delegated verged on outright interference. It was an intrusion even more unacceptable to those who saw Brownlee as "no grain man." Those who performed the essential functions of grain trading would have preferred he confine himself to a figure-head presidency and "grand old man" image. However, he was driven by his desire to use his knowledge and experience to solve the problems of his Company and those any member of his "U.G.G. family" might face. His perception, certainly not unfounded, was that "to him much had been given" so he had a greater duty than others to assume responsibilities. It was the same conception of leadership he had expressed in his college days and, on balance, it had served him well. However, it was a conception which was rapidly losing the popularity necessary to make it workable.

* * *

In June of 1957, Brownlee underwent the first of a series of major operations. He kept his medical problems to himself, letting his staff know he would be absent only a week before his surgery. He spent three weeks in Winnipeg General Hospital recuperating, plus an additional two weeks at the Royal Alexandra Hotel, before returning to Calgary. In both cities he was now assigned a car and driver. Bill Kwasnycia in Winnipeg, in particular, became his friend and confidant, bringing him newspapers, delivering letters and messages and always, despite Brownlee's protests, maneuvering the President's car so that Brownlee would have as few steps as possible.

Once at home in Calgary, there was further recuperation before the neighbours again saw the Brownlees, both assisted by canes, taking their accustomed quiet walk beside the Bow or sitting under the memorial trees which fringed its bank. It was about this time that Calgary traffic planners announced one of their periodic plans to clear aside the trees and lawns of Memorial Drive in order to add more pavement to speed a few more cars downtown in the morning rush hour. The residents were alarmed and sought ways of diverting the concrete conspiracy. Brownlee was consulted. He made one telephone call to the Mayor and the plans for widening Memorial Drive were dropped. There were many on the Drive who had little idea who Brownlee was or what his past accomplishments had been but they were impressed that the old man had been able to save their trees.

By the end of summer he was ready to resume his duties but he still required a good deal of assistance. His ability to remember details not associated with his work was now notoriously poor and when he left for a speaking engagement, for example, Florence would laboriously pack his large folding trunk to insure that every article of clothing he would need, from overshoes to hats, was included. Every compartment was labeled and inside was taped the location where he was speaking and detailed directions on how he was to get there. It was a family joke that all he had to remember to do was to open the trunk. More and more frequently he would telephone Florence from the office for some name or detail that had escaped his memory and when business associates visited their home, she would sit discreetly on the perimeter of the discussion, knitting and adding the occasional detail when required.

When it came to the details of office, however, his ability seemed unimpaired. Another study of elevator operating efficiency revealed the minimum handle was now in the 75,000 bushels per year range. With the use of trucks and cars confirming a growing farmer orientation toward larger centres, and with railway branch line abandonments likely to complicate matters further, Brownlee, with characteristic foresight, advised the Board that,

... the trend to deliver to large centres will continue and accelerate if surpluses disappear. As many as 20 percent of our points may be removed. We must pin-point strategic points for development and earmark points which will disappear. We must clarify our understanding with the Pools, if possible. What we do now and for the next ten years will influence our position 25 to 50 years hence.

Brownlee's management style had not changed either. Despite failing health and advancing years, he still worked longer hours than most executives. At Board meetings his style of chairmanship would have been instantly recognizable to any of his former Cabinet ministers. He would introduce the issue as a problem to be solved, list the possible solutions, and then invite comments. If the discussion that followed was long, he would put his hand over his eyes and slump back in his chair until there was some concern he had fallen asleep. However, at some point he would abruptly cut off discussion, succinctly summarize the points that had been made and call for the solution which usually was by this time obvious. Increasingly he neglected to invite even this modest amount of participation and junior Board members were chagrined to find they were merely expected to rubber-stamp decisions already arrived at by the Executive Committee. His approach worked well for questions with easy and clear cut answers, but for matters where the list of pros and cons did not produce an obvious answer the decision making process could be long and arduous.

One of the most difficult decisions concerned insurance for the Company's giant terminal elevator in Port Arthur. Although U.G.G. Securities wrote insurance, on a risk as large as a 5.5 million bushel elevator the common practice of spreading the risk was followed. The central question was whether the insurance should be "all perils" coverage, or the much lower cost "specified perils". Brownlee, ever frugal, challenged the Directors by stating that such an intelligent group should be able to list every possible peril and thus qualify for the lower rate. For weeks they grappled with the list, never quite satisfied that it was complete. Eventually, with impatience on Brownlee's part, they decided to adopt the safer course and take up the "all perils" insurance.

Besides such internal questions, Brownlee was still involved with the general problems of Western agriculture. The central problem was the large surpluses which were congesting the entire grain handling system. Export sales were slow and opportunities for new farm deliveries seemingly even slower. Most farmers were facing severely restricted delivery quotas and, as Brownlee had pointed out more than a decade earlier, farm stored grain which could not be marketed represented lost income. Once again there was the paradox of large production and low income although this time it resulted not from low prices but from a lack of markets and an inadequate grain transportation system. Finally, the new Diefenbaker Government responded to this difficulty by introducing a programme of cash advances on farm stored grain and a more aggressive export sales policy. The result was both short and long term relief for farmers whose income had been curtailed by sluggish grain movement.

Another spin-off problem from the large surplus was the criticism of box-car allocations. With farmers straining for every opportunity to market their grain, there was sharp complaint against both the Railways and the Wheat Board for not having sufficient box-cars in place to move grain from the local elevator. It seemed there was always another point receiving more cars and jealousies and complaints were rife. Some recommended a formula for box-car allocation so that each point would be assured of a definite number and farmers would have a definite standard against which to judge the allocations that did occur. Brownlee rejected this idea and in an impressive brief to the Commons Standing Committee on Agriculture, recommended that the allocation of box-cars remain the responsibility of the Wheat Board. He argued that it needed full authority in order to have the flexibility to fill export orders for certain grades.

Despite such continuing involvement in the agricultural issues of the day, Brownlee's time continued to be mainly spent in his role of President and Grand Old Man of the U.G.G. Whether at the opening of the world's most northerly grain elevator in Fort St. John, British Columbia, or welcoming the first box-car of grain in Vancouver direct from the Peace River country, whether leading a motorcade of staff over the new transcontinental highway to Banff for their annual picnic or reminding the Winnipeg office at the

Christmas banquet that the U.G.G. "was full of family spirit and mutual good will," his presence was a required and expected highlight. In keeping with his advancing years, he made frequent mention of the past but also he made many arrangements for the future, such as announcing a U.G.G. grant of $5,000 annually to each prairie university to assist agricultural research. He upgraded the Company's school for elevator agents and made continuing education an ongoing policy. He revised and improved pension plans and other Company benefits to employees. He worked and had little but his work, but always, when someone came into the office in the summer season, he asked the question so important to any true Westerner - "How are the crops?"

* * *

By 1959, the era of the steam locomotive had passed but the train was still a popular means of travel. So it was that on the evening of September 23, the U.G.G. Board and senior management bundled aboard at Winnipeg for a trip to Port Arthur. It was part of a programme, initiated by Brownlee, to bring the Company closer together by taking senior personnel into the field to see and be seen. The plan was to tour the terminal facilities, hold a Board meeting, and attend a banquet for staff. Brownlee had retired for the evening when a telegram for him was received at Kenora so P.C. Watt accepted it. It read simply, "Number 2 Annex slipped into Lake -- No Injuries." Brownlee was awakened and, shocked, blurted out to Watt, "Peter, this is the end of the Company."

By the next morning some composure had been regained, aided by the coincidence that within a few hours of this major disaster, almost the entire echelon of senior management was on the scene. Nearly one-half of the giant terminal, from the workhouse out on the lake-ward side, at about eight o'clock the previous evening, had sheered to one side and toppled into the chill waters of Thunder Bay. Fortunately, there was no ship in the slip alongside for it would have been instantly squashed to the bottom of the lake by the thousands of tons of concrete in the sixty-four, one hundred foot high bins which slithered and toppled into the lake in seconds. The collapse caused an instant tidal wave, over twelve feet high, which swept across the narrow bay beside the terminal, destroying boats and sheds on the opposite shore. Further along the lake front, tugs and pulpwood at the Abitibi Paper Still were swept ashore in a tangled heap up to 200 feet from the water line. As Brownlee and the Directors toured the devastation of what had been the second largest and second newest terminal on the Lakehead, they could well congratulate themselves that they had opted for the "all perils" insurance coverage. Despite a common belief that under water currents of the Current River, which empties into the lake near the elevator, had undermined the foundations, the official investigation concluded the cause of the collapse was "unknown". Therefore, it could not have been specified. However, while the elevator was covered, the question of responsibility for the loss of 2.5 million bushels of grain, conservatively valued at $2,500,000, proved much more difficult to settle. The U.G.G. said the grain belonged to the Canadian Wheat Board for which it had been merely supplying warehouse storage. The Chairman of the Wheat Board, on the other hand, declared the Board did not actually own the grain. He drew the analogy of money in a bank. If the specific bills the customer had deposited were destroyed in the bank, the Bank would still have to deliver the amount of money the customer had "stored", on demand. Brownlee admitted there was "some question of ownership" but the problem took a long time to resolve. In the meantime, over 1.5 million bushels was successfully salvaged.

In all the total losses, including damage to other property and loss of earnings through business interruption, were well over $5,000,000. Almost immediately after his first inspection of the site, Brownlee circulated a memorandum, "To Fellow Employees", detailing the losses, the insurance coverage, and promising that the Company would rebuild the terminal and "soon be in business ... at the Lakehead again in a larger way." Nevertheless, he later characterized 1959 as a year of "near disaster." Once the re-building was under way, he assured the staff, "We are in the battle and must have the spirit of an army in battle. Let the bugles sound and let us carry our banners high." However, John Brownlee was nearing his final battle. He underwent another operation and his bouts in hospital were now more frequent. Still he carried on.

In September, 1960, he appeared before yet another Royal Commission investigating a demand by railways to abrogate the statutory freight rates on grain. It was, indeed, appropriate that his last such appearance would concern an issue so closely bound up with the history, fabric and aspirations of Western Canadian society. In his submission, subsequently published under the title, In Defense of the Crow's Nest Pass Rates, he sketched the entire history of the West, pointing out that one could not simply consider the expenditures and revenues in the present day movement of grain. Millions of acres of Western land had been granted to the Railways out of which they continued to derive huge revenues. Millions of dollars in tax exemptions had also been granted the Railways. Westerners, directly and indirectly had had to replace those lost tax dollars. In short Westerners had made, and continued to make, huge payments toward a national transportation system out of which the statutory rates were their one and only clear benefit. Brownlee directly challenged the Railways' submissions, drawing attention to no fewer than eight fallacies in their arguments and recommending the rejection of their request. It was one of his strongest briefs on behalf of Western grain growers and, as he had so many times before, he contributed to a decision in their favour. It was a role which he enjoyed, presenting a submission to a none-too-sympathetic tribunal on behalf of his "clients" - the farmers of Western Canada.

In November, Premier Duff Roblin of Manitoba, the guest speaker at the U.G.G. Annual Meeting, inducted Brownlee into the "Order of the Buffalo Hunt", a device for honouring those who "have made a distinctive contribution to the life of Manitoba." It was an almost unique public recognition of his contributions over the years. In Alberta, the U.F.A., before slipping into obscurity, had awarded him an honourary life membership, and the Social Credit Government had grudgingly permitted his portrait to hang with that of the other premiers in the Legislative Building. Otherwise, in these latter years, John Brownlee was, for the most part, forgotten.

He received brief attention when the Diefenbaker Government named him as one of the twenty-five original members of the National Productivity Council, the forerunner of the Economic Council of Canada. Prime Minister Diefenbaker believed

Brownlee might be the man to head the Council but rapidly deteriorating health prevented him from attending any but the first meeting in Ottawa in March, 1961.

Also that spring in Ottawa, he attended the twenty-fifth annual meeting, of the Canadian Federation of Agriculture. His attendance was virtually forced by his friends who wanted him present as one of four (T. A. Crerar was another) who were being honoured for more than a half-century of service to farmer organizations. Indeed his record was an impressive one, stretching back to the earliest days of farmer owned businesses, through the organization of the Pools and Cooperatives, past the dislocation of depression and war and concluding as chief officer of the second largest grain handling business in North America. In length, variety, and permanence, his record could not be equaled. Later in the spring, he consented to a series of interviews by staff of the Glenbow Archives, the only extensive recording of his recollections. He spoke at that time of working on some memoirs in his favourite vacation spot of Victoria but it was not to be. He continued his duties until June before his tremendous weight loss and failing health made it obvious to all that the cancer within him could no longer be defied. On June 19, he announced the appointment of Louis Driscoll as General Manager and two days later submitted his resignation as President.

The Board of Directors of United Grain Growers Limited officially accepted the resignation of John Brownlee as of July 1, 1961. Two weeks later, on Florence's seventy-fourth birthday, July 15, 1961, as the morning sun caught the flanks of the Rockies and streaked across the endless prairie fields, he died.

The news went out across the West but its impact was nowhere as great as in the offices of the U.G.G. The telegram received in Winnipeg read simply, "The Chief is dead." Immediately the flag above the Hamilton Building was lowered to half-mast and the head office staff wept openly and unashamedly.

The funeral was held at Knox United Church in Calgary with an impressive assembly of dignitaries representing almost every sphere of activity or organization with which Brownlee had been involved. Later, a special two-car train took the body for burial north-east of Edmonton. Western papers editorialized about his passing. The Saskatoon <u>Star-Phoenix</u> was the most succinct, commenting,

> He was not inclined to become evangelistic about farming problems as popular causes to be exploited and placed out of proportion. He preferred a business-like, professional approach, and his personal policy of reasoned argument distinguished him in his public career.

<u>The Country Guide</u>, as befitted the publication which knew him best, was more fulsome, declaring,

> John Brownlee will not only be remembered for the breadth of his contribution, his dedication to duty and his legal, political and business acumen. He displayed other qualities. He was unusually charitable toward others, and showed a sympathetic understanding for the problems of the people with whom he worked and served. Through every experience he maintained his self-composure and often exhibited a fine sense of humour. People who met him for the first time invariably commented about his gentlemanly manners. But perhaps his greatest attribute of all was his humility. Few men of his stature display such modesty.
> ... Farmers across Canada have lost a devoted servant, an eloquent and effective spokesman and a wise counselor and friend. His presence will be missed greatly in the nation's agricultural and business councils. And while his work was primarily in the cause of the West, his concern was always for the nation as a whole. History will record that he was one of the truly great Canadians.

John Brownlee is buried in the rolling parkland of Alberta, a long way in space and time from the tiny Ontario village of Port Ryerse where over a century ago his life began. The cemetery, once miles from Edmonton in a fertile farming district, is now being consumed in the city's headlong urban sprawl. One can still see the crops growing in the distance from the graveside but when the wind changes the odours of giant petrochemical plants and refineries hang rancid in the prairie breeze. Albertans are virtually unanimous in their jealous determination to protect their province's jurisdiction over its natural resources yet not one in a thousand of those who whiz along the highway within sight of the grave knows, or cares, that Brownlee, more than any other individual, is responsible for their having that jurisdiction and the prosperity which has resulted from it.

Even among farmers, Brownlee is almost completely forgotten, although they still benefit daily from the things he achieved. When the Alberta Wheat Pool celebrated its fiftieth anniversary, one heard more of Aaron Sapiro than of John Brownlee, a fact which would have outraged the Pool's founding fathers or, more probably, simply amused them.

Considerable attention has recently been given to the "persons case" and the efforts of the "Famous Five" women of Alberta who successfully contested the right of women to be considered as persons at all levels of law and government in Canada. Never mentioned is the fact that the Brownlee Government was the only one in Canada to support their appeal and that he was a personal friend of all, and legal advisor of three of the women involved.

For years, when remembered at all, Brownlee was associated rather vaguely (except for his presumed guilt) with some scandal involving a secretary in the days before "Bible Bill". The MacMillan accusations blighted, and continue to blight, what might well have been an even more distinguished career. Such a career was, of course, not to be and instead the stain of scandal has long coloured the comments about him. For too long, even the scholars of Western Canadian history relegated Brownlee to an incidental footnote in the story of the rise of Social Credit. This current work, too, languished for a time due to the controversies involved in detailing his life. It is hoped that the publication, finally, of this, his biography, will begin the much needed honest evaluation of his career. Recently, United Western Communications Ltd. in their multi-volume history , <u>Alberta in the 20th Century</u> joined in acknowledging the significance of his career.

As a man who had an important career in law, politics, agriculture and business, John Edward Brownlee deserves his place in Canada's story.

The End

Bibliographical Note

The preceding is a shortened version of the author's Doctoral thesis of the same title, accepted by Queen's University in Kingston, Ontario in 1981. I have chosen not to inflict the general reader with thirty plus pages of notes. The reader should be reassured that every direct quotation in the preceding text is authentic and verifiable. The serious researcher is referred to my dissertation for a fuller treatment of several topics and the complete reference and bibliographical citations. Suffice it to say here that the work is based almost entirely on unpublished letters, reports, diaries and other primary materials. Four repositories are crucial to any study of Brownlee. The Provincial Archives of Alberta house his files as both Attorney General and Premier of Alberta. The Glenbow-Alberta Institute Archives have several valuable collections, including an impressive interview series with U.F.A. veterans, including Brownlee. The Head Office Library of United Grain Growers Limited, in Winnipeg, generously made available to this study, contains important information on Brownlee's non-political career. The T. A. Crerar Papers at Queen's University are also extremely valuable in this regard.

There are some secondary sources that are useful. The only extensive previously published reference to Brownlee is in The First Fifty Years a publication by the U.G.G. which he helped to write. Vital for a background on the economics of his era are Vernon Fowke's, The National Policy and the Wheat Economy and Paul Sharp's, The Agrarian Revolt in Western Canada. H. A. Innis' edition of The Diary of Alexander James McPhail and W. K. Rolph's biography, Henry Wise Wood of Alberta are also very useful studies of men important in Brownlee's life.

Index

Crerar, T.A. (Thomas Alexander),
32, 35, 42, 43, 45, 49, 51, 52,
53, 55, 69, 70, 71, 108, 116,
121, 129, 151, 165, 272, 303,
312, 315
Cuddy, Alfred, 86

Dafoe, John W., 151
Davis, Rev. William, 2
Davis, Justice, 272
Diefenbaker, John, 308, 311
Dinning, R. J., 107
Dodds, Jackson, 181, 222
Douglas, Major C. H., 89, 229,
230, 267, 268, 269
Driscoll, Louis, 312
Drury, E. C., 49, 71
Duggan, David, 188, 189
Dunning, Charles, 83, 96, 120,
143, 165, 166, 167

Edy, James N., 21
Edy, Mary, 21, 23
Elizabeth, H.R.H., the Princess,
286
Esdale, Matthew, 122, 123

Ferguson, Howard, 112
Forke, Robert, 121
Fream, E. J., 28, 29, 30, 31, 79, 94,
113, 131

Gahan, Frank, 272
Gardiner, James, 141
Gardiner, Robert, 53, 106, 182,
197, 220, 232, 263
Good, W. C., 222, 283
Govenlock, Isabella, 20
Greenfield, Herbert, 47, 52, 55, 59,
60, 61, 62, 64, 68, 69, 70, 71,
73, 75, 76, 78, 80, 81, 82, 83,
92, 96, 103, 111, 114, 115, 116,
120, 132, 133, 138, 147
Grisdale, Frank, 234

Gunn, Mrs. R. B., 122

Hall, William, 65
Harvey, Chief Justice, 260, 266
Hoadley, George, 54, 60, 62, 149,
166, 168, 221, 234
Horning, Emerson, 14
Howie, Frank, 297
Howson, W. R., 207, 214, 215,
217, 226, 231, 232, 263, 271
Hudson, A.B., 151
Huestis, Rev. Charles, 66, 67

Irvine, William, 47, 106, 133, 206,
232
Ives, Mr. Justice, 124, 248, 256,
258, 259, 261, 266

Jeffrey, J. W., 122, 123
Johnston, George, 111, 116

Kelly, Evelyn, 30, 36
Kennedy, D.M., 68
Keynes, John Maynard, 200, 217
King, William Lyon Mackenzie,
55, 65, 69, 71, 74, 80, 94, 114,
115, 116, 119, 120, 121, 122,
124, 125, 126, 127, 129, 131,
141, 143, 162, 165, 166, 167,
168, 169, 206, 225, 232, 263,
272
Kwasnycia, Bill, 305

Lambert, Norman, 206, 207
Lapointe, Ernest, 108, 115, 120,
125, 127, 168
Lassandra, Florence, 85, 86, 94, 95
Laurier, Sir Wilfrid, 6
Law, R. S., 22, 84, 85, 95, 138,
272, 283, 287, 288, 291
Lawson, Steve, 84, 85, 95
Layzell, Mr., 218
Leman, Beudrey, 217, 223
Lougheed, Sir James, 22, 45

Notes to Readers

History is always a work in progress. If you have additional documented and verifiable information which you believe should be part of this biography, we would be happy to review it. Also, photographs associated with Brownlee's life would be most welcome. Please mark clearly anything you wish returned and include your return address. Mail to:

Foster Learning Inc.
2904 - 58 Ave.
Lloydminster, Alberta
T9V 1X8

If you found this biography of interest, you are sure to enjoy <u>Alberta in the 20th Century</u>, a proposed "Journalistic History of the Province in Twelve Volumes". The first five volumes, filled with photographs, maps and drawings that bring our history back to life, have now been published. Volume Five, <u>Brownlee and the Victory of Populism</u> has just been released. Dealing with the decade of the 1920's, it makes an excellent companion for this biography. For more information about this series, write:

Alberta Report
17327 - 106A Ave.
Edmonton, Alberta
T5S 9Z9

To Order Copies of

John E. Brownlee: A Biography by Franklin Foster

photocopy this page, add the necessary information and
mail to:

Foster Learning Inc.
2904 - 58 Ave.
Lloydminster, Alberta
T9V 1X8

Let's share our history. This book makes an excellent gift for any
friend, relative or associate interested in Canadian history; or as a
donation to your local school or public library.

For each copy, the cost is:

$24.00 + $3.10 shipping and handling + GST = $29.00

Yes, I wish to order _____ copies of **John E. Brownlee: A
Biography** at $29.00 per copy.

I enclose my cheque for $_____ made payable to:
Foster Learning Inc.

Please ship to: (Print Clearly)

Name: _____

Address: _____

_____

Postal/Zip Code _____